The Cold War Years:
American Foreign Policy
Since 1945

Paul Y. Hammond
RAND CORPORATION

Under the general editorship of

John Morton Blum YALE UNIVERSITY

Harcourt, Brace & World, Inc.

NEW YORK / CHICAGO / SAN FRANCISCO / ATLANTA

All maps: Harbrace

ISBN 0-15-507880-1

Library of Congress Catalog Card Number: 75-79484

Printed in the United States of America

To Brett, Wendy, Robyn,
Spencer, and Clifford

Preface

Foreign policy has been the most distinctive feature of American history since World War II. This book examines American postwar foreign relations within the context of American public life as a whole, for its basic assumption is that our way of perceiving and dealing with external conditions is directly shaped by domestic public opinion, culture, and political life.

I have organized the book according to presidential administrations to reflect my conviction that the Presidency is the dominant influence on our foreign policy and the prime molder of public opinion about our foreign policies. As the preeminent national figure, the President is best able to dramatize foreign-policy issues and win public support for them at home. The main issues of postwar foreign policy, therefore, are examined in relation to each President's personal style and dominant political strategy.

My emphasis on the requirement for Presidential leadership in foreign policy reflects my skepticism of the common democratic assumption that great public attention to foreign policy would improve its quality. On the contrary, I think it can be demonstrated that some of the rigidities in our policies today are perpetuated by a highly attentive public that must be heeded on certain issues. The President who tries to mobilize active public support for specific issues may well find his options restricted later on by the domestic spotlight on his foreign policies. By contrast, the President who encourages broad public deference but less attention to specific policies often gains more latitude in handling complex foreign-policy issues than he would have in the face of strong expectations from a highly aroused public.

On the other hand, the administration that governs without active public support, relying instead on broad public deference, is vulnerable too, for public opinion can be aroused against it with the charge that it has been unconcerned about vital public issues. And in the long run an active public has an important constructive influence on policy-making: a change in the public's view forces the government to reassess its policies and helps in the reassessment process. Furthermore, a better-informed and more interested public is a distinct asset in international politics, where the strength of a democracy must often rest on the resolution of an informed public.

Many of the ideas and interpretations presented here were developed in the early sixties during a valuable two-year stay at the Washington Center of Foreign Policy Research. Part of this stay was supported by a Rockefeller Foundation fellowship. In the formative phase of writing I was particularly influenced by H. Bradford Westerfield and Frederick L. Holborn. Seyom Brown, John M. Blum, and Robert E. Osgood helped by commenting on the manuscript. The book, with its faults, is mine, but for its merits, I have depended upon these friends and colleagues in particular. Marjorie Schubert bore the main burden of typing and duplicating the manuscript. Finally, my children and my wife, Merylyn, felt the full weight of writing done in addition to my regular research duties.

Paul Y. Hammond

Contents

Chapter 4   Eisenhower: The Momentum of the First Term   59

Chapter 5   Eisenhower: The Inertia of the Second Term   95

The Cold War Years:
American Foreign Policy Since 1945

chapter **1**

Public Life and Foreign Affairs in Postwar America: An Introduction

In the United States the President normally towers above all other public figures in the handling of foreign relations. Whether we like it or not, he is the dominant "first" among "equals."

It is true that he has no monopoly in the formulation or conduct of foreign policy: Congress can legislate important changes in foreign relations, particularly through its control over federal expenditures. It often appropriates much less than the President requests for foreign economic assistance and has frequently added provisos to foreign-aid funds. A recent proviso, for instance, penalizes aid recipients who buy "sophisticated" military equipment from other countries.

The President also lacks exclusive control over the linkages with the external world. Some linkages, such as business and private communications, he cannot control at all for most practical purposes; most, such as the mass media—newspapers, radio, and television—he can manipulate only for a political price that may be high, for the press corps that interprets the news output of the government is diverse and suspicious. Yet no one but the President normally controls most external linkages for *any* price.

In foreign affairs, more than in any other area, the President is able to rise above party politics, or partisanship. This is not a statement about his virtues. Generally it is to his advantage to stand above partisanship when he can, for it adds to his congressional and public support. Yet he is never wholly disentangled from political concerns. The domestic constraints on his conduct of foreign relations are normally expressed in terms of political criticism and opposition, but not always along party lines.

These remarks do not set our foreign affairs apart from other kinds of political issues in this country. With domestic as well as foreign-policy issues, political leaders persistently compete for support across party lines. The lines of party identity are fluid, and political interest groups overlap. A textile worker, for example, may favor trade protection against Japanese and other imports, but he may want Japanese electronic and optical products to be fully competitive in the American market. He may be Polish or Hungarian and cling to the hope of a rollback of Communist power in Eastern Europe, while preferring a diplomatic settlement in Vietnam because he has sons of military age. He will then be a protectionist and a free trader, a "hawk" and a "dove," all at once.

In the chapters that follow, the President's role as political leader will be prominent in the explanation of national foreign-policy behavior. Certain aspects of public opinion, however, also influence our foreign policies. Opinion surveys and voting analyses indicate that the American voting public can be divided into several strata according to how much interest the voters normally have in foreign affairs, how well informed they are about foreign affairs, and how likely their voting behavior is to be influenced by foreign-policy issues. Normally, foreign affairs have distinctly lower priority for the voter than do most domestic issues. Usually, the constituency interested in foreign affairs and knowledgeable about it is very small; therefore, politicians correctly assume that domestic issues play a more important role in determining voting behavior and other political acts.

However, foreign issues cannot always be ignored, for they have played an important role in certain critical elections. In the 1916 presidential campaign the supporters of Woodrow Wilson played successfully on the growing public perception of a potential external threat by adopting the slogan "He kept us out of war!" Franklin

D. Roosevelt made a similarly successful appeal to the electorate in 1940. Both wars, it is clear, cut deeply into the public consciousness, though they ultimately had dissimilar effects on the political positions of the incumbent Presidents. Relating the issues raised by these wars to voting behavior is not easy with the available survey data. But we have rich and reliable data indicating that the Korean War, for example, was a salient political issue for millions of American voters in the 1952 presidential election. The messages in the mass media have a special impact when a personal followup occurs, such as the military draft. The economic recovery of Europe in the late forties meant little to millions of American voters. But the war in Korea was directly relevant because millions of voters or their kinfolk fought in it or expected to fight. It is also fairly clear that the more public attention Korea drew, the more impatient the public became. Protracted involvement was not popular, and many felt that we ought to end the war as soon as possible.

World War II, by contrast, generated a high degree of public unity in this country—mainly because once involved in that war, the United States went all out (or seemed to) to get it over with. The public remained united by the objective of early military victory. In order to develop and maintain this wide public consensus, Roosevelt's Administration excluded as wartime issues the nature of the postwar political settlement and the American postwar involvement in international affairs.

How much Roosevelt himself understood these postwar considerations is not our concern here, though the main lines of his wartime policy suggest that he did grasp them. Wartime planning in Washington, for example, was based on the accurate expectation that once the war was over, American public interest in foreign involvement—and support for it—would quickly subside. This expectation was reflected in Roosevelt's statement that the United States would not be able to keep troops in Europe after the war for more than two years.

An early wartime strategy was to create a network of legal commitments associated with what became the United Nations that would institutionalize the international role of the United States— in effect, to routinize and legitimize our role so as to put it above postwar partisan controversy. At the same time, these multilateral instruments would assure that international demands could be kept small. The United Nations, not the United States, would keep the peace and protect the security of its members.

Before the war was over, however, American officials began to interpret international events as requiring considerable unilateral American action—acts that required the mustering of public support for them. In attempting to generate this support, the President has often paid a substantial price in domestic politics. A major task of every postwar President has been the reconciliation of the demands of foreign affairs with the limitations of domestic politics, as he and his Administration assess both.

chapter 2

Truman's First Term: The Beginning of the Cold War

temp. alliance

The World War II coalition against Germany, Italy, and Japan had linked the United States with the Soviet Union as well as with Great Britain, the British Commonwealth, the exile governments of the defeated European states, and China. As the war drew to a close, Soviet-American relations began to deteriorate. Wartime cooperation had not been close, and the war provided no experience in conducting integrated multilateral operations with the Russians or in the mutual give-and-take that could absorb the stresses of the postwar adjustment.

operating several countries

The wartime collaboration had consisted almost solely of an expedient alignment against a common enemy. With the defeat of Germany, opposing perspectives and interests rapidly flared into open diplomatic conflict. Russia expected the defeat of Germany to bring security to her western frontiers through the establishment of friendly regimes in Eastern Europe. At the very least Moscow wanted Eastern Europe within her acknowledged sphere of influence. The British accepted in principle the concept of spheres of influence as a basis for postwar settlement, but since Britain had gone to war to save Poland from Germany she could hardly abandon the Poles to Russian control now.

As for the United States, the war with Germany had established an American interest in European security that included both the Eastern and Western sectors. Moreover, we disagreed with the British view that the establishment of spheres of influence could provide a stable basis for a postwar settlement. The U.S. State Department persistently advocated an ambitious new international system—what was to become the United Nations—rather than regional spheres. The American interest in Eastern Europe had domestic electoral origins as well: Roosevelt seriously thought that if he lost Eastern Europe to the Soviets he would alienate the Poles and other East European ethnic groups among the American voters. (In fact he was not far from the truth.)

Finally, the Soviet Union in 1945 was a totalitarian government in many respects more ominous than was Nazi Germany. This fact sharpened the conflict on both sides. For the Soviet Union, friendly governments in Eastern Europe had to be replicas of the Russian state. For the United States, the spread of Soviet police-state apparatus into Eastern Europe was more than Russia needed to assure her security—hardly an appropriate sequel to the defeat of Hitler. Finally, if Russia were to control Eastern Europe, Western Europe would be highly vulnerable to Soviet might.

The Soviet totalitarianism, moreover, did not limit its aspirations to the security of Russian territory and its approaches. As the wartime collaboration faded, Moscow drew local Communist parties into conflict with the nationalistic interests of their governments in Western Europe and even in the United States (where the Communist party became an irritant, though not a threat).

In its most precise form, then, the American perception of the Soviet menace at the end of World War II focused mainly on the actual or potential use of Soviet armed force, coupled with internal subversion, in areas along the Soviet borderlands where American interests were involved. At the same time, the United States was interested in the Soviet borderland because we sought a universalist postwar settlement. Russian regionalism and American universalism, as a result, collided head on, and this conflict was aggravated by the universalism of the Communist dogma. Walter Lippmann termed what followed the "Cold War"—a far-reaching hostility between the two "superpowers."

At the same time, other political factors were changing at a breathtaking rate. World War II had left Europe prostrate. In China the culmination of a civil war between Chiang Kai-shek's Nationalists and the Communists—postponed for a decade by the Japanese threat—now took place. Elsewhere in Asia and in Africa, the war had set loose forces of national independence and political revolution by demonstrating that Europe's political dominance on both continents could be challenged. The war catalyzed profound changes in the political patterns of the world and launched an era of decolonization that saw Southeast Asia, the Indian subcontinent, and most of Africa divide into a variety of independent states.

This was the setting for the development of postwar American foreign policy, the context in which American political leaders articulated the demands that they perceived as being imposed on the United States by external conditions. And they reconciled these demands with the requirements and constraints of domestic politics.

CLIMBING INTO THE SADDLE

Most major components of the United States Cold War posture were developed during the Truman Administration (1945–53), after Franklin D. Roosevelt's death in mid-April 1945 made Harry S. Truman President of the United States. Truman was an experienced but colorless politician. His political career had begun in the mediocrity of the Pendergast machine in Jackson County, Missouri, where he was a county judge for ten years, and most of his Senate career had been undistinguished. Truman gained national prominence, however, from his chairmanship of a Senate investigating committee established in 1941 to deal with mismanagement in the defense effort. His handling of the committee hinted at a deep concern with the larger purposes of public life that became more apparent later, and he was largely successful in his efforts to avoid excessive congressional zeal in overseeing the war effort. Truman's nomination for the Vice-Presidency on the Democratic ticket in 1944 left men of stronger views and bearing—among them James F. Byrnes, an able and ambitious South Carolinian, and Henry A. Wallace, the brilliant but erratic incumbent Vice-President—standing in the wings.

Truman came to the Presidency without the broad experience in urban (and urbane) politics that Franklin Roosevelt had gained by 1933, without the solid international and national stature that Eisenhower had achieved by 1953, without the dazzling success of Kennedy in capturing control of the national Democratic party by 1960, and without Johnson's demonstrated mastery of the Senate. Truman was not a heroic figure. He could be wrong; he could be petty; and he could be highly partisan. In the largest issues of his Administration, however, he rose to the occasion, acting out his own schoolboy image of great Presidents. "History taught me. . . ." he wrote and said many times. Sophisticated historians could quibble about the validity of the lessons that Truman learned from history, but these lessons were an important part of his public philosophy. They helped to make him an overachiever in the Presidency, a man made great, if great he was, more by his convictions than by his capabilities.

Truman became President as the European phase of the war drew to a close. The Allied armies from the west, under the command of General Dwight D. Eisenhower, and the Soviet armies from the east had converged on Germany. Men and materiel were already being transferred to the Pacific theater to complete the defeat of Japan. Germany surrendered in May, Japan in August.

The war operations required little direction from the new President at first, as did the effort already in full swing to structure the postwar international system with multilateral institutions. A more flexible international monetary system had been worked out at Bretton Woods in 1944, and arrangements had already been made for establishing a formal United Nations organization. In his first press statement as President, Truman announced that the San Francisco Conference, scheduled to begin two weeks later to write the United Nations Charter, would proceed as planned. The conference ended June 26, and the Senate ratified the Charter July 28. Meanwhile, Germany had surrendered on May 8, and Truman, arranging a meeting with Stalin and Churchill, had begun to address himself to the more pressing problems of the war's end.

The Big Three met in mid-July in the heart of defeated Germany to settle the outstanding issues of their wartime alliance —primarily the future of Germany. Roosevelt's meeting with Churchill and Stalin at Yalta in the Crimea in February 1945 had produced some optimism in the American delegation about working with the Russians. The mood of the American delegation returning from the Potsdam Conference five months later, however, was much grimmer. The diplomats had grappled with the issues growing out of the tightening grip of Soviet power in Eastern Europe—the question of what constituted a "broadly representative" government in Poland and the other new Soviet satellites, the exclusion of Western authorities from Eastern Germany, and the unwavering Soviet demand for large reparations from Germany. The American delegation had gone to Potsdam troubled by the developments in Eastern Europe but ill-prepared for the utter Soviet noncooperation that it encountered.[1]

Potsdam proved to be a holding action for the Big Three. It settled nothing of consequence. It did forestall head-on clashes over rival interests in Europe during a period when tragic outbreaks of violence between the two victorious sides were dangerously plausible. The heads of state dealt with most issues by referring them to a conference of foreign ministers or, as in the case of Poland, to future peace-treaty negotiations (which meant, on the whole, an acknowledgment of the Soviet-dominated status quo). Soviet behavior sharpened Truman's antagonism. But it was easier to resolve to "coddle" Stalin no more than to discover what steps would avoid "coddling" and to resolve to take them.

Yalta had already come under partisan attack, with the charge that Roosevelt gave Eastern Europe to Russia. Potsdam was to meet similar charges. A partisan breach thus opened in Washington over the wartime conferences. American negotiations with the Chinese Communists in 1946 (in an attempt to bring the Nationalists and Communists into a coalition government) served only to widen this breach.

Unfortunately, though attacking the Roosevelt and Truman records in negotiating with the Russians was fair politics, it did not face the central policy issue that was to confront this country over the next five years: what level and kinds of effort should the United States make to cope with what it perceived to be the Soviet threat? Equally important, though easier to lose sight of, was the question of

1 Paul Y. Hammond, "Directives for the Occupation of Germany: The Washington Story," *American Civil-Military Decisions,* Harold Stein, ed. (University, Ala.: Univ. of Alabama Press, 1962), pp. 434–435.

how to minimize antagonism between the United States and the Soviet Union. A single answer now came to be applied to both issues: the United States could get along best with the Soviet Union if it operated from a position of strength; any aggravation of Soviet hostility that American firmness would produce would be more than offset by the stabilizing effect of American strength. The analogy with the prewar appeasement of Hitler was often drawn in these early postwar years: giving in to aggressors only expanded their appetites.

The setting that Truman faced as a new President in 1945 was much like the one to be faced by the new President in 1969—a nation turning inward, tired of foreign burdens, yet aware of its central position as a world power. It became Truman's role to preside over the government in Washington while helping to recast public expectations substantially. And in 1945 he had few political assets, except good will, to help him carry out these tasks.

Truman was to lead the nation into the Cold War. His way of leading and the way the United States responded to what the public and its leaders perceived to be the threat of Soviet Communism undoubtedly contributed to the deepening bipolar hostility. A contemporary criticism leveled at Truman was that he had set a low standard for postwar Presidents. If nothing else, this criticism proved to be based on too optimistic a view of the future. For the standard of achievement in foreign relations that Truman set has not been surpassed by any other postwar President.

When the Truman Administration began in 1945, Washington anticipated a much smaller effort in foreign relations than was actually made over the years that followed. Wartime diplomacy had reflected President Roosevelt's expectation that American troops would not be stationed on the continent of Europe for more than two years after the end of the war. And in fact strong popular pressure to bring the troops home developed immediately after the Japanese surrender in August. As General Marshall, the head of the United States Army and Air Force, explained to a joint session of Congress a month later, "The rate of demobilization has been determined by transportation facilities. . . . It has no relationship whatsoever to the size of the Army in the future. . . ."[2]

2 Quoted in *United States Defense Policies Since World War II*, H. Doc. 85:1, No. 100, p. 5.

Roosevelt's postwar plans had hinged instead on the police-keeping powers of the United Nations. Truman at first accepted the architecture of these plans as part of the presidential office thrust upon him.

Churchill has written of the "deadly hiatus" between Roosevelt's fading strength and Truman's gradually tightening grip on world problems.

> *In this melancholy void one President could not act and the other could not know. Neither the military chiefs nor the State Department received the guidance they required. The former confined themselves to their professional sphere; the latter did not comprehend the issues involved. The indispensable political direction was lacking at the moment when it was most needed. The United States stood on the scene of victory, master of world fortunes, but without a true and coherent design.*[3]

The reasons for what Churchill saw as a "melancholy void" went beyond Roosevelt's illness, Truman's newness, and the tendency of the American military to avoid political issues and of the State Department to fix its attention elsewhere. Throughout the war, the State Department had been reduced largely to handling only the routine mechanics of diplomacy and writing papers about postwar policy, while the important external actions of this country took place overwhelmingly in the military sphere. The military, in turn, were anxious to keep their sphere of action as free of political constraints as possible. Roosevelt encouraged both Departments in their propensity to avoid settling the issues that grew out of the war because he, in turn, wanted to prevent these questions from intruding on the prosecution of the war itself. Finally, as long as he was Vice-President, Truman remained largely uninformed about the military and political issues of wartime negotiations because of Roosevelt's tendency to handle these matters personally.

When Truman became President, many government officials in the State Department and the armed services shared the view that it was essential to get along peacefully with the Soviet Union after the war. This belief was a carryover from a wartime judg-

[3] Winston S. Churchill, *Triumph and Tragedy* (Boston: Houghton Mifflin, 1953), p. 455.

ment that after the war the Soviet Union would be the dominant power in continental Europe. Cooperation with the Russians was a matter of prudence, a major necessity. It depended not on trust but on the expectation that the United States could not or should not maintain enough power in Europe to permit it to follow any other policy. As Churchill suggests, therefore, the State and War Departments both obstructed an early shift to a more belligerent posture toward the Soviet Union in the spring and summer of 1945.

But there were minority voices in the government who took a harder line toward Russia. Churchill and Averill Harriman, the American ambassador in Moscow, had been stating the case against the Russians, and Truman had unquestionably heard them. Harriman has recalled to Cabell Philips that he rushed back to Washington after Roosevelt's death to warn Truman about the Russians in order to stiffen our resolve to demand an independent government in Poland.

> I had talked with Mr. Truman for only a few minutes when I began to realize that the man had a real grasp of the situation. . . . He had read all the cables and reports that had passed between me and the State Department, going back for months. He knew the facts and the sequence of events, and he had a keen understanding of what they meant.[4]

Harriman and Churchill were not the only voices in Washington warning of the Soviet challenge to Western interests. Stimson and McCloy in the War Department talked in terms of power and interests in Europe. They and the Wall Street lawyers they had recruited to man the civilian posts of the vastly expanded military establishment hardly shared the euphoria about Russia prevalent in wartime Washington. Stimson and McCloy, fearing the creation of a power vacuum into which Russia could move, had opposed Secretary of the Treasury Morgenthau's proposal that the German economic apparatus be dismantled after the war. Still, they backed the Army Chief of Staff, General Marshall, in his insistence that postwar politics not interfere with the efficient winning of the war.

In May, during the closing days of the war in Europe, Eisenhower proposed to withdraw the Allied armies under his command

[4] Cabell Philips, *The Truman Presidency: The History of a Triumphant Succession* (New York: Macmillan, 1966), p. 79.

westward to the lines that would mark the occupation zones of Germany, established by agreement with the Russians eight months earlier. Eisenhower and the Joint Chiefs of Staff felt that United States compliance with the zone agreements would help to ensure Soviet cooperation in setting up the joint machinery for the administration of occupied Germany. When Churchill protested, Truman, according to his later account, responded that

> *we had no intention of extending ourselves beyond those zones. I took this position after consulting with our military chiefs. Russian tactics and aims were, of course, of much concern to us, and I agreed with Churchill on the seriousness of the situation. But I could not agree to going back on our commitments. Apart from that, there were powerful military considerations which we could not and should not disregard.*[5]

With a seemingly awesome task ahead of them in Asia, the military chiefs wanted to concentrate on defeating Germany. They insisted that the Soviet Union be brought into the war in Asia to help (Harriman wanted the Russians kept out). When it came to deciding in late July whether, and then how, to use atomic bombs, Truman's decision to drop them on Hiroshima and Nagasaki reflected the same dominant concern with military objectives and military costs, particularly in American lives.

Roosevelt—"Dr. Win-the-War"—had shared these views, but he had never venerated military advisers as much as Truman did. *It was Truman's propensity to follow his military advisers, rather than his slowness in perceiving a Soviet menace to our interests in Europe, that constituted the faltering of political leadership Churchill perceived when the military objectives of the war were reached in 1945.*

Furthermore, what Churchill perceived as a hiatus between Roosevelt and Truman was in part a gap between the Truman Administration's perception and its action. After the end of the war it became much more difficult to find practical ways to respond to the Soviet challenge to American interests that fit with the expectations in Washington about the postwar role of the United States in international affairs.

[5] Harry S Truman, *Memoirs*, Vol. I: *Years of Decision* (New York: Doubleday, 1958), pp. 298–299.

The Administration could not abandon in late 1945 or 1946 as easily as did its critics the viewpoint that cooperation with the Russians was a matter of necessity. The costs of losing all cooperation from the Russians were more immediate for officials who were responsible for administering occupation forces in Germany and Austria, who handled relief and rehabilitation problems in these countries, in Italy, and in the former enemy-occupied states of Western Europe, or who worried about the vulnerability of Greece, Turkey, Iran, China, or Korea to Soviet military threats.

Indeed, the postwar role of the United States, as visualized by the American public-opinion élites, assumed not only that Russia would be cooperative but that the international system could be stabilized with a minimum of American involvement, if necessary through the United Nations. Our conflict with Russia over postwar objectives provided a convenient impetus for adapting to a world that turned out to differ from the one we had anticipated in several other respects as well. American policy would have had to undergo substantial modification to expand our involvement abroad during the postwar era even without the conflict with Russian interests. But it was easier to perceive and present our modifications of postwar policy as responses to Communist challenges than as adaptations to a variety of changing or newly recognized conditions.

As evidence mounted after Potsdam, the perception of the Soviet Union as our enemy became increasingly strong in Washington and among the American public. In 1946 Russia exerted military pressure in Iran and against Turkey to gain special privileges in the use of the Dardanelles. In response, Truman dispatched the Sixth Fleet into the Eastern Mediterranean on a diplomatic pretext. This, the first American military reaction to a Soviet military threat in the postwar era, was limited to a redeployment of existing forces.

REACTING TO COLD WAR COSTS

The second phase in the Truman Administration's response to Soviet belligerence was its effort to reduce the costs that Soviet noncooperation was adding to America's economic burdens in Europe. Since the war, the four occupying powers (the United States, the Soviet Union, Great Britain, and France) had each governed a separate zone in Germany. Mindful of the imminent prospect that the four powers might not work together harmoniously, Byrnes had eliminated from the Potsdam protocol any wording that could provide grounds for direct Soviet collection of economic reparations in the Western zones. This, of course, did not eliminate the reparations themselves; it meant merely that they had to be delivered to the Russians by Western authorities. By the summer of 1945 it had become evident that the United States would have to prop up the economies of all three non-Soviet zones. Thus, much of the Western zones' share of the $10 billion in economic reparations that Russia demanded—and was getting—from Germany would, as Truman had bluntly told Stalin at Potsdam, be paid indirectly by the American taxpayer. Moreover, Soviet intransigence, combined with French determination to keep Germany divided, paralyzed the four-power occupation machinery. Together, these circumstances precipitated changes in American policy.

In May 1946 the United States zone commander, General Lucius Clay, suspended deliveries of economic reparations to the Soviet Union, thus ending Western cooperation with Soviet demands for reparations. In order to cope more effectively with the economic chaos of Germany, Byrnes offered to merge the American zone with the British and French and abandoned the agreed policy of holding German industrial production at 50 percent below the prewar level. At Stuttgart, in September, Byrnes gave a more positive tone to these steps: "Germany is a part of Europe and European recovery would be low indeed if Germany with her great resources . . . turned into a poorhouse." He thus gave support to long-held convictions in the State Department that reconciliation with Germany was in the interest of the United States. In January 1947 the British (but not the French) agreed to the merger—the first step in the establishment of the Federal Republic of Germany (which eventually gained the necessary French cooperation).

Merging the American and British zones did not mean that we were abandoning all cooperation with the Soviet Union in Germany but rather that we were seeking substitutes for Soviet cooperation to cope with Germany's political and economic collapse. The merger was intended to make Germany not only self-sustaining but useful in the economic recovery of Western Europe as a whole. It was not a commitment by the United States to extend its power to Europe but rather a move that would enable us to reduce our forces there. The merger pitted a policy of zonal action to reconstruct the German (and Western European) economy against a Soviet appeal for German national unity, which, with its concomitant demand for German plant, equipment, and current production as reparations, would have placed the German economy at the service of Russia. Implicit in the Russian plan was an acceptance of German and Western European economic chaos as compatible with Soviet interests.

Churchill, now out of power, gave classic expression to this phase in the break with Russia in a speech given at Fulton, Missouri, in March 1946. He referred to the new Russian imperialism as an "iron curtain" that had descended across Europe and advocated a "fraternal association" of the United States and Great Britain, French reconciliation with Germany, and European political integration. The American press hailed the speech for its candor.

Yet, it was one thing to sound the alarm and quite another to make effective responses. No one—and certainly not Churchill, whose country was economically prostrate—had recommended the remobilization of national power in any form.

MOBILIZING ACTION AND SUPPORT

Before the merger of the American and British zones of Germany could actually be accomplished in 1947, the Truman Administration had decided to increase its commitments in Europe, bringing it into the third phase of its response to Russia. Now it could exploit some of the advantages of its incumbency, but it also faced special problems in winning support from Congress and the public. In order to understand what those problems were we must go back and examine the domestic side of the foreign-policy debate that took place in 1945–46.

In September 1945, armed with a report from his war-reconversion director that predicted "an immediate and large dislocation in our economy,"[6] Truman had called Congress into

6 Quoted in Philips, *op. cit.*, p. 103.

special session and presented it with a staggering program of domestic legislation. He asked for strong powers to cope with reconversion problems, a modest tax reduction, a large increase in congressional pay, and a full program of basic social-welfare legislation and economic reforms—several measures to deal with unemployment and the stabilization of the peacetime economy, a huge housing program, and the expansion of programs for the development of our natural resources. Later, this program, somewhat restated, would be called the "Fair Deal." The breadth and magnitude of these proposals indicate the Administration's great concern about postwar domestic problems. (By contrast, when his Administration first came to grips with a peacetime military budget, Truman indicated that not more than a third of the federal budget, after paying interest on the national debt, was to be allocated for national defense.)

Republican leaders rightly considered Truman's legislative message the "kickoff" of the 1946 congressional campaign, for it was an aggressive partisan move by a President seeking a political base for his leadership—the first major indication that Truman intended to be more than just a caretaker President who would serve only through 1948. Truman's message also helped to alienate business leaders, who saw it (correctly) as an effort to perpetuate the significant powers that government had gained in wartime.[7] Finally, it cast a distinctly partisan shadow across the Administration's efforts to cope with inflationary wage and price pressures over the next two years. By indicating that he intended to extend New Deal social and economic programs and, above all, to take the initiative in domestic politics, Truman had fired the opening shot not only of the 1946 congressional elections but of postwar partisanship in domestic affairs.

But he was not permitted to pick his own grounds for partisan battles. Before the 1946 elections Truman's China policy came under partisan attack when a venerable Republican leader—former Secretary of War Patrick J. Hurley—came home from his post as ambassador to China to report in October 1945 and then resigned. In 1944 Roosevelt had sent Hurley to Chungking, the wartime Chinese capital, to help bring about political and military unity between Mao's Communists and Chiang Kai-shek's Nationalist

[7] *Ibid.*, p. 104.

government. Hurley had gone favorably disposed toward the Chinese Communists but had rapidly come to side with the Nationalist regime. After a year in China he had all but abandoned the effort to bring the two groups together. Having resigned, he charged (correctly) that State Department officials had been undermining his policies. His criticism was neither partisan nor ideological until he turned from questioning the personal loyalty of State Department officials to him and began to question their public loyalty, charging Communist sympathizing in the State Department. It was the beginning of a long and tragic vilification of the China specialists in the State Department in which distinctive and mediocre service alike were condemned.

Our China policy had been permitted to drift with Hurley's shift in attitude. To dispel the doubts raised by his disturbing and surprising resignation, the Administration now reaffirmed its goal of a "strong, united, and democratic China" and dispatched General Marshall as Ambassador to Chungking with instructions to broaden the base of Chiang's government by including representatives of other groups.

By March Marshall had negotiated a truce between Communists and Nationalists and returned to Washington for a visit. But the truce soon crumbled. By summer the Communist forces had gained substantial strength and confidence and paid little attention to the mediator from Washington. Thereafter, Marshall's role, like Hurley's, increasingly concentrated on the Nationalist government, persuading it to take measures of conciliation toward the Communists (which were ignored by Mao) and of reform in the hope of winning wider mass support.

By November 1946, when the congressional elections occurred, the situation in China was still too confusing to serve as an effective partisan issue, but it did add to the anxieties about international affairs and provided Republican candidates with an occasion to state their suspicions about the State Department. Republicans leveled their main criticisms of the incumbent government at Roosevelt's handling of the Yalta Conference and at Truman's negotiations at Potsdam for making legal concessions to the Russians —criticisms that implied that the Communist "menace" (as our conflicting postwar interests with Russia increasingly came to appear in the popular accounts) could be met without incurring costs to the United States. *It is quite clear that until after the 1946 elections both the Administration and its critics treated the objective of "getting tough" with the Russians as though it had little to do with the federal budget.*

After the elections, Truman replaced Secretary of State Byrnes with Marshall. It was a politically prudent move, with a Democratic Administration facing a Republican-controlled Congress for the first time in sixteen years, though it also reflected Truman's high regard for Marshall. Moreover, there had been vexing difficulties with Byrnes. They had climaxed after the Moscow Foreign Ministers' Conference in December 1945 when Byrnes attempted to arrange a radio address to the nation on the results of the conference without reporting first to Truman.

Two close observers of Byrnes's deteriorating relationship with Truman had been Dean Acheson, the Undersecretary of State, and John Foster Dulles, a special Republican adviser to Byrnes. Both men were to become Secretaries of State themselves, and both evidently learned from the firing of Byrnes that the Secretary of State is the President's man.

THE TRUMAN DOCTRINE: RESOURCES AND COMMITMENTS

With the convening of the 80th Congress in January 1947 under Republican leadership, it hardly seemed likely that the United States would make major new foreign commitments that would tax the federal treasury. House Speaker Joseph Martin promptly declared as a Republican goal a 20 percent cut in income taxes and commensurate spending reductions. The most reasonable prognosis was for two years of congressional dominance and financial retrenchment in Washington. Instead, what followed was a period of vigorous presidential competition with Congress in domestic affairs and strong (though often unchallenged) presidential leadership in foreign affairs that guided the United States into major foreign political and fiscal obligations abroad. Several circumstances produced this unexpected presidential success in foreign affairs: an economic crisis in Europe; the appointment of a new Secretary of State; and Truman's own leadership—often erratic, but tough in responding to the large issues of foreign policy and national security.

January 1947 brought a winter of record-breaking severity to Western Europe. The Labour government in Great Britain, faced with economic difficulties long anticipated but little acknowledged, had calculated the nation's fuel needs only for a normal year. The result was a shortage so severe that it slowed down the economy, causing further economic difficulties. The severe winter revealed economic and political weakness on the other side of the Channel, too. "Last week," Anne O'Hare McCormick wrote from Paris in *The New York Times* in mid-February,

> *it was suddenly brought home to us that we are now in the front line. . . . The crisis in Britain and France pointed up a truth the United States knows but shrinks from facing. They are primarily economic crises, signs of the difficulty of treating postwar breakdown by democratic means. They reveal how battered and shaken are the old strongholds of democracy in Europe, and how few these strongholds are. Most of all they throw the ball to us, giving notice that if freedom as we understand it is to survive it's up to the United States to save it.*[8]

In the same period, Marshall became Secretary of State and immediately began mobilizing the resources of the Department of State to meet the problems he saw. "Most of the other countries of the world," he told a Princeton audience in a Washington's-birthday address that year,

> *find themselves exhausted economically, financially, physically. If the world is to get on its feet, if the productive facilities of the world are to be restored, if democratic processes in many countries are to resume their functioning, a strong lead and definite assistance from the United States will be necessary.*[9]

This phase in our response to the postwar challenge of Russia depended upon a belief that Russia threatened vital American security interests through a combination of political and military subversion, backed up by military blackmail, in conditions of economic prostration. Such a perception of the Soviet menace led

[8] Quoted in Joseph M. Jones, *The Fifteen Weeks* (New York: Viking, 1955), p. 84.
[9] *Ibid.*, p. 108.

us to shoulder definite obligations and provide substantial resources, but we avoided a direct confrontation with Russia.

As the European national economies slumped we began to take rapid action in the spring of 1947 in order to bolster Europe's economic development and integration. According to the State Department's key memorandum on the proposals that were developed, the threat to Western Europe was due largely to "the disruptive effect of the war" rather than to Communist activities. But, before these ideas had come into focus, the slumping economy of Western Europe had produced a power vacuum in the Eastern Mediterranean that required further American action.

In late February 1947 the British informed Washington that their economic hardships would force them to reduce their commitment to Greece and Turkey after March 31. In less than three weeks President Truman had recommended to Congress a $400 million military-aid program for the two countries. Linked to it was the "Truman Doctrine," the tendentious and appealing idea that the United States must "support free peoples who are resisting attempted subjugation by armed minorities or by outside pressures," as President Truman put it in his nationwide radio address. "I believe," he went on, "that we must assist free peoples to work out their own destinies in their own way. I believe that our help should be primarily through economic and financial aid which is essential to economic stability and orderly political processes." The ideological cast of the Truman Doctrine was restrained, but unmistakeable. The President ended by saying:

> The seeds of totalitarian regimes are nurtured by misery and want. They spread and grow in the evil soil of poverty and strife. They reach their full growth when the hope of a people for a better life has died.
>
> We must keep that hope alive.
>
> The free peoples of the world look to us for support in maintaining their freedoms.
>
> If we falter in our leadership, we may endanger the peace of the world—and we shall surely endanger the welfare of our own nation.[10]

The Greek-Turkish aid program served a limited purpose: to help the Greek government against a Greek Communist guerrilla

[10] Harry S Truman, *Memoirs*, Vol. II: *Years of Trial and Hope*, p. 106.

war supported by Albania, Yugoslavia, and Bulgaria and to help the Turkish government withstand Soviet pressure for joint bases on the Dardanelles. It served as the dramatic beginning of the Truman Administration's successful effort to assume the task that Marshall had referred to at Princeton in February. Because its purpose was limited, military in nature, and urgent, the Greek-Turkish aid program was a highly satisfactory rallying point for overriding the congressional mood of severe budget cutting and tax cutting.

But the program was not too urgent to forego prior consultation with congressional leaders. Having resolved to act, Truman had Marshall and Acheson help him explain the need for the Greek-Turkish aid program privately to congressional leaders. Republican Senator Vandenberg garnered further support from among his party colleagues.

At two White House meetings Vandenberg had indicated that the price for congressional cooperation would be a "full and frank statement" by the President. In effect, Vandenberg was asking for two things: that the President strongly commit himself publicly to the aid program and that the rationale for the program be couched in the same language that had impressed the congressional leaders—with reference to Soviet aggressive interests in the eastern Mediterranean and beyond and the potential consequences for American security interests of not countering them. Vandenberg's first demand required only that the President play his presidential role, and Truman was happy to oblige. The second demand could have meant several things—a denunciation of historic Russian aggressiveness or of the world revolutionary aspirations of Communism; a description of the East-West struggle; an indication that the Greek-Turkish program was only the beginning of a larger and more costly effort; or reference at least to the trouble in Western Europe caused by economic chaos and domestic Communism. Vandenberg evidently meant something of all these things, for the distinctions among them were only just beginning to emerge. But what he meant primarily, and what his congressional colleagues meant when they supported him, was that the action was to be taken in pursuit of American interests, not humanitarian ideals, and that the easiest way to win political support for them was to talk about the threat of Communism. "The problem of Greece," Vandenberg wrote a congressional colleague at the time, "cannot be isolated by itself. On the contrary, it is probably symbolic of the world-wide ideological clash between Eastern communism and Western democracy; and it may easily be the thing which requires us to make some very fateful and far-reaching decisions."[11]

In his public message, Truman did not describe Soviet expansion in the same frank terms that he and Acheson had used privately with congressional leaders. He referred emphatically to the larger considerations that lay behind the Greek-Turkish program but without being specific. The result, paradoxically, was a landmark Cold War statement about the ideological and political challenge of Communism. But the program itself in no sense typified the thinking in the American government in the spring of 1947. For it was a narrow and defensive program to improve the military power of two rather poor examples of free or democratic government. The purpose of the public message was *not*, as it appeared to be, to generalize from the Greek-Turkish situation to the military threat of Communism everywhere. On the contrary, the purpose was to suggest the broader context of the response in Greece and Turkey, the political and economic problems of Western Europe, that were at that very time receiving intensive attention.

With Vandenberg's backing the program gained wide bipartisan support both in and out of Congress. Vandenberg also promptly alleviated anxiety that the program would bypass the United Nations by amending the aid bill to provide for withdrawal of American aid if the United Nations were to take equivalent action. After giving it much attention, Congress passed the Greek-Turkish bill in mid-May under the impetus of the Soviet-generated crisis in the Middle East and the breakdown of the Big Four Foreign Ministers' Conference in Moscow in April 1947.

THE MARSHALL PLAN

Meanwhile, Marshall had returned from the Moscow negotiations convinced of the Soviet Union's intent to aggravate the growing economic sickness of Western Europe and that the United

[11] Arthur H. Vandenberg, Jr., ed., *The Private Papers of Senator Vandenberg* (Boston: Houghton Mifflin, 1952), p. 340.

States had to act to bring about European recovery. He had found Acheson in agreement, convinced by the staff work begun in early March.

Their agreement was only one aspect of a remarkable convergence of informed opinion in Washington in the spring of 1947. Recognized Republicans had arrived at much the same conclusion and at a somewhat more methodical pace. Within the wartime Roosevelt Administration in 1945 Stimson and McCloy had struck out against the Morgenthau Plan to (in Churchill's term) "pastoralize" Germany, arguing that German industry was too great an asset for postwar Europe to be thrown away. Byrnes had adopted their view in his Stuttgart speech. In January 1947 John Foster Dulles, the Republican State Department Adviser, in an important speech cleared in advance by Vandenberg and by Thomas E. Dewey, the leader of the Republican party, had advocated the integration of the industrial potential of Germany into Western Europe in such a way as to advance the economic unification of Western Europe. Dulles subsequently accompanied Marshall to Moscow as a special adviser. While they were there, former President Hoover released a report on economic conditions in occupied Germany and Austria that also followed the Stimson-McCloy theme, emphasizing the common problems of the European economy and the need for restoring productivity. (Concern over what the German occupation was costing the United States launched the Hoover study.) Leading journalists—Lippmann in particular, as well as Reston, Childs, the Alsops, and the anonymous reporters of the weekly news magazines—wrote about European economic problems and the responsibility of the United States to act.

Acheson voiced the developing viewpoint of the State Department on May 8 at an obscure meeting in Cleveland, Mississippi. But it was Marshall's speech at the Harvard Commencement on June 5 that launched the effort and gave it a name: the Marshall Plan.

Despite the name his proposal acquired, Marshall made clear that there was no plan:

This is the business of the Europeans. The initiative, I think, must come from Europe. The role of this country should consist of friendly

*aid in the drafting of a European program and of later support of
such a program so far as it may be practical for us to do so. The program should be a joint one, agreed to by a number of, if not all, European nations.*

On a calculated risk that paid off handsomely, the Soviet
Union had not been specifically excluded from the invitation.
Neither France nor Britain was eager to include Russia in the
Marshall program. But the French government was hardly strong
enough to face a showdown with the French Left if the Marshall
Plan began to look like a Western coalition against the East, and
similarly, the Labour government in Britain had no desire to
divide Europe by making an issue of the Soviet Union's participation. For these reasons, Britain and France reluctantly invited the
Soviet government to a tripartite meeting in Paris in late June of
1947. It was a curious meeting. The Russian foreign minister,
Molotov, brought eighty-nine technicians and clerks and a rigid
position against a European program that all but ignored Marshall's speech. Bidault of France and Bevin of England insisted
upon a common European economic-recovery plan, accepting European economic integration in principle, whereupon Molotov and
his delegation, on a signal from Moscow, withdrew, taking with
them any prospect for the Soviet satellites' participation in the
Marshall Plan. Europe had been effectively partitioned—but without any onus on the British or French governments, and very little
on the United States. Sixteen states now set quickly to work.

Meanwhile, in Washington several prestigious government
committees helped the Administration tie down the case for aiding
Europe—one committee on natural resources; another to consider
the impact of foreign aid on the domestic economy; a third, composed of distinguished private citizens and chaired by Harriman,
who was now Secretary of Commerce, to advise on safe magnitudes
of assistance. In the House of Representatives, a Select Committee
on Foreign Aid, chaired by Massachusetts Congressman Christian
Herter, undertook a series of reports about the prospective aid
program. The select committee was a device for counterbalancing
the more conservative congressmen with seniority and power in the
standing committees. By December 19, 1947, when President Truman submitted draft legislation for the European Recovery Pro-

gram to Congress, a remarkable array of political pressures could be brought to bear upon the legislative process.

The Russians had already helped by walking out of the Paris meetings; they were to help again. The Communist coup in Czechoslovakia in late February 1948 and the suspicious death of the Czech Nationalist leader Jan Masaryk in March dramatized the European situation. Western anxieties over an impending Italian national election, in which the Italian Communist party stood a good chance of winning control of Parliament and the growing tensions over the status of West Berlin also helped. (The Soviet Blockade of West Berlin began on June 24 and was preceded by changes in Soviet behavior in Berlin that General Clay noticed and reported in early March.) Congress approved the European Recovery Program at the end of March.

THE BIRTH OF THE WESTERN COALITION

Another phase of the developing American response to the Soviet challenge—the making of military commitments to Western Europe—began at the end of 1947. As soon as Congress had authorized the Marshall Plan expenditures for the first year, the Administration, with the cooperation of the Republican leadership in the House and Senate foreign relations committees, began to lay the legislative groundwork for the North Atlantic Treaty, emphasizing bipartisan support, the goal of European unity, foreign self-reliance, and foreign initiative—factors that had made the Marshall Plan attractive in the United States. In June 1948, with a vote of 64 to 4, the Senate passed the Vandenberg Resolution, expressing support from both Republicans and Democrats for the collective-security measures taking shape in Western Europe. Ostensibly, the initiative for the North Atlantic Treaty came from the Republican side of the Senate; actually, the alliance had begun to take shape within the Administration early in 1948 through discreet diplomatic channels. The British had initiated the fifty-year Brussels Defense Pact, which, with Marshall's encouragement, would become the nucleus of the North Atlantic Treaty.

By October 1948 the United States had reached tentative agreement with the Brussels Pact countries (Britain, France, Belgium, the Netherlands, and Luxembourg) and with Canada on collective defense arrangements. These seven countries decided to invite Norway, Denmark, Iceland, Italy, and Portugal to join them. The twelve signed the NATO pact in Washington in April; the Senate ratified the treaty in July, more than a year after the Vandenberg Resolution. The treaty received broad public and congressional support in this country—partly because the Truman Administration carefully laid the groundwork for its acceptance, as it had done with the Marshall Plan.

When the North Atlantic alliance first took shape in early 1948 few American officials expected the treaty to be followed by an American military-assistance program to help the other members rearm. That summer, however, the Berlin Blockade put immense pressure on the airlift capacity of the United States and focused attention on the conventional Soviet military threat. Originally, the alliance had been intended on both sides of the Atlantic as a way to counter Soviet military blackmail used to promote political instability in Western Europe. The Berlin crisis, however, quickly turned official thinking to narrower military problems. And American officials became concerned about both Europe's military weakness and the limited American forces stationed in Europe. This would not be the last time that broader political considerations shifted to short-range military ones in response to a Cold War crisis.

By the following spring, when the North Atlantic Treaty was signed, plans to proceed with a military assistance program were already well advanced. As soon as the Senate had ratified the treaty on July 21 President Truman requested $1.45 billion for military aid, most of it for the treaty countries. The Truman Administration was now prepared to arm its allies against what was widely perceived in Congress, the executive branch, and among private-opinion élites to be the military menace of the Soviet Union.

THE CHANGE IN U.S. SECURITY POSTURE

In the thirty-four months from January 1947 until October 1949 the peacetime external posture of the United States changed dramatically. The Truman Administration had given up primary reliance on the United Nations for its security and had abandoned the expectation of cooperation with the Soviet Union to conduct a bipolar power struggle with the Russians. It had underwritten first the economic reconstruction and then the military security of Western Europe and had appropriated the first of the billions of dollars these tasks would require—this in spite of the congressional intent at the beginning of the period to cut the budget and taxes.

The vital votes on the Marshall Plan had occurred in 1948, when the prevailing view was that President Truman would not win reelection. These votes represented the high-water mark of postwar bipartisanship, with careful joint preparations between the Democratic Administration and the Republican leaders of Congress to win public support and legislative approval. The Administration could exploit the towering prestige of Senator Vandenberg on the Republican side and the high status that foreign affairs now enjoyed in both the Senate and the House. The behavior of the European states had made the political clearance problem in Washington easier. Their initiatives and visible interest in economic and military integration struck a responsive chord with American officials, who were inclined to see political and economic unification as the solution to Europe's weakness and chaos.

For the Truman Administration, the achievements of these thirty-four months should have been gratifying. Many of them had been approved before the 1948 election, while Truman's political standing was at a low ebb. He had appointed a nonpartisan Secretary of State, General Marshall, and had accepted (somewhat grudgingly) the nonpartisan role assumed by his Secretary of Defense, James F. Forrestal.

As the Administration moved into these massive commitments to Europe, it found the Republican leadership particularly cooperative. Senator Vandenberg, the venerated foreign-policy leader among congressional Republicans, and Thomas Dewey, leader of the Eastern and metropolitan Republicans who represented the party's presidential constituency, were both attracted by the growing link with Europe. If anything, the Eastern Republicans were ahead of the Administration in giving support for the components of the European recovery and rearmament programs—the acceptance of Germany as an essential part of the European economy; reconstruction in order to end American material obligations; and European unification to achieve stability and prosperity.

Formally, the cooperation between the two parties rested on the commitment of both to bipartisanship. But bipartisanship depended upon much more than close White House–Congressional cooperation. Truman's economic and military foreign-aid programs were ambitious enough to mute most claims that the Administration was neglecting the Communist threat abroad. They were constructive enough to appeal to some public idealism or vanity and to avoid charges that the United States was unduly belligerent. They were broad enough to make it difficult for their opponents to invent appealing alternative policies. Above all, they gave the Administration the initiative. *In the postwar era nothing more quickly won the sympathy of the public than a President who seemed to be dealing vigorously with what the public perceived to be an external threat to this country's interests.*

The alternative of greater patience and concessions to the Soviet Union, for which Henry Wallace came to be the leading spokesman, suffered from a special handicap. By 1947 Wallace had already been denied support from regular partisan leaders, so his only hope was to gain influence by winning public support for his policies. But the interest of a wider public in foreign affairs could more likely be aroused by a perception of external threats than by an appeal to patience.

Another choice—to aid Asia more and Europe less—was suppressed for the time being by the broad agreement in Washington that aiding Europe was urgent and primary.

A third choice, a more subtle and flexible one, was posed by the eloquent and prolific career foreign-service officer and Soviet specialist, George Kennan, in a widely read article published in July 1947 under the pseudonym "Mr. X." Kennan attributed Soviet conduct to historic Russian imperialism and to the ideology of Communism, both of which inclined the Soviet Union to be patient, flexible, and persistent in pursuing selected expansionist goals. As he made plain privately within the government, Kennan wanted to stop short of military involvement with Western Europe and, at the same time, not substantially rearm the United States. His view was rooted in a grand and traditional conception of diplomacy: American responses must be flexible. Only limited military force would be necessary. The balance of political factions within the Soviet Union must be taken into account; the militants must be discouraged by effective counterpressure from the West, not strengthened by Western militancy. These views were pushed aside by an Administration puzzled by Kennan's seemingly mystical faith in diplomacy and intent on winning public support for building "situations of strength" from which to negotiate with the Soviet Union. Whatever the merits of Kennan's views, his policy suggestions were never considered seriously during the Truman Administration, but his published statement *was* read for more urgent lessons about Soviet aspirations.

CONCLUSION

During the three years from Potsdam to the Democratic convention of 1948 the Truman Administration had laid the basis for a profound change in the character and magnitude of the American involvement in world affairs. The war had seriously undermined the economies of the major powers of Europe, including the Soviet Union, while it had forced the American economy to expand. By 1948 the fears of a postwar depression in this country had subsided and America's economic preeminence had become unmistakable.

The change in our involvement abroad was more than a matter of recognizing that we had interests outside the Western Hemisphere that required us to play a role in world affairs. Our type of role as a world power also changed. The instigator of the new role was Marshall, the professional soldier with the largest vision about the wartime effort. Characteristically, in 1947 he instructed the American officials assigned to develop a plan for Europe's economic recovery to "avoid trivia." By avoiding trivia Marshall had infused definite objectives into our enormous military effort during World War II, and in 1947, with commensurate vision, he set the guidelines for postwar American efforts to cope with external conditions by transforming them.

Traditionally (though with some important exceptions), American diplomacy, like British diplomacy, had been aloof and manipulative. Now, under Truman and Marshall, our diplomacy changed to bring American economic power directly to bear on Western Europe. The diplomat and his traditional functions of maintaining contact with foreign governments were pushed aside by new American officials—young economists, lawyers, and business executives— who established direct working relationships for their government with the budget and treasury offices in European capitals. Traditional diplomatic methods and objectives also gave way to deadlines and targets, to programs and their management. In turn, the costs of these efforts and the American stake in their success made our foreign relations far more dependent upon domestic political consent, which became an important element in our postwar experience as a world power.

3

Truman's Second Term: Apex and Nadir

THE 1948 ELECTION

The Truman Administration's response to the Soviet challenge and to Europe's needs during 1947 and 1948 represented towering achievements for any administration, but domestic problems within the Administration and the Democratic party had helped to bring Truman's popularity to a low ebb by the spring of 1948, as the presidential nominating conventions approached. The Democratic party was apathetic about Truman's nomination. He was able to thwart a "dump Truman" movement only because of his control over the party as President.

On the left, Truman had lost the support of many liberals in the party when he fired Henry Wallace from his Cabinet post (before the 1946 congressional elections) for disagreement with the Administration on foreign-policy issues. On the right, Truman lost the support of Southern Democrats by proposing a strong civil-rights program in early 1948. Both these groups broke away from the Democratic party to run their own presidential candidates: Henry Wallace on the Progressive ticket and Strom Thurmond on the States' Rights ticket. Nonetheless, Truman was able to hold together some elements of the New Deal coalition on the basis of his civil-rights commitment and his 1948 State of the Union message, which had included cutting taxes and proposals for spending $10 billion on social legislation.

After his nomination, Truman called the Republican-controlled 80th Congress back into session and challenged it to enact the legislative program called for in the Republican campaign platform. The challenge was an unprecedented act of partisanship, admired for its audacity as much as it was resented. Congress failed to respond, and the "Do Nothing Congress," as Truman dubbed it, became a keynote of his campaign. On the positive side Truman further detailed his State of the Union proposals for extensive social and economic legislation—what was to become "the Fair Deal"— and staked his campaign strategy on intensive whistle-stop speech-making tours.

Foreign-policy issues, ironically, had little impact on the conduct of the 1948 campaign or the electoral verdict. Bipartisanship prevented the President from capitalizing on foreign-policy achievements, although their impression on public opinion had been weak anyway. The public perception of a Soviet menace, however, had been stronger and had served Republicans to advantage in the congressional race in 1946. Because the President is in charge of the federal budget, he alone must make many difficult choices about the allocation of national resources. This constraint had kept the Truman Administration from adjusting as expeditiously to the Soviet challenge as its critics had wished. But by the 1948 campaign Truman had made up for this deficiency, and the Republican presidential candidate, Thomas E. Dewey, did not find the President sufficiently vulnerable to make the "soft on Communism" charge a prominent part of his campaign attack on Truman. Dewey campaigned with the posture of the front-runner, using a strategy that was designed to appeal to Democrats and Independents while holding together the divergent elements of his own party. Attacking his opponent's record would only open schisms in what seemed to be a winning Republican coalition. Given these Republican inhibitions, the bipartisan and anti-Communist emphasis of the Truman Administration's foreign policy served to keep it from a prominent place in the Republican-Democratic debate.

Henry Wallace's campaign as the Progressive-party candidate

for President attempted but failed to raise the saliency of foreign-policy issues for the 1948 electorate. Wallace had lost his place in the Cabinet over a speech in September 1946 in which he had attacked the nascent Western alliance and the prospects of postwar American rearmament. Just about everything the Truman Administration had done in foreign relations since then had run contrary to Wallace's position. Wallace did make foreign relations—particularly the growing antagonism with Russia—a campaign issue, but he intermingled it with a program for obscurantist though radical domestic reform. Dewey, with his lofty bearing, made little effort to drive Truman and Wallace together and thus left Truman free to ignore Wallace. Truman chose Los Angeles, where Wallace seemed to have made the greatest inroads into Democratic ranks, to lash at the Progressive party's Communist ties (though not at Wallace's own loyalty). Elsewhere, however, Wallace drew neither Truman nor Dewey into debate on foreign affairs.

In a decisive upset, Truman won the election with a 2.2 million-vote plurality over Dewey, and the Democrats handily reversed the Republican majorities in the House and Senate. It seemed as though the Administration would now be able to seize the partisan initiative by instituting the domestic-welfare program Truman had generated to hold the Roosevelt coalition together.

But appearances were misleading. In fact, the election represented mainly a personal victory for Truman and only a tenuous public endorsement of his domestic programs. The election in no sense endorsed Truman's foreign policy, since such issues had played little part in the campaign. Moreover, the low voter turnout —one of the smallest percentages of eligible voters since the emergence of the modern two-party system after the Civil War—reflected the lack of public interest in either electoral issues or political personalities.

Even more important, the Administration soon found that the federal budget had to accommodate prior foreign-policy commitments before it could assume new domestic expenditures. The Marshall Plan and the foreign military-assistance program for Europe cost us $5 billion in a federal budget that totalled $39.5 billion for the fiscal year beginning in mid-1949 and included heavy fixed obligations. This large a sum for external commitments could not help but undercut the prospects for the social-welfare expenditures outlined in Truman's Fair Deal program. It is ironic that Truman's electoral victory was largely on the basis of his projected domestic programs rather than his past foreign-policy record, and yet throughout Truman's second term the Administration's growing financial and political commitment to foreign problems was ultimately to force the sacrifice of his contemplated domestic program.

At the same time, the prospects for presidential success in foreign policy also diminished after the 1948 election. Bipartisanship is, among other things, an agreement among the leaders of the two major parties not to bother the public with disputes about policy. It induces public confidence, but with it, public inattention as well. However, in order to win the 1948 election Truman had had to arouse public attention with a slam-bang partisanship that strained the relations with Republican leaders upon which bipartisanship in foreign relations rested. His partisanship also aroused voter interest and engaged public attention with domestic and political matters to a degree that was incompatible with the public inattention that bipartisanship required (and produced). Yet the practice of bipartisanship lingered on and continued to be the principal method by which the Truman Administration sought and kept political support for American foreign policy.

After 1948, however, bipartisanship was under severe stress as both parties turned toward more partisan foreign policies. Dewey's defeat not only left the leadership of the Republican party in the hands of congressional leaders who were narrower partisans than Dewey but it diminished the political value for the Republicans of bipartisan agreement on foreign affairs. Senator Vandenberg might have been able to prevent the trend toward partisanship in foreign policy, but his health began to fail. The strongly conservative Senator Taft of Ohio became "Mr. Republican" in foreign as well as domestic affairs, his partisanship enhanced by Dewey's defeat and his own ten years in the Senate opposition to Democratic administrations.

The Administration, too, assumed a more partisan stance in foreign affairs after the election. Acheson, a life-long Democrat with no popular national standing, replaced Marshall as Secretary of State. Louis Johnson, a politically ambitious right-wing Democrat, replaced Forrestal as Secretary of Defense. Later, in 1950, when the Korean War shifted the principal immediate issues of foreign

Europe to Asia, the Administration found itself
ly from the Republican leadership in Congress but
ant Democratic legislators as well.

IMMUNISM AND CORRUPTION

The Republicans discovered that the lack of active public support for our foreign-policy programs gave them a chance to make
partisan gains by raising issues that would undermine public confidence in the Truman Administration itself and thus—by this indirect route—in the Administration's foreign policy. It is this
plummeting of public confidence in the Truman Administration
(as contrasted with the high confidence in the Eisenhower Administration later on) that explains why, paradoxically, the Truman Administration was to become so vulnerable on foreign-policy issues
after it had in fact developed an impressive Cold War program
abroad.

What factors contributed to the loss of public confidence in the
Truman Administration? The Republicans were successfully able
to rally public support on two major issues after 1948: the "mess in
Washington" and the fear of Communist subversion. The "mess"
consisted of a series of disclosures, mainly through congressional
investigations, of corruption and unethical behavior in the government on the part of Truman's military aide, his appointment
secretary, and other members of the White House staff. "Influence-
peddling" to gain business loans from the government-owned Reconstruction Finance Corporation and to "fix" tax investigations
were the most invidious scandals. The Bureau of Internal Revenue,
staffed by political patronage, was particularly susceptible to influence peddling. The opposition understandably exploited these
scandals, and Truman was pathetically loyal to his friends under
attack. At the end of 1951, with evidence of the RFC and tax bureau scandals accumulating, he attempted to reorganize these agencies and to conduct a cleanup campaign within the government.
Truman's efforts—a comedy of errors—collapsed a few months later,
just in time for corruption to figure prominently with Communism
in the Republican campaign charges in the 1952 election.

The charge of being "soft on Communism" had been a political issue since the wartime alliance with the Soviet Union began to sour early in 1945. It had been used effectively in congressional campaigns as early as 1946. That year the Republican Party won control of Congress for the first time since 1935 with a campaign that featured a pledge to clean communists and fellow travelers out of the government. Through the late forties, the subversion issue continued to develop.

President Truman established the Federal Employee Loyalty Program in 1947 in order to forestall the 80th Congress from setting up more stringent surveillance over federal employees. Truman's program screened the vast majority of federal employees rather than concentrating on the small number of officials employed in jobs that directly affected national security or even on the somewhat larger number of government employees having access to classified documents. The mere existence of the loyalty program stigmatized the federal service and invited suspicion about government officials. But without the more sensational spy confessions and trials the loyalty program would have made little impression on public opinion.

Before 1948, two principal cases of possible espionage had come to light within the government. Both were initiated by FBI investigations; both remained inconclusive. One involved *Amerasia,* a scholarly journal with a propensity to favor the Chinese Communists. This case produced the arrest, but not the conviction, of a senior foreign-service officer. The second case involved a government official named Harry Dexter White. He was Assistant Secretary of the Treasury in 1946 when the FBI presented their report about him to the President. With insufficient evidence for prosecution, Truman decided merely to keep him under special FBI surveillance. The next year he was called before the House Un-American Activities Committee, where he denied charges leveled at him, but died suddenly before the investigation could go further.

It was a third case, however, that caused the government real trouble. Alger Hiss had left an impressive fourteen-year career in the State Department in 1947 to become the President of the Carnegie Endowment for International Peace. In mid-1948 the House Un-American Activities Committee learned of testimony then being given to a federal grand jury by two former Communists, Whittaker Chambers and Elizabeth Bentley. The committee called them as witnesses in public hearings, and Chambers named Alger Hiss as a Communist agent in his testimony. Hiss denied the charge under oath and challenged Chambers to repeat his charges where he was not immune from prosecution. Chambers did, and Hiss promptly sued for slander. Chambers in turn produced stolen government documents and microfilm copies of other documents that the Justice Department then used to convict Hiss of perjury for denying under oath that he had passed State Department papers to Chambers. (Hiss was never prosecuted for espionage itself.) Hiss's conviction for perjury in January 1950 gave Republicans the evidence to charge that the Truman Administration was "soft on Communism."

By early 1950 the anti-Communist pot was boiling. The Senate Internal Security Subcommittee had reopened the *Amerasia* case. The Communist party had been convicted of criminal conspiracy. Judith Coplon had been proved a spy while employed in the Internal Security Division of the Justice Department. And Harry Gold and David Greenglass were under arrest, implicated with Klaus Fuchs, the confessed British nuclear-scientist spy.

The junior Senator from Wisconsin, Joseph R. McCarthy, joined the ranks of the congressional Communist-hunters, adding to the partisan clamor his special talents as a virtuoso demagogue. In his first speech on the subject (arranged by the Republican National Committee for the Republican Women's Club of Wheeling, West Virginia, in February 1950), McCarthy drove straight into the dark corners of public suspicion. "The reason why we find ourselves in a position of impotency" in the world, he told his listeners, is "because of the traitorous actions of those who have been treated so well by this nation." He singled out the State Department, where "the bright young men who were born with silver spoons in their mouths are the ones who have been most traitorous. . . ."[1] Said McCarthy: "I have here in my hand a list of 205—a list of names that were made known to the Secretary of State as being members of the Communist party and who nevertheless are still working and shaping policy in the State Department."

The technique of the alleged proof, the wild charge, and the "hit and run" tactics were formidable weapons in McCarthy's hands. He did not answer charges: he issued them. The Senate set

[1] Quoted in Eric F. Goldman, *The Crucial Decade* (New York: Vintage, 1960), p. 141.

up a distinguished subcommittee under Senator Millard Tydings, a respected conservative Democrat, to hear McCarthy's charges. He won overwhelmingly a publicity contest with this subcommittee, driving it to charge him with fraud, and the Senate to support the charge, on a strict party-line vote. Even Senator Margaret Chase Smith, who had been the first Senator to rebuke McCarthy on the floor of the Senate, fell into line. Finally, McCarthy was instrumental in the defeat of Senator Tydings in the Maryland elections that November, as well as in that of the Senate Majority Leader, Scott Lucas, in Illinois. With this demonstration of nerve and potency, McCarthy cowed his opposition. Throughout the remainder of the Truman Administration, McCarthy was the most militant opponent of Truman's foreign policy and a scourge on the State Department.

Like the corruption scandals, the danger of Communist subversion had some substance in fact. No doubt some American citizens recruited into Russian espionage rings have worked for the government. And probably our protections against Soviet espionage were improved because internal security became a partisan issue. On the other hand, the internal threat of Communism was blown up out of all proportion for its political value and dealt with by costly and ineffective means. No one was convicted of espionage or related crimes from evidence disclosed either by the elaborate Federal Employee Loyalty Program or from the congressional investigations of the late forties. Yet the effect of these investigations on the federal service—lowered morale, inhibited initiative, overly "safe" advice, and recruitment troubles—was profound, overwhelmingly negative, and long-lasting.

THE LIMITS OF BIPARTISAN ENGAGEMENT

The Truman Administration's foreign policy became particularly vulnerable to partisan attack in this atmosphere of suspicion and low public confidence. The Republicans discovered that by charging corruption and subversion they could make foreign policy salient to a considerably larger segment of the voters than could the Atlantic alliance or economic assistance. For these charges linked the public's perceptions of external threats and difficulties with concepts with which they were more familiar—conditions at home and the loyalty and patriotism of Americans.

The Republicans were particularly successful in attacking the Administration's neglect of Asia, which they attributed to subversion in our government. In politics, the charge of subversion is a terrorist weapon because of its indiscriminate destructiveness. In leveling this charge against the government congressional Republicans felt confident that their Democratic colleagues would stand by or even cooperate in the attack—particularly since the Administration had neglected to secure the endorsement of even the congressional Democrats for its China policy.

After 1946 the Truman Administration decided to put its money on Europe. The decision reflected three assumptions: that Europe was more vital to American interests than was Asia; that the money we could spend abroad was limited; and that the political effectiveness (and hence the future) of Chiang Kai-shek's regime in China was uncertain. Truman's decision was, in short, a calculated neglect of Asia in favor of Europe, much as the strategy of World War II had been to concentrate first on winning the war in Europe and then in Asia.

Truman's emphasis on Europe reflected a fundamental choice of long-range priorities and objectives—one of the few made by any Administration in the postwar era. Yet the Administration suffered heavily for deciding not to pour more resources into China while it gained little politically for saving Europe. Quite understandably, Republicans as well as Democrats, the Congress as well as the Executive, got credit for saving Europe. Because of the criticism over China, however, deciding against foreign actions became unpopular.

On the other hand, if Truman had attempted to associate some of his potential critics with his decision to neglect China, the Administration would not have been so vulnerable to criticism. For example, the Truman Administration missed an important opportunity to link Congress with its policies through lax execution of the China Aid Act of 1948. This election-year bill was passed by congressional Republicans and Democrats alike in an effort to clear themselves of responsibility for the declining fortunes of the Nationalist Chinese government, and the act passed Congress with wide majorities in both houses. In fact, the additional aid it provided the Nationalist government could hardly have saved it from collapsing on the mainland in 1949. But by apparently lax execution of the statute's provisions, the Truman Administration permitted Republicans and Democrats alike in Congress to disassociate themselves from its Far Eastern policies. The result was not a cleavage between the two parties, but a cleavage between the executive branch and the Congress.[2] As the Communist forces in China took increasing control of the Chinese mainland in 1949 while the Nationalist regime moved to Taiwan, the Truman Administration came under heavy attack for abandoning Chiang Kai-shek.

EUROPE FIRST AND DEFENSE CUTBACKS: THE AMBIVALENT STANCE

In the earliest phase of the postwar response to the Soviet challenge, the Truman Administration had been at a disadvantage in meeting demands that it shift more quickly from alliance to opposition, for critics could advocate change without having to find the additional resources required to implement it.

Once the perception of a Soviet threat to postwar American interests in Europe had become widespread, however, the Administration would have found public support readily forthcoming had it chosen to allocate resources for direct American rearmament. But this was not the response the Administration decided upon. It concentrated instead on the economic recovery and then the minimum military rearmament of Western Europe. Only after the Korean War started did the Truman Administration throw itself into American rearmament, and when it did, as we shall see, public demands for ambitious military efforts continued to outpace its effort. From March 1947 until 1951 the Truman Administration was inhibited in its search for popular support for its response to the Soviet challenge by the quite justifiable fear that the public response might get out of hand and force the Administration to rearm the United States at the expense of its support for European recovery and rearmament.

Deciding against American rearmament as a means of meeting

[2] H. Bradford Westerfield, *Foreign Policy and Party Politics: Pearl Harbor to Korea* (New Haven: Yale Univ. Press, 1955), pp. 266–268.

the Soviet challenge, the Administration exploited the popularity of economizing in our military establishment at the same time that it rested the case for its foreign commitments on the less popular strategy of building foreign defenses against the Soviet challenge as it was popularly perceived.

The early emphasis of the Truman Administration on economizing in the military establishment would make it highly vulnerable to partisan attack later when it reversed that policy. And two key appointments to the Truman Cabinet after the 1948 election served to accentuate that reversal when it came: Johnson, as Secretary of Defense, flamboyantly exploited the political appeal of budget cutting in the Defense Department from his appointment in early 1949 through April 1950. Acheson, as Secretary of State, drew into focus a quite different trend of thinking within the executive branch that began a year before the Korean War started. It emphasized a much expanded rearmament effort for the West although still favoring the rearming of Western Europe first because the main prize—and hence the main threat—was there.

Johnson had been instructed by the White House to hold the defense budget to a low ceiling of $12.5 billion and had resolved to make the most of his mandate to economize. His severe budget cuts exacerbated service rivalries, which, in turn, exploded into an acrimonious public row between the Navy and the Air Force. Johnson defended his economy cuts, and the two armed services both asserted their rival claims to funds and functions in congressional hearings a few weeks after the Soviet Union detonated its first atom bomb. The hearings demonstrated a preoccupation with large-scale nuclear war fought on our side almost exclusively by American forces at the expense of less glamorous conventional warfare (such as they would be conducting within a year in Korea). The claims of all three armed services were tuned to the predilections of their congressional and public audiences. The economizing pressures had forced them to concentrate on being able to perform the tasks that were easiest to justify and that least required the allocation of American resources to her allies. The result was an anachronism: we were increasing our reliance on a deterrent military posture based on an American nuclear monopoly without figuring the new Soviet nuclear capacity into the strategic equation. Congress remained preoccupied with the Navy–Air Force rivalry over strategic air power, but the anachronism did not escape notice within the government.

The plight of the American military posture and Europe's military weakness had become apparent to the U.S. officials planning the military-assistance program for Western Europe in mid-1949. As a result, Acheson had assigned State Department planners to take a fresh look at military requirements and examine whether our economy could carry the burden of increased defense expenditures. The Soviet detonation gave urgency to the State Department's inquiries and touched off a bitter secret wrangle over whether to proceed with the crash development of a hydrogen bomb. The wrangle ended in January 1950 when Truman directed the scientists to proceed, but the fight left several high-ranking civilians in the government doubtful about military strategy and policy. Acheson had been an advocate of the bomb's development, and the heat of the dispute produced one of his strongest Cold War statements:

> *The only way to deal with the Soviet Union, we have found from hard experience, is to create situations of strength. Wherever the Soviet detects weakness or disunity—and it is quick to detect them—it exploits them to the full. . . . When we have reached unity and determination on the part of the free nations—when we have eliminated all the areas of weakness that we can—we will be able to evolve working agreements with the Russians. . . . It is clear that the Russians do not want to settle those issues as long as they feel there is any possibility they can exploit them for their own objectives of world domination. It is only when they come to the conclusion that they cannot so exploit them that they will make agreements, and they will let it be known when they have reached that decision.[3]*

The Truman Administration had difficulty presenting a united front in its response to the Soviet nuclear detonation. Democratic Senators Brien MacMahon and Millard Tydings wanted to start ambitious summit negotiations with the Soviet Union, while Acheson belittled the value of any negotiations at that time. Louis Johnson had been carrying out the President's mandate to hold down defense expenditures, only to find Acheson building a case for higher defense budgets.

[3] Department of State *Bulletin*, 22 (March 20, 1950), pp. 427–429.

Furthermore, Truman's decision to proceed with the H-bomb had given presidential support to Acheson's reassessment of military requirements, thereby widening the gap between the economizers and the mobilizers within the government. By April Truman had on his desk a report reflecting Acheson's view and urging a huge increase in military spending. It gave top priority to building up the conventional forces of our European allies, but it asserted that the American economy could carry a much larger military budget without faltering. The report recommended that we begin assuming this burden, since it predicted that the Soviet Union would have nuclear weapons deployed for fighting within an estimated two to four years. And by that time, the report recommended, the United States would have to be able to fight small, conventional wars.

When the Korean War began two months later NSC-68 (as the report was called) became the basis for a worldwide rearmament supported by the United States. Our involvement in Korea lent substance to the opposition's charges of neglecting American interests in Asia; the broader rearmament that Korea triggered confirmed the accusations that Truman had neglected the Armed Forces.

THE KOREAN WAR AND THE LOSS OF PUBLIC CONFIDENCE

From World War II the United States inherited the occupation of the southern half of Korea up to the 38th parallel, facing a Soviet-occupied North Korea. Unable to agree on the terms of unification, the two occupying powers established separate regimes. The South Korean government more closely reflected historic Korean nationalism, but it was dependent upon American security guarantees against the North Korean government.

By 1948 Korea had become an embarrassment to the United States. With our limited military forces stretched thin around the world, the Joint Chiefs of Staff judged available American forces inadequate to defend Korea and recommended our withdrawal. They also proposed that we establish a "defensive perimeter" in the Pacific off the Asian mainland—that is, a line drawn for purposes of strategic planning that would demarcate those countries in the

Pacific we planned to defend in case they were attacked. Truman approved both recommendations.

Sixteen months later, with the American withdrawal from Korea completed, Truman and Acheson drew attention to the import of the new offshore deployments. In January 1950 the President indicated that the defensive perimeter did not necessarily include Formosa. Acheson, speaking at a press-club luncheon, was more explicit: the line of American defense in the Pacific ran from the Aleutians through Japan and the Philippines, excluding Korea and the Asian mainland. Korea must depend for its defense, he indicated, upon the United Nations.

In June 1950 North Korea launched a well-prepared invasion of South Korea. Syngman Rhee's government in Seoul appealed to the United States and the United Nations for help. President Truman promptly committed American forces to the defense of South Korea in the belief that if we failed to respond to so obvious an aggression we would encourage further Communist expansion in Asia. First, however, American diplomats had won ambiguous U.N. sanction for the American intervention: the Security Council swiftly convened and called for the withdrawal of the North Koreans to the 38th parallel. Two days later the Council authorized U.N. members to aid South Korea. Russia failed to exercise her customary veto in the Security Council because she was boycotting the Council and was caught by surprise. By the time the Soviet delegate returned to tie up the Council's deliberations the basis for the United Nations Command in Korea had been laid.

In his first acts to aid South Korea, Truman had ordered the Seventh Fleet to protect the island of Formosa, the new home of Nationalist China. There were military justifications for protecting Formosa, but not strong ones. More important was the political significance of the action, since it effectively committed the United States to the continued existence of Nationalist China. The move embarrassed U.N. member participants in the Korean War because it indicated to them that the United States was willing to act unilaterally to gain its objectives in the region. On the other hand, the action probably did soften the domestic recriminations over our treatment of the Nationalist Chinese government.

Truman's decision to defend South Korea and protect Formosa against invasion with American naval power raised the level of the

American military commitment abroad to sums roughly equivalent to those contemplated in NSC-68. But the Administration again stopped short of a military escalation that could have stilled some of its critics in the new circumstance of war. By September 1950—even before the Chinese intervention—the Administration was resisting the critics who were demanding full mobilization.

General Douglas MacArthur, the commander of American forces in the Far East and proconsul of the United States occupation of Japan, directed the American forces in Korea and also became head of the U.N. Command, which consisted predominantly of American troops coupled with American-trained and supported South Korean combat forces. The Communist attack swept down the Korean peninsula. American forces were quickly deployed from Japan and later directly from the United States. Unable to stop the advancing enemy, MacArthur chose a strategic enclave defense on the East Coast at the bottom of the peninsula around Pusan. When he had received sufficient reinforcements, he struck back at the Communists, following up with a landing on the West Coast at Inchon that caught the North Koreans by surprise. His break-out from Inchon went sufficiently well to put the North Korean forces to flight. On October 1 South Korean troops crossed the 38th parallel. A week later, a United Nations resolution instructed MacArthur to "take all appropriate steps . . . to ensure conditions of stability throughout Korea." This resolution appeared to give him the authority to unify the entire country by force of arms, and he proceeded to attempt this task.

The new drive was short lived, however. Reinforcements of Red Chinese troops began to appear among the North Korean units in October, and in November a Chinese offensive struck the separated columns of MacArthur's advancing forces, sending them reeling. Once again troops from the North swept down the peninsula, though this time their advance was soon checked. The Chinese involvement forced both Washington and the U.N. General Assembly to fall back on the more modest objective of repelling the invasion of South Korea.

The Korean War added immediately to the partisan fires in Washington. Acheson's press-club speech the previous January was singled out as an American invitation to attack South Korea, and a leading Republican Senator charged that "The blood of our boys in Korea is on his shoulders, and no one else." The Administration's abandonment of the Nationalist Chinese regime came under new fire as being the cause of the Korean War. Finally, critics justly blamed the Truman Administration for defining the defense perimeter in the Pacific to exclude Korea.

The decisive behavior of Truman won him immediate public support, but the opinion surveys revealed that his popularity began to trail off in August 1950 as the limited scope of our rearmament became apparent.[4] In September Truman called General Marshall back into the government, this time as Secretary of Defense to replace Johnson. After the Chinese intervention House and Senate Republicans also asked Truman to replace Acheson as Secretary of State because "he had lost the confidence of the country." The attacks on Acheson were to persist, and even State officials such as Lieutenant Governor Knight of California denounced him.

The principal campaign issues of Republican candidates for the congressional election that November were inflation, Communism, and corruption—all familiar domestic themes played with varying emphasis in 1946 and 1948—and, in addition, the Korean situation. Robert A. Taft, the leader of the Senate Republicans, blamed the Administration for high prices, high taxes, the loss of China to the Communists, and the Korean conflict itself. Former Governor Stassen and Senator McCarthy added to the campaign the charge of Communist subversion in Washington.

The election can be considered only a moderate defeat for the Administration if we take into account the historical tendency in this country for the President's party to lose seats at the midterm elections. The Republicans gained only five seats in the Senate and twenty-eight in the House. But outside the conservative (though Democratic) South, the Republicans held a 196–126 seat advantage in the House after 1950, and Truman's domestic legislative program lost all its momentum.

By early 1951 General MacArthur had stabilized the front just south of the 38th parallel. American casualties had reached 40,000. In the next six months, ending with a cease-fire agreement

---

[4] For statistics on answers to the question "Do you approve or disapprove of the way Truman is handling his job as President?" in polls conducted by the American Institute of Public Opinion (AIPO) from 1945 through 1952 see *Public Opinion Quarterly*, 25 (Spring, 1961), p. 135.

and the beginning of armistice negotiations, the struggle in the midsection of Korea cost the United States another 35,000 casualties and produced stronger demands in the United States for breaking the military stalemate by bombing bases in Manchuria and taking other military actions directed at Red China itself. The Administration, aware of the vulnerability of its supply lines and staging areas to air attack, was fearful of expanding the conflict, and, in addition, Truman was sensitive to the views of our U.N. allies, who wanted to restrict the fighting as much as possible.

The Administration offered its critics another rallying point as well—General Douglas MacArthur. Left in charge of the Japanese occupation after the war, MacArthur had maintained an extraordinary independence from the Administration. Truman was displeased with MacArthur's propensity to ignore directives from Washington, but not enough to remove him from command. Truman even shrank from a proposal to confine MacArthur to Japan and have the Joint Chiefs deal directly with the field commander, General Matthew B. Ridgeway.

However, on April 10, 1951, Truman finally did remove MacArthur, after House Minority Leader Joseph W. Martin, Jr., read a letter from MacArthur on the floor of the House that challenged the Administration's Korean policy on several points. For months MacArthur's views had created lively partisan debate in Washington and embarrassment among our allies. In the Martin letter MacArthur failed to refer to the United Nations, speaking only of "Red China's entry into the war against us in Korea. . . ." Previous public statements from MacArthur referring to "abnormal military inhibitions" and other differences with the U.N. allies had, as Secretary Marshall later testified at the Senate Armed Services and Foreign Relations hearings, "aroused their fears, their uncertainties, and made it all the more difficult for us to deal with them."[5]

The dismissal of MacArthur helped to overcome the crisis in U.S. relations with our allies caused by the Martin letter. But, as Truman anticipated, his action set off a crisis in American domestic affairs instead. For General MacArthur returned to the United States for the first time in fourteen years to tour the major cities as a dissident national hero.

[5] Hearings, *Military Situation in the Far East*, I (1951), p. 349.

highly independent field commander could have been. These plications were the result of common but indefensible temporiz-

But the Truman Administration's shortcomings in handling e Korean War are overshadowed by the immense political disdvantages inherent in maintaining a balanced and restrained American war-fighting posture. Full American war mobilization probably would have popularized the war domestically if war mobilization had been accompanied by commensurate American militancy somewhere in the world. If, for example, the Truman Administration hesitated to upset the worldwide balance by becoming highly militant in Asia, then it would have had to become more militant in Europe and endured all the complications *that* would have produced in our NATO alliance and the conflict with Moscow.

The militancy would have engaged the attention of increasing numbers of the American public faster than the Korean War actually did, probably accelerating the mood of the reaction that actually occurred—growing militancy and impatience to get it over with. The Truman Administration decided against this course of action, fully aware that it was denying itself a domestic political opportunity, though it was wrong in its belief that it could popularize its choice of limited war. *The largest lesson of the Korean War—and indeed the legacy of Truman's Presidency—may well be that American political leadership, out of courage or ignorance, is willing to manage wars as it thinks they should be managed, despite the domestic political forces that are set loose.*

NATO AFTER KOREA

The Korean War strained the Truman Administration's relations with Western Europe, but it also helped to translate the North Atlantic Alliance into an organized military effort. The North Atlantic Treaty Organization (NATO) as a whole and its principal area command, the Supreme Headquarters of the Allied Powers in Europe (SHAPE), under the Supreme Allied Commander for Europe (SACEUR), were supposed to provide the military capability to defend Europe through supranational military planning and

He addressed a joint session of Congress on April 19, displaying an oratorical skill fully equal to the dramatic occasion. In his speech, and later in his testimony before combined hearings of the Senate Armed Services and Foreign Relations Committees, he challenged the Administration's emphasis on Europe, its willingness to accommodate allies, its reluctance to widen the scope of the war, and its assessments of the costs of doing so. MacArthur wanted Nationalist forces to be used in Korea and to attack the mainland of China. He wanted to blockade the Chinese coast and use American air power on the Chinese interior. He estimated that the enactment of these measures would require no increase in American ground strength and only a small increase in our air and naval forces.

MacArthur's recommendations touched vital emotional chords in American public life, but in fact his proposals got nowhere. As there had been quadrennially since the 1930's, there was a flurry of Republican interest in him as a presidential candidate in 1952. But although he delivered the keynote address at the Republican convention that June, nothing more developed. Moreover, although MacArthur supplied the Republicans with eloquent strategic arguments to be exploited in the 1952 election campaigns, he was actually to influence the reformation of defense policy under Eisenhower very little.

As for Truman, the most remarkable thing about his dismissal of MacArthur was how few direct consequences the action had. And to his supporters, Truman came across well in defending his constitutional position as Commander in Chief of the American Armed Forces. Indirectly, however, the MacArthur incident may well have helped to weaken popular confidence in the Administration by calling attention to the erratic course of American foreign policy before and during the Korean War.

It seems likely that the Administration's periodic switching of signals contributed to the new low in public support for our conduct of the war during 1951. First the Administration had defined its Asian defense perimeter to exclude Korea; then it had reversed this decision when the North Koreans attacked and Seoul appealed to us for help. Once American forces and prestige were committed Washington's objectives soared in a few weeks from holding and defending South Korea to "liberating" North Korea; then our goals were sharply trimmed back to defending the South and settling for the *status quo ante.* The Administration raised public expectations only to dash them again. Adding to the frustrations of this erratic course were the inhibitions imposed by our U.N. allies, although press and broadcasting accounts showed the American public that the actual fighting was mainly a Korean-American affair. Finally, there was the calculated decision of the Administration to fight a limited war rather than to go to a "total" war footing and bring overwhelming force to bear against our enemies, as we had so successfully done in World War II.[6]

All these factors contributed to the unpopularity of the Korean War, and some of them could not even be openly debated with Administration critics. To defend its decision against extending the air war to North Korea and China, for example, the Truman Administration would have had to publicize American military vulnerabilities, such as our extended supply lines from the United States through Japan.

Even the arguments that could be offered publicly by the Administration were inconclusive because they rested on disputable strategic plans and contingencies that ranked Korea as a lesser part of a large strategic whole. A military engagement in Korea was regarded by the Chairman of the Joint Chiefs of Staff as "the wrong war, at the wrong place, at the wrong time, and with the wrong enemy."[7] This evaluation may have shown a commendable resolve not to overreact. But it was also disputable, for it rested on a comparison between a real military challenge in Asia and a potential one in Europe. No less an authority on Soviet behavior than George Kennan considered the potential military threat in Europe exaggerated. He argued that the Russians, believing that history and politics were on their side, could afford to be patient and that their record showed that in practice they were cautious in their pursuit of foreign objectives.

Had the Administration taken Kennan's view about the Soviet

[6] It should be noted that during the Korean War U.S. defense expenditures rose from $11.9 billion in 1950 to $43.6 billion in 1953. But the American economy, rather than faltering, expanded enough to absorb the increased military costs. During the Korean War the American public got both guns *and* butter.

[7] Hearings, *Military Situation in the Far East* (1951), pp. 731–732.

threat to Europe, it would not have been
defenses in Europe or elsewhere in orde
Korea—that is, unless it also shared Kenn
pinned down militarily anywhere. Korea sho
Administration was willing to answer a Comm
side Europe but reluctant to get pinned down
jeopardizing America's European and other inter
Truman Administration worried about the worl
threat of Soviet Communism, it was unable to re
heartedly to particular Communist threats. Once agai
earliest phase of the postwar response to the perceived
Soviet Communism, the Truman Administration suffered
advantages of having to decide how to allocate limited m
resources because it was in charge of foreign policy.

What had not been apparent in 1946, however, was the infl
bility that was associated with the broad involvement of the Unite
States in world affairs by 1951. The United States had thrown itself
into two world wars in the twentieth century untroubled by the
prospect that it was neglecting other international commitments.
The Korean War was different because it involved distinctly limited
American interests, but also because the United States had established many other distinct interests. Truman's critics were able to
argue that he was not responding sufficiently to a bold act of military aggression in Korea without having to commit themselves to
the increased risks of thinning our defenses elsewhere and without
sharing responsibility for the consequences of escalating the war in
Asia. Just as the Truman Administration was inhibited by its role
from exploring alternatives to its Korean War policies, its critics
were inhibited in weighing all the consequences of the ventures
they proposed.

Nonetheless, the unsteady course of American policy in Asia
could partly have been avoided, even without changing our European priorities. The strategic military-planning decisions of 1948
ought to have been compatible with the political-military decisions
of the President in 1950. The escalation of war objectives during
autumn 1950 and the complications they would cause—the intervention of China and the discrediting of MacArthur's strategy by Truman—could not be specifically anticipated, but the general dangers

command. In practice, their main function became one of helping to win the support of domestic political audiences on both sides of the Atlantic by giving authoritative endorsements for national military-rearmament programs.

SHAPE was the product of three converging forces: first, the growing anxiety about the inadequacy of Europe's defense capabilities; second, the growing concern about how to integrate West German troops into NATO so as to make German rearmament palatable to its European allies; and third, the eagerness of Europeans for visible, permanent commitments by the United States to the defense of Europe.

An integrated military force in Western Europe was discussed only in extremely general terms before the beginning of the Korean War, but the subject was pursued in greater detail as European rearmament became more urgent in light of the war. At the NATO Council meeting in May 1950, more than a month before the war started, the members unanimously approved the creation of a permanent executive committee. Headed by an American, this committee was to coordinate the national economies of NATO members so as to plan for a balanced collective force that could be paid for without disrupting national recovery programs. Two Americans with high prestige in Europe were mentioned: Averill Harriman, by now head of both the American military- and economic-assistance programs abroad and a man with a towering bipartisan reputation in Congress, and General Eisenhower, the hero of European liberation in World War II. At the time, the United States opposed the establishment of a supreme military command. The following December, however, the NATO Council worked out a supreme command for the central front as part of the arrangement for German rearmament.

An integrated supreme command under an enormously popular international figure such as Eisenhower would offer several advantages on the domestic front for European governments: SHAPE would appeal to the centrist and right-wing political groups who were eager to rearm in the face of what they perceived to be a threat from the East; at the same time, national military expansion could now take the name of European integration through NATO, and governments could use the appeal of internationalism to counter opposition to rearmament from the leftist groups in their own countries. SHAPE also blunted the edge of left-wing criticism by demonstrating that the European governments were in fact gaining by their dealings with the United States—that they were not simply being "dragged too far behind the wheels of American diplomacy," as British Labour-party leader Aneurin Bevan had declared when he resigned from the government in April 1951.[8] And finally, SHAPE was established at a time when American prestige from the accomplishments of the European recovery program (despite the Korean War) could have an important impact on the military sphere.

In January 1951, immediately after his appointment as Supreme Commander, Eisenhower toured the capitals of the NATO countries. His triumphal return to Europe became a rallying point for NATO. The French government showed new confidence in dealing with the extreme left by blocking a Communist rally that threatened to interfere with the Eisenhower tour. Meanwhile, the Labour government in London announced an ambitious plan to expand the British armed forces. In the aftermath of the trip, in a burst of enthusiasm that was not fully sustained, the Netherlands (which had been criticized by the United States for its alleged low level of military effort) increased its defense budget. Back in Washington, Eisenhower assured Congress that Europe was determined to bear its share of the military burden of fighting Communism. Returning to Italy in April, Eisenhower spurred the Italian defense effort as well.

But European governments quickly discovered that their efforts to share the burden of rearmament had high political costs. In Britain, for example, the drain on the budget imposed by the Labour government's plan to expand the armed forces ultimately split the party and led to its electoral defeat in October 1951. Similarly, in May 1951, as Frenchmen began to realize that their social-welfare programs were being cut back to pay for the ambitious military expansion undertaken by the French government before and at the beginning of the Korean War, the Defense Minister Jules Moch lost his seat on the Socialist party's national executive committee for supporting defense requirements at the expense of social-welfare objectives.

8 487 *House of Commons Debate 38* (April 23, 1951), as quoted in Leon O. Epstein, *Britain—Uneasy Ally* (Chicago: Univ. of Chicago Press, 1954), p. 242.

Similar problems existed in other NATO capitals. Unavoidably, the political interests of the governments had become tied to the European recovery program. Officials feared that their own tenure in office and the future prospects of political stability in their own countries were dependent upon the success of their national economic recovery. As Dirk U. Stikker, the Dutch Foreign Minister, posed the problem presented by precipitous rearmament in the North Atlantic Council meeting in New York on September 18, 1950: "any further lowering of the present living standard in Europe without the prospects of a rise in the near future will endanger the social peace on the home front which is so essential to our defense effort."[9]

As Supreme Commander, Eisenhower immediately established himself as a broker, mediating between his European clients and the United States to encourage their support of a common undertaking. But by autumn of 1951 it had become necessary to adopt a new device for dealing with the bickering that had developed among member nations over a fair division of military burdens. In October the NATO Temporary Council Committee, meeting in Paris for its first session, appointed a committee of three—"the three wise men"—representing the United States, Britain, and France, to work out objectively an equitable distribution of burdens among the NATO allies.

This committee of three is often referred to as a major milestone in the integration of NATO, and it was. The committee obtained in unprecedented detail political and economic data from the NATO member countries, laid down criteria for establishing the division of military burdens, and produced a report that applied these criteria quite concretely. But its most significant function was to remove from direct intergovernment dispute the issue of burden sharing that had caused so much discord in NATO relations.

Throughout 1950–51 communications among NATO members abounded with published threats and counterthreats. Typically, American spokesmen in Congress stipulated that the United States —specifically, Congress—would not appropriate economic or military funds for NATO members if they did not meet some specified standard of performance. The European recipients of American aid,

9 *The New York Times,* September 19, 1951, p. 6.

on the other hand, stipulated that they could not meet the standards of military support expected of them if additional economic support were not forthcoming from the United States.

All these demands could have been made privately, but stating them publicly demonstrated a government's determination not to back down and thus strengthened its bargaining position. Moreover, this public dialogue was intended for the ears of a wider audience than just the foreign offices of the NATO members: it was intended to show each government's domestic constituency the relationship between American assistance and their own efforts.

It was here that the Truman Administration performed competently the political function of winning consent and support for its foreign endeavors. What was said privately evidently kept the American public threats from carrying too strong a sting in European capitals. The need for the Administration to placate Congress was a fact of life the Europeans had to live with.

NATO, SHAPE, and SACEUR all served to ease the political burdens of Washington as well as those of Europe. Eisenhower played a skillful role as international military leader, validating the common military effort for governments on both sides of the Atlantic. That role ended in May 1951, when he resigned as Supreme Allied Commander to seek the Republican presidential nomination.

CONCLUSION

Truman left the White House in 1953 as he had entered it in 1945: major negotiations with elements of the Communist bloc were still pending. In 1945 neither the Soviet nor the Western bloc had taken definite shape. But Europe soon became divided between East and West, and parts of Asia looked either to Moscow or Washington.

The United States government had been the major force in developing the Western alliance against Communism. In part our efforts represented responses to hostile Soviet or Communist initiatives. But the converse was also true: the Communist coup in Czechoslovakia and the Berlin Blockade of 1948 were partly generated—possibly even directly triggered—by the Marshall Plan and the development of NATO. Doubtless the Warsaw Pact, a multi-lateral military alliance with a combined command structure, was largely what it appeared to be—a mirror image of NATO. It is plain enough, then, that after 1945 the growing American hostility to-ward the Soviet Union in turn helped harden the Soviet posture toward the United States. It would indeed be extraordinary if the Soviet-American rivalry did not have this reciprocal effect.

Yet, it is unlikely that a change in American behavior could have done much to modify Soviet behavior. In the first place, there is no evidence that the Russians expected to reconcile their political or ideological interests after the war with those of the West or the United States. Second, given the German invasion of Russia in 1941, it is understandable that the Russians emerged from the war with an enhanced determination to eliminate any European threat to their national security. Expectations of revolution in Western Europe reinforced this determination (as did the later hope that Russia could benefit from the chaos and aspirations of the underdeveloped world). Finally, the morbid suspicions of the Soviet dictator Joseph Stalin assured that conciliatory gestures from the West would be largely discounted in Moscow.

But ideologies change and rulers pass away. The U.S. govern-ment needed to make clear that it was dealing with a dynamic polit-ical system that would not necessarily go on behaving the way it said it would. The Truman Administration needed to make its own predictions about Soviet behavior independently of Soviet predictions.

The main obstacle to making such reassessments came from the domestic political environment. There was little risk that any American political figure would be criticized for being overly anti-Communist, while it was difficult to make the point to a large and relatively inattentive public that, despite what the Russians charged about the capitalist West, they were likely to make certain accommodations to us as expediencies.

Both Harriman, the wartime ambassador in Moscow, and Kennan, who was also in Russia then, had warned Washington in 1945 about the difficulties of dealing with the Russians. If the United States was tough and firm, they argued, the Soviet Union would eventually see that it would have to accommodate the United States. In the end, we would be able to settle the outstanding issues with Moscow.

Their advice was to be firm with the Russians—but to remain willing to negotiate. Above all, they said, Washington should not adopt a policy that precluded negotiation, since, even if the Russians did not want a settlement, it was our task to put them in a political and strategic position in which they *would* want one.

Yet, by the end of 1951 the Truman Administration's efforts to mobilize the American and foreign publics against the Communist threat had in fact frozen American posture toward Russia into a rigid stance to counter aggressive Communism and develop positions of strength from which to negotiate with Moscow without trying to specify for itself—and certainly not for the public—what the terms of a satisfactory negotiating position, to say nothing of a satisfactory settlement with the Russians, would be.

4

Eisenhower: The Momentum of the First Term

THE MANDATE OF THE 1952 ELECTION

"I shall go to Korea." This dramatic eleventh-hour campaign promise made by Dwight D. Eisenhower in October 1952 appealed strongly to the American public's impatience with the stalemate in Korea. And in fact the 1952 election represented an odd postscript to the Truman era as well as a mandate for new leadership.

In 1952 both parties passed over regular party leaders to nominate candidates with potentially strong extrapartisan appeal. Eisenhower's career as an eminent military commander in World War II and as Supreme Commander of SHAPE had won the confidence of the American public to a unique degree, and the Republicans saw in him a relative outsider to partisan politics who could win votes from Independents and Democrats, thus offsetting the numerical advantage of the Democrats as the majority party in this country since 1932. By nominating Eisenhower over Robert A. Taft, Senator from Ohio, the Republicans moved away from the conservative wing of the party and suggested that the electoral issues raised by their candidate would not reflect the criticisms leveled by Republican Congressmen against Truman's foreign policies.

The Democrats too chose to minimize partisanship in this election in order to reduce their identity with the Truman Administration. They selected the incumbent governor of Illinois, Adlai E. Stevenson, a man who, like Woodrow Wilson, had been drawn into state politics on a reform ticket. And like Eisenhower, Stevenson was a fresh face in his party's leadership ranks who had little connection with the partisan controversies over foreign policy that preceded his nomination. In fact Stevenson had refused to campaign for his party's presidential nomination. He had no connections with Truman before the campaign and labored to avoid them during it.

The voter turn-out in 1952 (62.7 percent) was much greater than in 1948 (51.5 percent), attesting to the stronger appeal of both candidates as well as to the degree of political controversy surrounding Truman's second term. Election survey interviews do indicate that few voters associated their negative feelings about Truman with Stevenson, who seems to have been relatively successful in avoiding the handicap of the Truman legacy. But while the partisan controversies of the past Administration did not directly affect the contest for the Presidency, they helped to mobilize increased voter participation in the 1952 election by raising public anxieties and attracting public attention to government affairs.

The winner in presidential elections usually gets barely more than 50 percent of the popular vote, but Eisenhower won 55 percent of the votes in 1952—a landslide not achieved since Roosevelt's victory in 1936. (Eisenhower was to surpass his own record in 1956.) The result attested to his unique popular appeal as a trustworthy and likeable public figure. Foreign policy issues weighed more heavily in the 1952 campaign than they had in 1948, but domestic issues were still paramount.[1]

If Eisenhower was so popular, if he had special status as someone who could settle the Korean War, and if foreign policy was *not* the most important factor in the election's outcome, it would then appear that the low public confidence in the Truman Administration and the partisan attacks on its handling of Korea, China,

[1] A. Campbell, G. Gurin, and W. E. Miller, *The Voter Decides* (Evanston: Row, Peterson, 1954), pp. 58 and 67. In open-ended survey questioning, domestic issues were mentioned from two to three times as often as foreign-policy issues. *Ibid.*, pp. 49–50.

and the internal Communist menace had little to do with the Republican victory in 1952.

To a surprising degree this is true. Foreign policy issues affected the outcome of the 1952 election mainly because of Eisenhower's presumed personal ability to resolve them effectively. It helped that he was a Republican, since voters almost universally attributed to the Republican party the superior ability to deal with international problems. But this strong public belief apparently did *not* reflect judgments about the Truman Administration's performance and the opposition's attacks on its handling of Korea. In fact, the opposition's criticism of Truman's China policy had little direct impact on the voter in 1952, and even charges that we had Communists in the government made very little impression in comparison with the domestic issues of internal corruption and excess government spending.[2]

Why, then, such an interest in Eisenhower for his probable capacity to settle the Korean War? The issue of Korea was vastly different from that of Communism or China because it was a war. For two years the general public had been exposed to grim evidence that the United States was fighting a war on the mainland of Asia with American troops while its public leaders disagreed about the war's purpose. Evidently Eisenhower appealed to the general voting public as a President to whom it could delegate with confidence the complex issues that irritated and alarmed it. Despite partisan efforts, *specific* foreign-policy issues had not become salient. But the partisan clamor had predisposed the voters to want solutions, particularly in Korea. "A central aspect" of Eisenhower's appeal "was his presumed ability to do something personally about Korea. . . ."[3] It was not, as Kenneth Waltz has shown, an unreasonable assignment for the electorate to give its President.[4]

[2] "The most interesting fact . . . is that only 3 percent of the population mentioned the argument that the Democratic administration had been 'soft on Communism' and was 'infiltrated with Communists,' in spite of the fact that this argument was very prominent among the campaign stimuli to which the voters were subjected." *Ibid.*, p. 52; for additional evidence see Samuel A. Stouffer, *Communism, Conformity, and Civil Liberties* (New York: Doubleday, 1955) pp. 86–88.

[3] Campbell, Gurin, and Miller, *op. cit.*, p. 67.

[4] In James N. Rosenau, ed., *Domestic Sources of Foreign Policy* (New York: Free Press, 1967), p. 282.

THE EARLY PROSPECTS FOR CHANGE

Normally, the inauguration of a newly elected President provides the occasion for departures in public policy. New ideas have been generated in the campaign; the electoral results reveal new popular constraints and mandates for the Congress and the President; and new faces appear in key positions of the executive branch. Eisenhower's accession to the Presidency was no exception. His was the first Republican administration in twenty years, and the campaign had provided even more than the normal opportunities for policy changes.

It is true that Eisenhower's 1952 victory, unlike that of Roosevelt in 1932, did not mark a massive shift in party identification. Eisenhower's landslide brought the Republicans only one seat in the Senate, giving them a bare majority of 48 to 47 and 22 more in the House to give them a majority of eight there. Two years later the Republicans were to lose control of both houses of Congress and remain under Democratic leadership for the rest of Eisenhower's Presidency.

Nonetheless, Eisenhower's prospects for broad congressional support were better than those faced by Truman at the beginning of his term. Since Eisenhower's popularity stretched well beyond party lines, cooperation with him in Congress was a feasible and attractive prospect for Democratic Congressmen. Moreover, they were not inhibited by their past record, for they had avoided taking much responsibility for the Truman Administration's Asian policy —the foreign-policy area in which it was most vulnerable—and they had taken no more responsibility than the Republicans for the other aspects of Truman's foreign policy. Thus congressional Democrats were free to help Eisenhower reshape our foreign policy. Finally, no President in the twentieth century has enjoyed greater public confidence—particularly in his ability to conduct foreign relations—than did Eisenhower, at least during his first five years.

Administration officials and congressional leaders alike were disposed to make changes or give the appearance of change, if only to slough off the liabilities of being associated with the preceding administration. Some prominent Republican leaders wanted radical change—major cuts in the budget, major reductions in foreign commitments and operations, and major changes in foreign relations. Reflecting the general public's mood of frustration over the Korean War, Republican spokesmen wanted to achieve a great deal more in foreign relations for much less money and with fewer commitments than had the Truman Administration. Senator Taft, for example, the leading contender against Eisenhower in 1952 for the party nomination, expected major cutbacks in domestic programs. Senator William F. Knowland, who was to succeed Taft as the Floor Leader of Senate Republicans after a fatal illness hospitalized Taft in 1953, wanted to promote a Chinese Nationalist invasion of Red China and expand the Korean War, while reducing the federal budget. Taft and Knowland were both strong partisans who had elbowed their way to the top of their party in Congress when the Republicans were the party of opposition and hammered out vivid alternatives to contemporary policy. John Foster Dulles, who would become Eisenhower's first Secretary of State, had talked about taking the "psychological and political offensive," and insisted that the United States openly declare its intention to liberate the captive peoples of Eastern Europe.

Given the impetus for change in the Republican Party, the general impatience over Korea, the public confidence in Eisenhower, and Eisenhower's appointment of men who wanted to make changes—particularly Dulles, and Admiral Arthur W. Radford as Chairman of the Joint Chiefs of Staff—major changes *might* have occurred. But they did not. In this chapter we shall examine some examples of Eisenhower's early initiatives in foreign policy along with the ultimate failure of the Administration to meet its own expectations for change in its first term. The main reasons for this failure can be outlined here.

In nominating Eisenhower, the Republicans had opted against radical change. Their candidate identified with the internationalist wing of his party and with two major tenets of Truman's foreign policy—the American commitment in Europe and the strategic primacy of Europe over Asia. Eisenhower's nomination guaranteed that a Republican administration would seek to conclude the Korean War rather than involve the United States further in Asia by escalating it.

Foreign-policy changes, furthermore, would have required strong presidential leadership and additional government activity. Eisenhower had the political support for both but the inclination for neither. His own views about the proper role of the President, coupled with his conviction that government had already over-shadowed the private sector, restrained him from asserting strong leadership in domestic matters. In foreign as in domestic affairs, Eisenhower's special concern over public expenditures limited his leadership. Eisenhower accepted a conservative economic view that (1) the federal budget should be balanced and (2) federal taxes should be cut. His desire for a tax cut reflected his belief in the limited utility of public over private expenditures. A balanced budget was the objective of an economic school that sought economic stability through a "sound" dollar (i.e., one that would remain constant in value) and economic growth through improvement of the climate for business investment with tax cuts and the complete elimination of inflation. This theory about the behavior of business investors became widely discarded by the early sixties in favor of one which held that the government could play a positive role in creating pressure for expansion in the economy.

Finally, the Republicans had unrealistic expectations about changing foreign and domestic policies. In 1953, for the first time since the Hoover Administration, a Republican administration had to come to terms with the constraints and frustrations of governing. In no sector of public policy had conditions changed more or had the difference between governing and opposing the government become greater than in that of foreign affairs.

We shall look at the development of foreign policy during Eisenhower's first term in greater detail from three aspects: (1) Eisenhower's early leadership, (2) his domestic problems, and (3) his attempt to recast foreign policy and construct new relations with allies and enemies, including his nurturing of a new disarmament policy for the United States.

EISENHOWER'S EARLY LEADERSHIP

The 1952 campaign had suggested two issues on which the Republicans if elected could be expected to take decisive action.

The first was the settlement of the Korean War. Prior to Eisenhower's election, armistice negotiations with North Korea and the Chinese Reds had dragged on for more than a year before being suspended in October 1952 at Panmunjom. When Eisenhower took office he faced the major stumbling block to agreement: the question of whether the repatriation of war prisoners should be forcible or voluntary. The United Nations Command had insisted upon the right of prisoners *not* to return home if they did not wish to. Negotiations resumed in April. When they appeared to be breaking down again in late May, the Administration advised the United Nations Commander, then General Mark W. Clark, that if the Communists did not accept our final offer or if they made no constructive counterproposals he was authorized to break off the negotiations and "carry on the war in new ways never yet tried in Korea." Within less than two weeks the Communists accepted the final proposals from Washington and signed an agreement on the repatriation issue. The armistice went into effect on July 27, and with the settlement of the Korean War the public agitation over foreign relations that had plagued the Truman Administration subsided.

The second issue, that of the "captive peoples" of Eastern Europe, had emerged from the rhetoric of the Republican campaign. The foreign-policy plank of the 1952 Republican platform had denounced the "negative, futile and immoral policy of 'containment'" and promised to "repudiate all commitments contained in secret understandings such as those of Yalta which aid Communist enslavements." The platform had also promised to "wage peace and to win it." In the ensuing presidential campaign, to Eisenhower's dismay, Dulles talked of liberating the "captive" states of Eastern Europe without indicating that he meant by peaceful means.

The captive-peoples issue seemed ideally suited for demonstrating the differences between a Republican and a Democratic administration, particularly since nothing more than verbal declarations were required to underscore this point. Shortly after his inauguration, President Eisenhower said in addressing Congress that he would ask it to "join in an appropriate resolution" to recommend liberation of the East European states by peaceful means. But meanwhile Dulles had been learning in the State Department of the utility to the United States of the Yalta and Potsdam protocols. The Russians alleged that the Yalta agreement on democratic governments for Eastern Europe meant the acceptance of Soviet satellite regimes. But Yalta and Potsdam also underwrote the legal status of West Berlin and, indeed, of West Germany. The resolution, when finally drafted, merely referred to "violations" of the "clear intent" of unnamed wartime agreements and proclaimed "hope" that captive peoples would one day be free. The proposal languished in both the House and Senate from lack of Republican enthusiasm. With the death of the Soviet dictator, Joseph Stalin, on March 5, 1953, the Administration arranged to have further action on the resolution postponed indefinitely on the grounds that future Soviet action was now uncertain.

The Eisenhower Administration quickly learned that although "captive peoples" was a valuable political issue for the Republicans as an opposition party, it had become an embarrassment for them once in office. The Administration's handling of the Polish and Hungarian revolts three years later was to demonstrate how much it had reduced its efforts to win and hold public attention with specific foreign-policy issues.

Ironically, the two early examples of Republican initiative led to a reduction in Administration efforts to base foreign policy on a broad and active public consensus. The Korean settlement promptly reduced the visibility of foreign policy to the public, while the Administration itself hardly wanted public attention called to the fact that it had abandoned the popular idea of rolling back the Communist empire and liberating captive peoples. Public attention to foreign affairs declined, and even opinion leaders increasingly accepted without question the Administration's handling of foreign relations.

Eisenhower's political status and style, coupled with his deference to Dulles, accentuated this trend. Eisenhower disliked partisan politics. He had a confidence bred by success in politics, yet he preferred to take important matters out of politics. Whereas Truman had relished the role of the national leader arousing the public to support the government in time of crisis, Eisenhower wanted to routinize the execution of foreign policy so that problems would not have to be treated as crises in order to win the political support needed to deal with them. The burdens of foreign affairs had to be limited to commitments that could be sustained over the "long haul," and their handling would have to be better organized.

The application of these views, however, depended on what turned out to be Eisenhower's most important foreign-policy commitment, at least in his first term: his confidence in John Foster Dulles, his Secretary of State from 1953 until 1958.

Eisenhower held Dulles in high esteem and treated him as the government's expert on foreign policy. He was consistent (with one important exception[5]) in delegating the authority for foreign relations to Dulles. This was not a new experience for Dulles, who had long been recognized as a leading authority in foreign affairs by the Republican party. In 1948 he had awaited a Republican victory that would certainly have made him Secretary of State.

Dulles was less confident than Eisenhower about being able to control the forces of public opinion. He had been a highly successful New York corporation lawyer but an unsuccessful political candidate. When he became Secretary of State he resolved to get along with Congress better than had Dean Acheson. Dulles had served briefly as an appointed United States Senator in 1950, and he evidently hoped to hold the support of the powerful Senate Foreign Relations Committee. His relations with the Committee began on a cordial note, but by 1954 the Committee's hearings had become rough and contentious, setting back his effort to win selective political consent and support for his policies.

Dulles also differed from Eisenhower in his inclination to handle political relationships as adversary proceedings, to be conducted by manipulation and maneuver rather than by accommodation and compromise. It was a style that did not endear him to Congress. It may well have reflected his experience as a corporation lawyer and lack of experience as a business or government executive. Eisenhower's record as a leader of military coalitions, on the other hand, showed him to be highly skilled in conciliation and in accumulating the support and confidence of diverse groups.

"PACTOMANIA"

The new Administration reflected a Republican resolve to pay more attention to the seriousness of the non-European threat of

[5] See pp. 84–85.

Communist aggression. It saw Communist China as the obedient agent of the Soviet Union. When this premise of Sino-Soviet unity was coupled with the Republican determination to do better in Asia, the objective became "completion" of containment—that is, the building up of our defense capabilities from NATO's right flank in Greece and Turkey, through the Middle East, across South and Southeast Asia, and up through the Western Pacific offshore line to Korea.

At the same time the Republicans were determined to meet the Communist menace with a lower cost in manpower and material resources to the United States than had the Truman Administration. Eisenhower shared with a large proportion of his party the aspiration to make the profile of the national government less prominent and, in doing so, to lighten the burden, as they saw it, that government commitments imposed on the private sector of the economy. According to this view—one to which Truman had subscribed until the Korean War—the economy could not carry the burdens of external affairs and domestic welfare without being weakened by the effort. (This simple view of political economy was to be modified in both parties in the late fifties as Western European governments demonstrated that, under certain conditions, national governments could, with deficit budgets and other devices of fiscal and economic policy, force feed their economies to achieve extraordinarily high rates of economic growth.) For the moment, however, the view held, as it had for President Truman, a vital political meaning: that any administration must come to terms with the political as well as the strictly economic limits of national policies.

The Truman Administration's policy of containment assumed that time would erode the cohesion and hostility of the Communist bloc. Yet the most eloquent expositor of this view, George Kennan, considered the Truman Administration's policies needlessly belligerent, while the more militant Acheson wanted to create "situations of strength" in the Western position in order to demonstrate to the Russians that they would have to come to terms with the West. Acheson had seen the threat in Asia declining as Sino-Soviet unity disintegrated. Most of Eisenhower's advisers on foreign affairs, however, rejected both Kennan's view that the Soviet regime would change from within and Acheson's prediction of friction within the Soviet bloc. They considered Russia's control over the bloc too firm to permit its breakup.

The post-Korean American effort to achieve flexibility in Asia, much like the pre-Korean one, emphasized the use of indigenous forces coupled with strategic reinforcement—now, however, with regional allies providing the reinforcement. Along with disengagement in Korea, the Eisenhower Administration undertook to build up local military forces in Taiwan, the Philippines, Vietnam, Thailand, Pakistan, Iraq, and Iran. In Korea, the United States kept two American divisions, mixed with ROK (South Korean) forces, because of distrust of the militant President of South Korea, Syngman Rhee. Our distrust grew out of an incident that had occurred during the drawn-out truce negotiations: in early 1953, as a long deadlock in the negotiations appeared to be breaking, Rhee released North Korean prisoners of war. By doing so, he made it impossible for the United States or his own government to expatriate these forces, forcibly or otherwise, and jeopardized the success of the negotiations. His action served to remind American officials that with his long dedication to national independence for Korea, Rhee did not share the American interest in an armistice that would leave the country divided roughly the way it had been before the North Korean attack in 1950. On the contrary, he had an interest in catalytic military ventures similar to that of the other revisionist American ally in Asia, Nationalist-ruled Formosa.

The United States signed a bilateral defense treaty with South Vietnam in October 1953. It went into force a year later. A defense treaty with the Chinese Nationalists followed soon after. Neither bilateral arrangement was supplemented by a multilateral treaty. Southward and westward, along the Sino-Soviet periphery, however, the arrangements that were concluded had both a bilateral and a multilateral component. At Manila, in September 1954, the United States signed a loosely knit collective-security arrangement with the United Kingdom, France, New Zealand, Australia, and three Asian countries—the Philippines, Thailand, and Pakistan—that came to be known as the Southeast Asia Treaty Organization (SEATO). This treaty covered aggression (privately, it was understood to be only Communist aggression) in a territory that also included non-SEATO members Taiwan, Cambodia, Laos, and South Vietnam.

Early in 1955, around the western rim of Soviet power, two states on the "Northern Tier" of the Middle East, Turkey and Iraq, signed the Baghdad Pact. They were followed by Pakistan, Iran, and Britain in an alliance that came to be known as CENTO (Central Treaty Organization). Dulles had promoted the idea of a "Northern Tier" treaty, and the members had joined with the expectation that the United States would sponsor and support their common effort. Dulles' object had been a military alliance against the Soviet Union that would avoid embroilment in Arab politics and be independent of the British. At the insistence of the British, however, he did include Iraq, a prominent Arab state, in his proposal. When Colonal Gamul Abdul Nasser, head of the new Nationalist regime in Egypt, denounced the treaty because it rivaled his aspirations for Arab unity, Washington decided to keep our participation as inconspicuous as possible. Rather than signing the treaty, the United States remained only an informal participant.

Both Dulles and Defense Department officials saw Pakistan's common membership in SEATO and CENTO as a vital link between two chains. Also, since NATO membership already had been extended to Greece and Turkey (in 1951), Turkey linked CENTO with NATO. Critics charged that the Eisenhower Administration overvalued the benefits of open military alliance and undervalued the importance of such neutral states as Indonesia and India. These critics dubbed the new interest in military alliances "pactomania."

Military and economic aid from the United States played an important role in our relationships with all the Asian members of the two alliances—the Philippines, Thailand, Pakistan, Iraq, Iran, and Turkey (though not with New Zealand and Australia), and with South Vietnam. Although they were intended to add flexibility to the American policy in Asia, the military-aid programs and the multilateral treaty chain stretching from the Philippines through the Middle East and Europe and across the Atlantic to Canada became a literal-minded and rigid application of the policy of containment, with no alliance member inclined to question whether the level of American effort was too high or too low or whether our efforts should be oriented in another direction altogether.

DOMESTIC PROBLEMS OF THE FIRST ADMINISTRATION

The "long haul" meant two things for the Eisenhower Administration: recognition that the Soviet challenge was a long-term one and adoption of policies that Congress and the American public would support over the long term. The new Administration undertook to deal with the problem of domestic support for the stand against international Communism in characteristic fashion: by economizing in defense outlays and manpower (so that fewer sacrifices would be asked of Congress and the public) and by deferring to Congress—permitting it to play a more prominent role in governing than it had come to play during twenty years of Democratic Presidents. Both economizing and presidential self-constraint were prominently (though hardly exclusively) Republican ideas.

As the Eisenhower Administration discovered, deferring to Congress was not necessarily a way to win friends on Capitol Hill. Congressmen are not interested simply in getting their views adopted as foreign policy: they are interested more broadly in governing, and that includes the delegation of authority and the fixing of responsibility. When the President leads, he assumes responsibility; when he defers to Congress, he may be seeking to share a responsibility that Congress does not want to accept. Moreover, while Eisenhower evidently doubted that the constitutional role of Congress was resilient enough to withstand pressure from an assertive modern Presidency, and while Dulles worried about the power of a hostile Congress to block the President's policies and immobilize the Secretary of State, both men wanted to maintain the full reach of legal discretion in foreign relations that they had inherited. They soon found themselves defending presidential discretion in foreign relations against the onslaught of the Bricker Amendment, a proposed constitutional change originated by the American Bar Association that would substantially restrict the power of the President to conduct foreign relations. The proposal, championed by Republican Senator John W. Bricker of Ohio, took several forms from the time of its introduction in 1953 until it faded from serious public concern in 1956. It was propelled into national attention by a cluster of varied interests—conservative leaders of the American Bar Association who opposed the growth of presidential power, particularly in treaty making; a wider group who distrusted summit meetings, such as Yalta and Potsdam, and the power of the United Nations; and certain East European émigré groups who blamed the Yalta agreements for the Soviet domination of their homelands. Dulles and Eisenhower insisted on the importance of presidential discretion in foreign relations, expressed interest in modifications of the proposed amendment and substitutes for it, and rode out the enthusiasm for it until it died.

Eisenhower and Dulles used much the same method to deal with Senator McCarthy, though with different consequences. Eisenhower had avoided conflict with McCarthy during the presidential campaign of 1952, and he continued to do so in office. When the Republicans gained control of the Senate in 1952 McCarthy became head of the investigating subcommittee of the Senate Government Operations Committee and continued to pursue his earlier charges that the State Department was riddled with Communists.

Biding its time with Bricker and his associates had cost the Eisenhower Administration very little, but avoiding a showdown with Senator McCarthy severely undermined the operations of the State Department. The inept handling of political appointments had put the State Department security post in the hands of Scott McCleod, a friend of McCarthy who pressed his charges from inside the Department. Dulles permitted McCleod and McCarthy to work together, and the morale of the State Department—already low—plummeted further.

Dulles' failure to defend the State Department against irresponsible attacks was not the only source of friction between the Secretary and his subordinates. He was inexperienced in delegating responsibilities, insistent that everything be cleared through him, and inclined to manipulate and maneuver—all of which helped suppress State Department initiative and responsiveness. Increasingly, foreign policy became a matter handled by Dulles at a level where, for the time being, it was least vulnerable to public or congressional scrutiny.

McCarthy was later to shift his investigation to the Army and ultimately to offend the Senate, bringing down a motion of censure against him in 1954 for his behavior toward his fellow Senators.

His influence was negligible after his fall from grace in the Senate, and he died in 1957. His demise ended the bitter controversy between those who supported Eisenhower's hands-off policy, arguing that McCarthy had had only minor impact on the quality of performance in the executive branch and on the lives of the people he had attacked, and those who argued that the tolls on both fronts had been very great and that Eisenhower should have taken a stronger stand.

MILITARY STRATEGY AND DEFENSE ALLOCATIONS

The Eisenhower Administration's effort to recast our defense posture and military doctrines was a puzzling combination of moves and intentions. When Dulles became Secretary of State he had been acting for more than four years as the principal Republican spokesman for foreign policy and strategy. Dulles' criticisms were those of an opposition leader—more precise in specifying errors than in drawing up alternatives. He talked of taking the "psychological and political offensive." He adopted the much-voiced views of air-power advocates (given increased appeal by our possession of nuclear weapons). He argued that the United States should use the threat of aerial atomic retaliation of any size and in any place as a deterrent to Communist aggression or expansion. The air-power reference opened old wounds for an Army man. Eisenhower insisted that Dulles' statement about atomic retaliation be deleted from the Republican platform and criticized in his campaign the air-power enthusiast's advocacy of exclusive reliance on retaliatory air power.

At the same time, Eisenhower was skeptical of the claims made by the armed services about what forces and equipment they needed. (Since he had once been Army Chief of Staff, he could claim some basis for his skepticism.) He also wanted to economize in the government and cut taxes. He did not flinch when George Humphrey, his Secretary of the Treasury, advocated a one-third cut in the budget, "using a meat ax" where necessary, as he put it.[6] Sixty percent of the federal budget for the fiscal year ending in mid-1953 was scheduled to be spent for defense; of the domestic

[6] Emmett J. Hughes, *The Ordeal of Power* (New York: Atheneum, 1963), p. 72.

portion, half was for fixed obligations. Eisenhower understood this and accepted its implications: most of the cuts in the federal budget would have to be made in the area of defense. His views about how to accomplish this reflected air-power beliefs in cutting down ground and sea forces. As might be expected, however, he believed that ground forces were still important. His aim was to provide a cheaper way to get them.

The defense of Europe against Russia was still the central strategic problem for the United States beyond its own borders. It was important that the United States not permit its forces to get pinned down again as they had been in Korea. This conclusion reflected the worries of the professional military about meeting additional threats. But it also reflected the anxiety shared by both the military and the politicians about mobilizing and maintaining domestic political support for prolonged combat overseas. In the campaign Eisenhower had talked of a defense posture that would "keep our boys at our side instead of on a foreign shore."[7] This idea evidently meant to him that the United States should withdraw forces from overseas—primarily from Asia—and hold them in reserve. After the election he found that Admiral Arthur W. Radford, the Commander in Chief of the Pacific Fleet, shared his resolve to effect major economies in the defense budget and to withdraw American ground forces from overseas. He called Radford back to Washington and named him Chairman of the Joint Chiefs of Staff.

For Radford, however, bringing the troops home and cutting the defense budget held a different meaning: a nearly exclusive reliance on strategic air power—the very thing that Eisenhower opposed—which made it unnecessary to build up a central military reserve—the very thing Eisenhower favored. Yet, as a practical matter, Eisenhower did not disagree with Radford about budgets and manpower requirements because he doubted that the military's estimates of its requirements were sound.

It was Radford's views about military strategy, articulated and rammed through the opposition of the armed services (particularly the Army) that became the "New Look," a headline term

[7] Glenn H. Snyder, "The 'New Look' of 1953," in Warner R. Shilling, Paul Y. Hammond, and Glenn H. Snyder, *Strategy, Politics and Defense Budgets* (New York: Columbia Univ. Press, 1962), p. 390.

for the new Administration's revamping of defense policy. The New Look cut the Army and increased the size of the Air Force, substituting local foreign-defense forces, trained and provisioned if necessary by the United States, for American troops. (Equivalent U.S. forces, the argument went, could be several times as expensive to maintain.) The New Look substituted long-range bombers and missiles carrying nuclear warheads for ground and sea forces armed with conventional (non-nuclear) weapons. It tried to take advantage of new weapons technology in order to save money and manpower.

Dulles was at first dubious about cutting defense spending by relying more on nuclear weapons. At a cabinet meeting in March 1953, responding to a plea for massive federal-budget cuts, he had pointed out:

> *It's all very well for us to balance our budgets, but we have to remember that every other NATO country would like to do the same thing. If we tidy up our own shop nicely, they aren't going to take kindly to our insistence on their defense buildups, leaving them stuck with unbalanced budgets.*

Before the year ended, however, Dulles joined Eisenhower and Radford in emphasizing that the changes he advocated in strategy meant direct savings in defense spending. In May 1953, while touring the Middle East, he had adapted his views on strategy to accommodate Eisenhower's interest in local military forces by discovering that the "Northern Tier" of states, Turkey, Iran, Iraq, and (excluding Afghanistan) Pakistan, had certain military traditions akin to the developed states of Western Europe and a traditional fear of Russia. Even without the economic strength of Western Europe, he considered them potential members of an effective regional security system like NATO and invited them promptly to organize one, promising American support if they did. That was the beginning of his "pactomania." CENTO and SEATO were designed to meet two aims of the United States: to specify to the potential aggressor what areas came under U.S. protection and to substitute local military capabilities for American soldiers. But even while promoting these alliances, Dulles wanted to free the United States from reliance on local forces. Reflecting a crucial de-

8 As quoted in Hughes, *op. cit.*, p. 73.

cision by Eisenhower at the end of 1953 that permitted the military-contingency planners to count on using nuclear weapons, Dulles restated in January 1954 his preference for strategic air power, linking these ideas about strategy with economizing: "We need allies and collective security," he said in a speech in New York. "Our purpose is to make these relations more effective and less costly. This can be done by placing more reliance on deterrence power and less dependence on local defensive power."

Instead of endorsing the emphasis Dulles and Radford placed on strategic air power and deterrence, Eisenhower preferred to stress local defense forces, strengthened if necessary by American forces from the central military reserve. "Our first objectives," he indicated in a policy directive to the Defense Department at the beginning of 1955, "must be to maintain the capability to deter an enemy from without and to blunt [such an] attack if it comes. . . . To provide for meeting lesser hostile action—such as local aggression not broadened by the intervention of a major aggressor's forces—growing reliance can be placed upon the forces now being built and strengthened in many areas of the free world."

Eisenhower, then, did not agree with Dulles' strategic ideas but he did not repudiate them, just as he did not repudiate Radford's unabashed dogmas of strategic air power, even where they ran against his own convictions about a central military reserve.

Radford, for his part, pushed the conventional-force cutbacks through the military establishment with single-minded determination while promoting with equal vigor military-assistance agreements to build up local forces in Asia. Dulles, in turn, was well aware that the New Look would encourage our NATO allies to weaken their conventional forces while our policy was to get them to strengthen these forces; yet he, too, supported the New Look.

Eisenhower and Dulles never explained these disparities between their convictions and their policies or even acknowledged that they existed. They both evidently accepted the New Look as the product of a realistic assessment about the resources available to buy military strength. Dulles treated the negative European reaction to the New Look as something he must minimize. Eisenhower shielded from public discussion behind his authoritative general endorsement of Radford's defense policies the disparity between his skepticism about air power and his acceptance of air-power-dominated force postures. Neither Dulles nor Eisenhower would have gained much from exposing these disparities unless they were prepared to recast public discussion on foreign relations. Both would have had to acknowledge that economic and political constraints played an important role in the determination of defense policy, and had they done so, defense policy would have become a much more partisan issue. Both preferred instead to claim a more authoritative basis for the determination of military and foreign policy. Military budgets and forces could be justified on the grounds that they were what was "necessary" to meet the "requirements" of national security. Similar considerations applied to foreign relations. In this way, Eisenhower and Dulles avoided the arousal of public anxieties and the attracting of public attention to the intractible problems of foreign policy.

Their style was consistent with one interpretation of Eisenhower's electoral popularity: the public wish to turn foreign relations over to a trustful figure so that public attention could turn elsewhere. It also reflected the inclination of any incumbent Administration, when it is not optimistic about its capacity to explain foreign policy to the public, to minimize public involvement in foreign relations.

COPING WITH FRIENDS AND ENEMIES

The New Look had a direct impact on our conduct of foreign policy—particularly on our ability to cope with our friends and enemies abroad. As we have seen, the Eisenhower Administration's shift in emphasis from conventional to nuclear power helped the United States to maintain the initiative in its foreign relations with a strong posture of prestige and influence, as the settlement of the Korean War and the extension of American power around the rimland of Asia demonstrated.

At the same time, however, the priorities underlying the New Look made it more difficult to exert American influence in other areas. Four areas of particular difficulty deserve attention here: (1) the failure to revive NATO rearmament without additional American commitments; (2) the decision not to apply the "massive retaliation" doctrine in Indochina to extricate the French forces from defeat there; (3) the first Taiwan Straits crisis; and (4) the problems of recasting disarmament negotiations with the Soviet Union.

NATO, EDC, AND GERMAN REARMAMENT

The difficulties with NATO had several origins. One was, as Dulles had anticipated, the New Look. The further development of NATO required its members to increase the size of their conventional forces. American military manpower and defense-expenditure reductions could only make it difficult for NATO allies to carry their own armament efforts further—and even more difficult for the United States to press them to do so. In fact, European armament efforts leveled off in 1954 (coinciding with the decline of American military assistance). For the rest of the decade, Washington would concern itself over the failures of other NATO members to meet their commitments.

Another basic problem with NATO was the disparity in the economic and military power of the alliance members. Secure beside the towering strength of the United States, no other NATO member worried much about its own lack of military readiness to defend itself.

This difficulty of reactivating NATO rearmament was accentuated by the decline of anxiety over the Soviet threat after 1953, brought about by the armistice in Korea and by developments in the Soviet bloc. When the Eisenhower Administration came to power, the Soviet bloc was a tightly knit military and economic alliance (although Yugoslavia, expelled from the bloc in 1948, had firmly established by 1953 that it could survive as a Communist state outside Russia's aegis).

In early 1953, however, the death of Soviet dictator Joseph Stalin led to a protracted but restrained struggle for leadership of Russia. At the beginning of this struggle Moscow's grip on the East European satellites slackened, and a riot flared in East Germany. But after the first tensions of the succession crisis passed, Soviet foreign policy became more flexible and conciliatory as a program of "de-Stalinization" got under way.

The Soviet Union displayed its new flexibility by increasing its support of nonbloc nationalist forces (at the expense of local Communist movements) and went into the foreign economic- and military-aid business. A tour by Soviet Chief of State Bulganin and Soviet Premier Khrushchev of Burma, India, and Afghanistan, followed by economic-aid missions, scored diplomatic gains that were sobering to Washington. For Afghanistan, in the literal-minded geography of the Baghdad Pact, breached the Northern Tier between Pakistan and Iran and India had been passed over in early 1954 in favor of Pakistan as a reliable ally. The Chinese Communist regime, following suit, modified its opposition to non-Communist governments in Asia and Africa. Shortly after the Geneva summit meeting in 1955, Czechoslovakia completed an arms-for-cotton agreement with Egypt that added considerably to Anglo-Egyptian tensions over the future of the Suez Canal. Increasingly, the United States found itself caught between its military commitments and its Asian political interests.

Moscow's new flexibility in dealing with underdeveloped areas meant that the United States had a more effective, though perhaps less menacing, competitor in these areas. The Soviet Union's apparent shift from military to economic and diplomatic initiatives was underscored in May 1956 when Moscow announced the reduction of Soviet armed forces from 4 million to 2.8 million men and depicted this as a major unilateral step toward disarmament. Western skeptics saw it instead as a belated effort to effect economies in the Soviet military establishment as part of the de-Stalinization campaign—much like the New Look in Washington. Nonetheless, the net impact of the Soviet thaw was to reinforce the sentiment of our West European allies that the military need for NATO rearmament was less urgent than Washington claimed.

Before taking office, Eisenhower and Dulles had resolved to force the issue of what form the German military contribution to NATO should take. A treaty establishing a European Defense Community (EDC) had been signed in 1952, but ratification of it had been stalled by France and Italy. It provided for a unified defense force that would permit the rebuilding of a German army only as part of an integrated Western European force. As President-elect, Eisenhower used a public New Year's greeting to set the unification of Western Europe as a major objective of American foreign policy. The message was clear enough in Western Europe.

"Within my first few hours in office," Eisenhower has reported, "I had read messages from both Bonn and Paris describing meetings between Chancellor Adenauer of Germany and Foreign Minister Georges Bidault of France in which assurances were given of the support of both their governments for the principle of the European Defense Community."[9] On his first foreign trip as Secretary of State, Dulles was dispatched to Europe at the end of January to press the case of EDC. (In the next six years he was to travel more than half a million miles on similar errands.) On the eve of his departure, in a nationwide television address, he made his object clear. After referring to the massive financial assistance ($30 million) the United States had given to Western Europe since World War II, he warned: ". . . if it appeared there were no chance of getting effective unity, and if in particular, France, Germany and England should go their separate ways, then certainly it would be necessary to give a little rethinking to America's own foreign policy in relation to Western Europe."[10]

At the year's end, although Dulles had taken every opportunity to press the case privately with European officials, EDC remained an unratified treaty. He now threatened publicly again, and a bit more pointedly, that if EDC was not ratified, the United States would have to undertake "an agonizing reappraisal" of its commitments to Europe.

The threat caused a flurry of anxiety abroad and criticism of French and Italian leaders by their publics. Statesmen in Paris and Rome did not appreciate this public criticism. After all, they wanted EDC too, but, as they saw it, their parliaments were the obstacles. American public threats could only make their work more difficult by inflaming nationalist feelings. Dulles, however, evidently felt that these leaders needed public prodding. The United States Senate added pressure by denying mutual-security funds in 1954 legislation to countries that had not ratified the treaty.

Eisenhower, sensitive to the domestic problems in Europe that he had helped to moderate as Supreme Allied Commander, prom-

9 Dwight D. Eisenhower, *The White House Years*, Vol. II: *Waging Peace, 1956–1961* (New York: Doubleday, 1965), p. 140.
10 *Ibid.*, p. 141.

ised in April a long-term commitment of American ground forces in Europe, provided the EDC treaty was ratified. But neither sticks nor carrots were sufficient. On August 30 the French National Assembly rejected the EDC treaty, for all practical purposes killing it.

Washington's bluff had been called. When EDC failed, Dulles offered to make the long-term troop commitment anyway, providing an alternative arrangement could be found. The arrangement turned out to be a loose aggregation of military forces, incongruously called the Western European Union (WEU). This union satisfied Washington because it established a means for bringing West Germany directly into NATO membership under certain armament limitations administered by WEU.

The Eisenhower Administration had attempted by threatening sanctions to expedite the building of the military capabilities of the NATO alliance without additional American commitments. In the end, it had, like the Truman Administration before, carried NATO along only by entangling itself further. The threats were ineffective, in part because they were not believed: the United States wanted a strong NATO as much as anyone did. In fact, the "agonizing reappraisal" Europeans might well worry about would be the one that would have occurred *after* EDC had come into effect. For Washington supported political integration and EDC in order to reduce Western Europe's dependence on it, while an important attraction of NATO to most of its members was that it tied American military might to their defense. EDC, moreover, by providing an effective conventional military force on the central front in Europe, would have permitted the United States to concentrate even more on nuclear weapons, saving itself the cost of conventional forces. The effort to win acceptance of EDC, then, was a new departure in foreign policy for the Eisenhower Administration (1) in the way it influenced other NATO members, (2) in economizing on American military commitments to NATO, and (3) in furthering the United States effort to specialize in nuclear military forces. The extent of the United States failure to make these shifts can be seen in the death of EDC, the increase in American military commitments to NATO that followed, and later, in the wasteful duplication of nuclear-weapons armament in Great Britain and then France.

THE INDOCHINA CRISIS OF 1954

The limits of the New Look military posture were further underlined by the Eisenhower Administration's handling of the French appeal for help in Indochina.

Early in 1954 the American position was that Indochina should not be permitted to fall into the hands of the Communists. As the situation deteriorated, Radford proposed carrier-based air strikes. His plan was duly processed in the National Security Council. Eisenhower approved, as did his principal advisers—Dulles, Radford, Secretary of the Treasury George Humphrey, and Charles Wilson, the Secretary of Defense. But key Congressmen, consulted privately, demurred: if the President expected support from a joint congressional resolution, he should line up foreign allies first.

Now the Administration shifted ground. Eisenhower accepted the Congressmen's proviso and insisted on British support as a prerequisite. Dulles might have considered the Indochinese situation an opportunity to apply his doctrine of "massive retaliation." Instead, at the first signs of British disapproval, Dulles abandoned the Radford proposal because he feared that pressure on Britain over Indochina would jeopardize British approval of the Southeast Asian security pact. Eisenhower also backed off, partly because he found the Army's rebuttal of Radford persuasive. The rebuttal also convinced Humphrey, who shrank from the prospective cost in conventional forces that rescue of the French in Indochina now seemed to require.[11]

Radford's forceful advocacy of an air-power venture in Indochina had won strong but only temporary endorsement. Eisenhower had been concerned about the tactics of winning congressional endorsement for a major step in foreign relations. Dulles' attention had been on his bargaining position with the British. Radford could regard the abandonment of his proposal as merely a tactical setback. Yet Washington's failure to act could not help but be re-

11 Chalmers M. Roberts, "The Day We Didn't Go to War," *The Reporter*, XI, No. 4 (September 14, 1954), pp. 3–4; Dwight D. Eisenhower, *The White House Years*, Vol. 1: *Mandate for Change, 1953–1956*, pp. 331–340; Peter F. Whittereid, *The Chairman of the Joint Chiefs of Staff: An Evolving Institution*, M.A. thesis, University of Virginia, 1964, pp. 101 ff.

garded abroad as just that. Despite the Administration's resolve to exploit American strategic superiority and military flexibility, it had in effect demonstrated that the New Look had hampered its ability to deal with what it certainly perceived to be Communist initiatives along the containment perimeter.

Dulles had provided a way to avoid the test of his new doctrine in advance. Before the French appeal for American air strikes he had stated that deterrence through strategic air power did not apply to Indochina because there had been no open aggression. In this way, however, he had ruled out the applicability of "massive retaliation" in meeting the main challenge in Asia.

When direct American military intervention did not materialize, and the French bastion at Dien Bien Phu fell, the French government settled at Geneva with the representatives of Ho Chi Minh for a North-South partitioning of Vietnam at the waist and completed armistice arrangements for Cambodia and Laos—the other two states composing French Indochina. Neither the United States nor the South Vietnamese government signed the agreement on Vietnam.

The Geneva agreements provided for elections in South Vietnam within two years, an arrangement that many delegates at Geneva interpreted as a graceful way to let Ho win. Washington, however, quickly became determined to save the anti-Communist government in South Vietnam. Dulles also pushed ahead with his plans for a Southeast Asia Treaty Organization, in part to internationalize the defense of South Vietnam.

The Indochinese crisis underlined the disparity between military power measured in technical terms and military power that was politically usable. An ally had appealed for American intervention, suggesting that American air power could be used without further U.S. involvement. The United States government, concluding that air power would not achieve the stated objectives and would lead to further American military involvement, carefully limited its military intervention.

The New Look and the new strategy that went with it had reduced our military expenditures but had not ensured us the capacity to act without incurring heavy costs. Our doctrines had become more flexible but our military capabilities had not—and our allies found this disparity quite unattractive.

THE EFFORTS TO DISARM

In its early disarmament negotiations with the Soviet Union, the Truman Administration had at first taken the position outlined in the Baruch Plan in 1946: that the United States would not give up its nuclear-weapons monopoly unless it could have absolute assurance against nuclear proliferation in return. The effect, of course, would be to keep Russia from getting nuclear weapons. Faced with this plan at the negotiating table, the Soviet Union needed only to delay agreement until, as a recognized nuclear power, it could get better terms. Disarmament negotiations had degenerated in the face of this deadlock into a propaganda battle, soiling the record of good intentions for both sides.

The United Nations established a Disarmament Commission in January 1952, and the Western powers began developing a new disarmament program. But the American position remained unchanged on the vital issue of nuclear control: an acceptable agreement would have to provide a reliable method of accounting for all nuclear-fuel production (and hence, for all nuclear weapons).

United States experience in negotiating with the Soviet Union had shown that Russian negotiators were kept on a tight rein by Moscow. It also became clear as the negotiations dragged on interminably that Western negotiators did not always have the attention of their own governments. Getting the heads of state together for a "summit" meeting, therefore, seemed like a good way to open up new avenues on both sides. The prospect of a summit meeting thus became linked early in the Eisenhower Administration to the rejuvenation of disarmament talks.

Once hopes for improved relations with the Soviet Union began to rise in 1953, prospective summit meetings became politically important. In France, and particularly in Britain, a summit meeting promised enhanced status for the heads of state who attended.

Eisenhower was distinctly more hopeful about negotiating with the Russians than was Dulles, and as a result he put far more faith than Dulles did in the efficacy of disarmament negotiations and summit conferences. This difference of views led Eisenhower to establish a separate avenue for initiating proposals in these areas— the one exception to his almost complete reliance on Dulles' handling of foreign-military matters. Throughout most of Dulles' tenure, Eisenhower kept a man in the White House to work on proposals that might change the United States relationship with the Soviet Union—in particular, proposals for disarmament and summitry. The first presidential aide to play that role was C. D. Jackson, who took Eisenhower's own idea for the "peaceful atom" and developed it into the proposal that Eisenhower presented to the United Nations General Assembly in December 1953. Eisenhower's proposal recognized that it was no longer possible to safeguard disarmament by trying to account for all nuclear fissile material. It simply provided that nuclear powers would contribute to a United Nations pool of nuclear fuel. The weight of the new plan rested on the quantities that would be disclosed and put under international control rather than on the impossible task of accounting for all fuel possessed by the nuclear powers.

Though widely hailed, the Eisenhower proposal had no effect on our relationship with the Soviet Union and, for a while, little effect even on the United States Atomic Energy Commission. The actual negotiating position of the United States did not change for nearly two years, and when it did, even our new position was outdated. As a result of the Eisenhower proposal, however, a United Nations Atomic Energy Commission was established to direct nuclear cooperation for peaceful uses.

The U.N. Disarmament Commission meetings continued in London into 1954, but since the American negotiating position failed to reflect Eisenhower's speech of the previous December, these meetings could hardly be more than a propaganda forum. Despite the fact that the Soviet delegation had been attacking Western proposals since long before the "Atoms for Peace" speech, Moscow indicated in the fall of 1954, after the Commission meetings had ended, that it was willing to reconsider some of the Western proposals. Both sides were having considerable difficulty in addressing the same issues at the same time, doubtless in part because disarmament remained a secondary objective to both. It looked as though a summit meeting would be necessary if disarmament negotiations were to be fruitful.

Soviet agreement to an Austrian State Treaty in April 1955 raised the hope in Bonn for German reunification, though Washington feared the consequences of overextended hopes. Eisenhower, forced mostly by British enthusiasm into a Big Four summit meeting in Geneva in July 1955, made a dramatic proposal to the Soviet delegation at that time: that the United States and Russia exchange complete blueprints of their military establishments and permit one another to make aerial-photo reconnaissance flights over the other country's territory in order to reduce the prospect of surprise attack. This "open skies" proposal was an appealing and powerful propaganda move in its own right as well as effective insurance against the possibility of Soviet propaganda gains. But the proposal did not offset the fact that the disarmament meeting itself indirectly undermined the military esprit of NATO by making the threat from Russia seem more remote. For the German Federal Republic, moreover, the meeting dashed its hopes for reunification, causing trouble for the aged Premier Konrad Adenauer, whose party suffered embarrassing defections. The summit had in fact served to complicate the politics of NATO, much as Dulles had feared.

Summitry had suffered a setback. But Eisenhower continued to shelter an independent office for the development of new disarmament ideas in the White House. Nelson Rockefeller had succeeded Jackson as its head, and it was the Rockefeller staff that had, with virtually no clearance from the State Department, prepared the "open skies" proposal that Eisenhower presented at Geneva.

Once again, the American negotiating position on disarmament failed to reflect Eisenhower's proposals. This time, the American position was simply suspended, and it was not until Eisenhower's second Administration that the U.S. disarmament delegation was prepared to reenter serious negotiations.

THE SUEZ CRISIS

PRECRISIS DISCORD

The Suez War brought the Anglo-American relationship to its postwar nadir and fueled French resentment over Britain's special relationship with the United States. For both Britain and France the Suez incident was an act of defiance against the United States. For France, it was a desperate venture that reflected the stress of domestic political instability and the strain of a contracting empire. For Britain, which was more stable domestically and more reconciled to her shrinking world status, Suez revealed her deteriorating relations with the United States and the personal alienation between Dulles and the British Prime Minister, Sir Anthony Eden.

Eden had never been an admirer of Dulles. Mutual hostility grew as Dulles set about separating American interests from British interests in the Middle East, making special overtures of friendship to Cairo and pressing the British to close their huge naval base in Suez.

Dulles' efforts to secure a military alliance in the Middle East became a point of particular antagonism. Dulles wanted to break away from a British plan and build a military alliance with the non-Arab states on the Soviet borderlands. Eden persuaded him to follow the British plan by including Iraq in his proposal for a "Northern Tier," assuring Dulles that Egypt would not object. When Egypt condemned the resulting Baghdad Pact because Iraq, her main rival for Arab state leadership, was a member, Dulles was annoyed with Eden for his reassurances about Egypt; Eden, in turn, resented the United States failure to join the pact. "Worse still," Eden resented "the fact that Dulles tried to take credit" for not joining the pact in capitals, such as Cairo, that were hostile to it.[12]

The French were also antagonistic toward Dulles. They resented the pressure he had exerted on France to ratify the EDC Treaty, and they remembered his role in their withdrawal from Vietnam. Dulles had in fact intentionally played a detached role in the Geneva negotiations partitioning Vietnam in 1954, but his detachment was more apparent in Washington than in Paris. The French saw him as presiding over the dissolution of their Asian empire—and picking up some pieces for the United States in the process (for this country quickly became involved in consolidating the rule of a new regime in South Vietnam).

The deterioration of American relations with Britain and France was due to other factors as well. By the mid-fifties NATO no longer commanded the priorities it had at the beginning of the decade on either side of the Atlantic. One indication of this change was that the United States was more willing than before to allow

[12] Anthony Eden, *The Memoirs of the Rt. Hon. Sir Anthony Eden: Full Circle* (Boston: Houghton Mifflin, 1960), p. 139.

its policies in the underdeveloped areas to conflict with British and French policies.

Nowhere was the potential conflict between two foreign "constituencies"—the former colonial powers in NATO and the former colonies outside Europe—better illustrated than by the response of our allies to the new regime in Egypt. Britain had commercial and strategic interests in the Suez Canal, but perhaps even higher stakes in its own national prestige. French commercial interests were also heavy. France's position in Lebanon and Israel was threatened by the ambitions of the Nasser regime, and, moreover, Egypt had become an important source of arms for Algeria in its fight against France. The United States, in its efforts to ingratiate itself with the Egyptian government, seemed to be encouraging Nasser's aspirations.

THE SUEZ WAR

Egypt's monarchy had been deposed in 1952 by the Egyptian Army, intent on modernization and reform. Nasser came to power in a colonels' revolt that followed in 1954. He set out to make Egypt the dominant and unifying force in the Middle East, exploiting popular resentment toward Israel's statehood and British control over the Suez Canal and the Sudan. To pursue development and reformation he adopted a "positive neutralism," seeking help from both the Communist and Western power blocs.

In July 1956, after the announcement of an Egyptian arms agreement with the Soviet Union, Washington (followed by London) backed away from a major commitment for economic aid to Egypt to help build the Aswan Dam. Nasser responded on July 26, 1956, by nationalizing the British-controlled (and partially French-owned) Suez Canal. Britain and France demanded in turn that the Canal be put under an international authority. Dulles played a major role in devising schemes for international control, but he undermined the impact of threats from London and Paris issued to Nasser in an effort to win Egypt's compliance. Eden saw Nasser as another Hitler. Impatient with the delays introduced by the United States, he resolved to act.

On October 29 Israeli forces swept across Egypt's Sinai Peninsula toward Suez. Britain and France quickly joined in thinly veiled collusion with Israel on the pretext of protecting the Canal. Their object was to seize the Canal and shatter the Nasser regime. President Eisenhower immediately condemned the tripartite action, took the matter to the United Nations General Assembly, and applied monetary and military pressures. With American support, the General Assembly approved a resolution calling for a ceasefire, while American naval and air forces in the Mediterranean harassed the British invasion forces.

As for monetary pressures, Britain proved to be more vulnerable than France because the pound sterling was one of the world's reserve currencies. Fearing that the British government would devalue the pound because of trade difficulties stemming from the war—caused in particular by the embargo on oil by the Middle East—holders of sterling credits rushed to convert them to dollars or gold. Only the International Monetary Fund could save the pound, but the United States withheld the Fund's help, promising to aid Britain only after she had accepted a ceasefire supervised by the United Nations. When Moscow threatened a nuclear strike against France and Britain, Washington responded ambiguously and then cut off further communication with British officials. Under these combined pressures, Eden caved in. The French Premier, Pineau, followed suit.

The war ended within eight days of the initial attack and hardly more than hours after the actual engagement of British and French landing forces. Among the many mistakes the British, and to a lesser extent the French, made in the Suez crisis was their calculations about the timing of the attack in relation to the American presidential election of 1956. The nearness of the election (it was only a week away), rather than helping to bring the United States in on their side, did quite the opposite.

Dulles had thrown himself into the complicated negotiations that followed Egypt's takeover of the Canal, attempting to protect the interests of the users and to avoid British and French belligerence. The decision to attack showed a dramatic loss of confidence in Dulles as conciliator. The British and French mistakenly expected that the United States would not block an Anglo-French effort—a colossal misunderstanding of American intentions. London attributed the "misunderstanding" to Washington's deliberate deception,

while Washington interpreted it as the product of puzzling stu-
pidity on the part of Britain and France.

To top it off, the British attack suffered major failures in execution. The British invasion force took a week longer to mount its
attack than Prime Minister Eden had been led to believe. The delay
was critical, for it permitted Washington to bring pressure to bear
in stopping the attack.

London and Paris evidently missed a major point about American behavior throughout the crisis. By attacking Egypt without
U.S. approval, Britain and France were challenging American leadership in the Atlantic alliance and the American role in the Middle
East. Washington reacted with genuine indignation. Eisenhower, in
a national television address, appealed to the rule of law in the
world community, condemning aggression "no matter who the
attackers, no matter who the victim."

It was the attack on Egypt per se, not her possible defeat, that
had challenged United States leadership. Whatever Washington
had to do to minimize the damage to its position in the Middle
East, Africa, and Asia and to maintain its leadership of the Atlantic
alliance could be done more palatably to victorious allies. Dulles
had given the strong impression in London that Britain and France
might have to resort to force. But what Britain and France mis-
understood was that the United States was not willing to sacrifice
its bloc leadership and its world esteem to permit them to do it.
Evidently British and French officials equated Dulles' hinted willingness to let them use force to his permitting them carte blanche.

Blame for the failure of both London and Paris to understand
our viewpoint lay with both sides. Dulles must have been insensitive
to the personal anxieties and stresses under which Eden and Pineau
labored. And they, in their hostility toward Dulles, may well have
underestimated his grasp of the American interests at stake in the
planned venture and his determination to pursue these interests.
At any rate, there is no reason to doubt the report that when Sel-
wyn Lloyd, the British Foreign Minister, went to see Dulles after
it was all over, the first question Dulles asked him was, "Why did
you stop?"[13]

The Suez War made the Baghdad Pact a source of embarrass-

[13] Richard Gould-Adams, *The Time of Power: A Reappraisal of John Foster
Dulles* (London: Weidenfelt & Nicolson, 1962), p. 222.

ment to the United States, left NATO in disarray, and antagonized many neutral states. Countries that nursed anticolonial grievances condemned the war as a revival of the old colonial-power aggression. At the same time, the caving in of Britain and France displayed the weaknesses of these states, diminishing the prestige of the NATO powers and of the United States, which suffered indirectly through its traditional association with the French and British.

The American role in the Suez crisis was to have severe long-term consequences for the cohesion of NATO and for Franco-American relations, as the next chapter will show in greater detail. The failure of the Suez venture brought down Eden, though not the Conservative government. The French government, already annoyed by Britain's special ties with Washington, resented Britain's submission and Washington's aid to the British afterward. These events added to the fiercely nationalistic, anti-American, and anti-British attitudes upon which De Gaulle would soon draw.

Nowhere has the American status with the public of its allies suffered so severe a setback as it did with the French and British publics over Suez. Conversely, Nasser's standing in the Middle East skyrocketed, and the Soviet position in the region improved, partly because Britain and France had agreed to a U.N. ceasefire order the day after the Soviet nuclear threat. The apparent knuckling under of Britain and France to Soviet nuclear power in turn diminished the confidence of Europeans in the American strategic umbrella.

The effects of the Suez crisis on European cohesion, however, are difficult to isolate from the events occurring in the Soviet Union and Eastern Europe at that time.

THE HUNGARIAN REVOLUTION

In the struggle for succession after Stalin's death in 1953, the new ruling group in Moscow had helped to stabilize its collective leadership by denigrating the myth of Stalin's greatness. Premier Khrushchev accelerated this effort early in 1956 at the Twentieth Party Congress with a remarkable secret speech telling of Stalin's malevolence and abuse of power during his reign. The contents of this speech not only became known throughout the

West but sent tremors reverberating throughout the regimes of Eastern Europe. All the East European Communist leaders had depended heavily on Moscow during the Stalin era. All had relied on the Soviet government as a model to legitimize their own authoritarian rule. Thus, to discredit Stalin was to discredit those Communist officials in the satellite regimes who were the most closely associated with Stalin and his narrow autocratic model. If, as Khrushchev claimed, Stalin had abused power, had not the lesser Stalins of Warsaw and Prague, Budapest, Bucharest, and Sofia also been abusive? In solving the succession problem within the Soviet Union, the Russian leaders were creating other problems for their satellites by discrediting Stalin.

In June 1956 workers in Poznań, Poland, struck against a regime that had only recently been "democratized." Their violence —three days of open rebellion—set off a national upsurge that installed a new regime and withstood Russian threats of intervention in October.

While the Soviet leaders were still dealing with the challenge to their authority in Warsaw, Hungarian students touched off a revolt in Budapest. Soviet troops intervened but were quickly forced to withdraw. As they left Hungary, Imre Nagy, the new premier, pledged free elections, an end to the one-party system, and "no interference in our internal affairs"—in effect a repudiation of Soviet hegemony that went well beyond the Polish stand. Four days later massively reinforced Soviet forces returned, quickly installed a new regime, and began a ruthless purge that Nagy, among others, did not survive. If the concessions to Polish nationalism marked the potential liberalization, the brutal repression of Hungary marked its limits.

Dulles correctly concluded that bringing American pressure to bear in support of Poland would only have hurt the Polish cause by provoking the Russians into retracting the concessions they had already made; in Hungary, on the other hand, it would seem in retrospect that little more could have been lost if Dulles had put pressure on Moscow to moderate its actions there. In fact, the United States inadvertently became involved in the Hungarian Revolution despite the Administration's general policy. Radio Free Europe, a CIA-supported private propaganda organization that proved unresponsive to the hands-off policy adopted in Washington, encouraged Hungarians to expect American intervention. The result was that the United States was correctly blamed for provoking Hungarians to take futile risks while Washington had actually adopted a policy that could in no way lend support to the courageous Hungarian stand.

The disappointing American policy in regard to Hungary, it should be noted, cannot be attributed to the New Look. It was rather the consequence of more fundamental limitations upon U.S. policy. Without a vastly greater military force swiftly deployable into Eastern Europe *and* a much greater inclination to risk war with Russia in Europe, the United States could not expect to do much more than it did.

The Suez crisis upset the Atlantic bloc; the Hungarian crisis, the Soviet bloc. Both crises resulted in the bloc leader temporarily asserting his dominance.

Both crises produced severe setbacks for long-term American foreign-policy goals. Suez badly strained the alliance pacts of Washington with Western Europe and throughout the Middle East into Asia. American inaction in behalf of Poland and Hungary not only demonstrated the Eisenhower Administration's abandonment of all efforts to liberate the "captive peoples" of Eastern Europe, but also showed Washington to be helpless while Russia tightened her grip on Eastern Europe.

On the other side, however, the repression of Hungary in 1956 only temporarily set back the prospects for a liberalized Soviet bloc. Moscow could not tolerate the repudiation of its dominance in the bloc, but neither was it pleased with the inept and costly regimes run by little autocrats such as Ulbricht in East Germany that a Stalinist grip on the bloc produced. Once the repression of Hungary had marked the limits of permissible de-Stalinization in the satellites, Moscow could then permit political liberalization within its European satellites with increased assurance that they would remain within limits tolerable to Moscow.

CONCLUSION

Our responses to Poland and Hungary were the most dramatic acts of restraint in the Eisenhower Administration's first term. But

Eisenhower had been restrained from the beginning of his term in settling the Korean War, in reducing our defense expenditures and modifying our military posture, in refusing to save the French military position in Indochina, and in avoiding involvement in the Middle East over the Egyptian seizure of the Suez Canal or the Anglo-French attack on Egypt. Dulles had considerably expanded our foreign commitments by spreading our legal and fiscal military obligations along the borders of China and Russia through the creation of SEATO and the offer of American military assistance to its members and to the Baghdad Pact members. Yet, behind these legal and fiscal forms and the rhetoric of international activism, the Eisenhower Administration had quietly constrained its foreign action when confronted with some notable chances to act. As a result, the reasons for action were highly articulated, while the reasons for inaction remained largely unarticulated. As we will see in the next chapter, this disparity was ultimately to cause public disillusionment over the failure of the Eisenhower Administration to live up to its articulated goals.

chapter 5

Eisenhower: The Inertia of the Second Term

INTRODUCTION

Three events—the Suez War, the Hungarian Revolution, and, a year later, the launching of the first satellite, Russia's "Sputnik"—marked a change in the Eisenhower Administration's posture in foreign affairs and in turn affected its domestic status. Eisenhower was to write to a friend in November 1957:

> *Since July 25th of 1956, when Nasser announced the nationalization of the Suez, I cannot remember a day that has not brought its major or minor crisis.*[1]

This comment effectively distinguishes the second phase of Eisenhower's foreign policy from the first. In the first phase, the United States worked actively to impose its policies on foreign affairs; in the second period, our policy making seemed to consist mainly of responses to events.

The 1956 elections might have been a time to move into a new

---

[1] Dwight D. Eisenhower, *The White House Years*, Vol. II: *Waging Peace, 1956–1961* (New York: Doubleday, 1965), p. 226.

orientation toward international affairs. The Korean War had long since been settled. The public anxieties over it had subsided. McCarthyism had died with a whimper. Broad public confidence in government had grown. The shibboleths of Republican opposition had been put aside. Eisenhower's self-restraint in partisanship and his style of governing had created an era of good feeling that the election of 1956 only confirmed.

Yet the election itself was no occasion for innovation. The Administration did not use it to imbue the public with a new understanding of foreign affairs but rather to play established popular themes. Eisenhower may have been confident of his capacity to win elections, but he did not display high confidence in his capacity to persuade the public that he was right. The Eisenhower administrators took public opinion in foreign relations mostly as they found it—and indeed one does not expect more from a popular government.

The 1956 presidential campaign reflected this quiescence in public debate. The Democrats again nominated Stevenson. In order to win he needed to arouse the public—even to alarm it—over Eisenhower's conduct of public affairs. Before the Suez War began he accused the incumbent of "irresponsibility and deception" in foreign affairs and of stating only half the facts on questions of war and peace. In late October, barely two weeks before the election, U.S. press and television news headlined the outbreak of war in the Middle East and uprisings in Poland and Hungary. Stevenson charged the Administration with "mistake after mistake" in the Middle East, terming Eisenhower's reassurances on that subject "tragically less than the truth." By the eve of the election it had become amply clear that Washington had frustrated the Anglo-French (though not the Israeli) effort against Egypt and had stood motionless while the Soviet Union crushed the Hungarian revolt. These events might have caused a wavering of confidence in Eisenhower for not better controlling international conditions or for not responding with greater energy to perceived threatening situations. But for the time being, the public reaction was, if anything, quite the opposite. The electoral results, which gave Eisenhower an even larger majority than in 1952, showed that Stevenson had not shaken public confidence in the President. In fact Suez and Hungary actually contributed some votes to the Eisenhower landslide, confirming the partisan value of Eisenhower's strategy of political leadership in foreign relations and reflecting the reduction in public interest and attention in foreign affairs. Eisenhower started his second term with 79 percent of the public approving of his handling of the Presidency.

Foreign-policy debates are normally confined to a narrow compass of public attention (compared with the size of the electorate). But in 1957 the prospect of a broader audience, which could become responsive to the cues of opinion leaders, affected the behavior of both the government and its critics—the "ins" and the "outs." Issues that had little public appeal now became the basis for a controversy among the public-opinion élites that was harsher than in the first phase of Eisenhower's foreign relations. The President's ability to articulate issues and explain policies to the opinion élites and the attentive publics now became far more important.

SPUTNIK AND THE DECLINE OF AMERICAN CONFIDENCE

In the mid-fifties Moscow and Washington each made secret decisions about the pace at which it would develop two successive new generations of weapons: liquid-fueled and solid-fueled nuclear rockets of intercontinental range. In 1957 it became clear in Washington that Moscow had developed powerful and relatively accurate liquid-fueled rockets and that the Soviet Union had the technical and economic capability to produce enough nuclear-tipped missiles to destroy or seriously weaken the capacity of the United States to retaliate. If the Russians concentrated on developing their capabilities further, they might well be able to neutralize an American second-strike nuclear deterrent, thus allowing a safe Russian nuclear strike at the United States, or it might be able to deter a nuclear attack *from* the United States so effectively as to free *conventional* Russian arms to undertake aggression.

By 1957 the Eisenhower Administration had committed itself to a limited deployment of liquid-fueled intercontinental ballistic missiles (the Atlas and Titan) in order to press on with the development and deployment of the solid-fueled missiles (the Minuteman and Polaris) with their promise of greater economy and better performance. The earliest Administration decisions in favor of the solid-fueled missiles evidently reflected an estimate that the Russians were far behind us in strategic nuclear strength. However, surprisingly rapid advances in Soviet missile technology posed the alarming prospect in 1957 that the Russians might build a missile force that could deliver several times more explosive power than the American force could.

Two groups faced this issue in 1957. The Gaither Committee was a study group of eminent private citizens based at the White House, with access to many government secrets. It concluded that the prospect of growing Soviet strategic nuclear capability raised the requirements for American armed might. The other group was privately sponsored by the Rockefeller Brothers Fund, though its views also reflected information gathered from secret government reports. It came to similar conclusions and advocated several annual $3-billion increases in the defense budget.

The Rockefeller report was not published until January 1958, after Sputnik. The Gaither Committee, however, had submitted its secret conclusions to the White House before Sputnik. When Eisenhower failed to act some members of the committee became restless and leaked their findings to the press, indicating their hope that the President would implement them. Because the Gaither activists were severely inhibited by their obligations as presidential advisers, they never drew much public attention. But privately, they contributed, as did the Rockefeller report, to a restlessness among active and authoritative public opinion élites.

Sputnik I, the world's first artificial earth satellite, was launched by the Soviet Union on October 4, 1957. Six weeks earlier Moscow had announced the successful test of an intercontinental ballistic missile. American reports on the missile test indicated impressive accuracy. Two days after lofting Sputnik I, the Russians tested "a mighty hydrogen warhead of a new design," as they put it. A month later Sputnik II, weighing 1300 pounds, carried a dog into orbit, demonstrating a very large payload capacity for Soviet rockets.

The impact of the Soviet space feats on public opinion throughout the world was immense. Among the literate or listening public in every country for which survey data is available, Soviet scientific and technological prestige soared dramatically—at the expense of the United States. The impact caught both Washington and Moscow by surprise. The Soviet Union exploited its space achievements for maximum propaganda impact and launched a diplomatic offensive by threatening the Western status in Berlin once again. Premier Khrushchev indicated that Russia might negotiate a separate peace settlement with East Germany and called for a summit meeting.

Even in the United States, opinions changed dramatically. Sputnik brought a new awareness—and new illusions—of Soviet scientific prowess. It also destroyed some old illusions about America's technological superiority. What was more important, Sputnik had a profound effect on public inattentiveness to external affairs by posing a symbolic as well as a military threat. By shaking the American belief in U.S. technological superiority, upon which our feeling of security in part depended, Sputnik raised the prospect that the United States was vulnerable. And, by raising the public perception of threat from abroad, Sputnik diminished public confidence in the Eisenhower Administration.

This reduction in confidence was accentuated by a public awareness that the Eisenhower Administration's response to Sputnik was essentially that of a government that was improvising its response to a perceived threat rather than one that was taking major initiatives to meet a serious long-range crisis.

The Eisenhower Administration further disconcerted the public by emphasizing that, regardless of Sputnik, it would continue to permit only limited government expenditures and limited presidential leadership. Privately, Eisenhower talked of the public reaction to Sputnik as revealing the "psychological vulnerability of our people" and producing "a measure of self-doubt." He hoped that this stimulus would reduce congressional "balkiness" in supporting his legislative programs. Dulles too found a bright side to Sputnik. In an address in January 1958 he referred to the public reaction to Sputnik as a mood that was producing "a more serious appraisal of the struggle in which we are engaged and an increasing willingness to make the kind of efforts and sacrifices needed to win that struggle."

The orbiting of Sputnik had in fact caught the Administration in the middle of an effort to reduce its defense programs. Between January and August of 1957, as Defense Secretary Wilson had estimated, the total price of defense programs had jumped 5 percent. The rate of defense spending had been abnormally high. Now, faced with the choice of whether to stabilize our military programs at this new rate of expenditure or to normalize our rate of expenditure by cutting back on our programs, the Administration chose the latter course. It cut out weapons-development programs, cut back and stretched out production, ordered military manpower cut 7 percent, and closed military installations.

Sputnik did not alter the situation much. "The informed word from the Defense and Treasury Departments," a press report immediately after Sputnik read, "was that the Administration's economy effort had not been abandoned."[2]

Nonetheless, the Administration did undertake a series of limited responses to Sputnik. It reorganized the Defense Department and established a special agency to manage nonmilitary research in outer space. These steps did not shift any government priorities, but their immediate impact was to demonstrate Administrative concern over Sputnik. In November, shortly after Sputnik, Eisenhower declared, "Our people will not sacrifice security to worship a balanced budget." Yet his budget message to Congress in January asked for only small increases in defense outlays. Within the fixed ceiling of the defense budget, however, substantial funds were shifted to military research and development. For the next five years, "R and D" would be a popular category of budget expenditures.

Finally, the Administration attempted somewhat unsuccessfully to shore up NATO's military and diplomatic defenses against the newly revealed Soviet missile capability and a new Berlin crisis. First, it sought to strengthen NATO's nuclear might by locating Thor and Jupiter intermediate-range ballistic missiles (IRBM's) on the territory of NATO allies. But the offer of IRBM's produced embarrassingly lukewarm responses and developed surprisingly strong opposition. An arrangement was already under consideration with the British for Thors that was completed only after further delays. Much later, Italy and Turkey acquired Jupiters. No other member would accept these missiles.

Second, the Administration put much advance emphasis on

2 *The New York Times,* November 1, 1957, quoted in Samuel P. Huntington, *The Common Defense* (New York: Columbia Univ. Press, 1961), p. 96.

the semiannual NATO ministerial meeting, scheduled in Paris in early December 1957, to transform it into a heads-of-government meeting. Eisenhower's attendance, despite his having suffered a stroke barely three weeks earlier (his third illness in twenty-six months), added to the meeting's drama. Yet, anticipated as an opportunity to prepare for the new Berlin crisis, the meeting in fact produced very little.

In short, the steps taken by the Eisenhower Administration in response to Sputnik did not convey a picture of government concern grave enough over new Russian technological strength to offset the public anxieties raised by Sputnik. In fact the tendency of the Administration to handle foreign affairs after Sputnik by offering limited responses to crises but no major initiatives was to transform this public anxiety into prolonged malaise.[3]

Moscow had detonated its first hydrogen bomb in 1953, less than a year after the United States test. In exploiting the worldwide reaction to Sputnik, Soviet leaders now claimed to have rapidly growing missile strength based on the Soviet nuclear prowess and the awkward but powerful rockets that had launched the orbital satellites. Khrushchev gave the erroneous impression that Russia had undertaken a crash program to build and deploy these first-generation ICBMs.[4]

In Washington, the January budget messages in 1959 and 1960 indicated that the Eisenhower Administration still labored under arbitrary defense-budget ceilings. They gave the impression that military needs were not being met on their merits but on the basis of arbitrary decisions about keeping the size of the federal budget compatible with a sound economy.

The Truman Administration had confronted similar problems with fluctuating public moods about national-security expenditures, particularly in its last two years. Confidence in the Administration declined, while pressures to increase the level of its military effort mounted. Challengers of orthodox fiscal assumptions had insisted in 1949 and 1950 that if federal expenditures for defense doubled, the economy would not be jeopardized but would simply be forced into a general expansion. After Sputnik, similar challenges arose.

---

[3] See Appendix A at the end of this chapter for a public-opinion survey analyzing this trend.

[4] Allen Dulles, *The Craft of Intelligence* (New York: Harper & Row, 1963), p. 163.

Senate Democrats, for example, pointed to the fact that certain European governments had used deficit spending to achieve high rates of economic growth—in Italy and France, for example, the growth rates were more than double the American rate in 1958.

Defense issues have the potential of attracting—though not necessarily sustaining—broad public attention, and both the President and Congress must cope with this potential volatility. In the mid-fifties, Eisenhower usually coped with it by tamping it down; Congress usually coped by appropriating more for defense than the President requested or would spend. In this way, Congress took out political insurance against possible charges of negligence in defense matters, should some future event arouse public anxieties about national security. (This forethought did not extend to congressional appropriations for foreign economic assistance, for this issue was unlikely to arouse public anxieties very much.)

Before Sputnik—in fact, before the Democratic presidential nominating convention of 1956—Senator Stuart Symington had publicized the fears of Air Force generals that Russian air power would overtake and surpass U.S. air power. But the generals succeeded neither in spreading alarm nor in helping Symington win the Democratic nomination. After Sputnik, air-power enthusiasts returned to this issue. They carried Congress beyond its normal impatience with the executive budget into a tough and energetic (though not always coherent) attack on Eisenhower's defense program and, through the defense program, to the Administration's conduct of foreign relations, and finally, to the inflexibility and complacency of Eisenhower and Dulles themselves. As congressional demands for substantially increased defense expenditures developed, Eisenhower argued that there could be no "security" without "solvency." That year and the next (1958–59), the Administration rode out congressional pressures for major defense increases, but the severe congressional scrutiny and certain alterations in defense programs by Congress left a residue of public anxiety. These successive years of apparent underresponse to perceived external threats eroded the confidence of Congress and of other public-opinion leaders in Eisenhower's external policies.

The moods of broad public opinion fluctuated noticeably after Sputnik. After the first impact of Sputnik on public opinion, attention and anxiety declined through the spring of 1958, to be aroused again in December by Khrushchev's announcement that he would sign a peace treaty with East Germany that would turn over control of the Western access routes to Berlin to the East German regime. Nonetheless, the Administration's critics had lodged with at least a small, attentive public the suspicion that arbitrary budget ceilings prevented the government from considering foreign and defense policies on their own merits.

Eisenhower could deny—as he did in a television address in March 1959—that he was subordinating defense to budgetary considerations and that defense was based on the "best composite judgment available." But public statements by military spokesmen had already provided contrary evidence. No composite military judgment considered the American defense posture adequate. Furthermore, no less an authority than Army Chief of Staff Maxwell D. Taylor had testified that the Administration permitted military experts to judge defense issues only within the confines of rigid budget ceilings imposed in advance.[5]

Taylor retired as Army Chief in 1959 to publicize his disagreements with the Eisenhower Administration. He and his criticism gave authoritative support to charges that had been voiced intermittently from 1954 on—that the New Look had abandoned flexibility. By Taylor's account, the American capacity for low-level conventional military responses had been eliminated in favor of sole reliance on strategic air power on the basis of budgetary considerations and without acknowledgment by either the military chiefs or the President's civilian advisers that this concentration was wise. Without conventional-force flexibility, reserve flexibility was possible only if our allies agreed that the United States should specialize in capital-intensive nuclear forces while they concentrated on manpower-intensive conventional forces. Yet no such agreement existed.

Eisenhower's effort to buy flexibility for less money had failed. Taylor wanted to buy flexibility with yet higher defense expenditures. Stevenson had argued in the 1952 campaign that lesser costs were possible only through disarmament agreements. Three factors bounded the national armaments question: (1) relations with Russia; (2) the values placed on having what Taylor called a "flex-

[5] Hearings, Senate Armed Services Committee, *Major Defense Matters*, Part I (1959), pp. 44–45.

ible response" capability; and (3) the need for economy in defense spending. It is clear that Eisenhower appreciated the values of all three factors, but he traded flexibility for economy.

The Korean rearmament had expanded the group of industries that depended for much of their revenues on government arms contracts. Rearmament had started a series of new ventures in technology which, by the late fifties, promised virtually a glut of varied weapons for the Army, Navy, and Air Force. The Defense Department labored under the pressure from interests vested during the research and development stage of the weapons-acquisition process to go ahead to the lucrative production phase. Sputnik gave these firms an opportunity to vent their frustrations over the government's indecision. The result was that the Administration got the worst of two worlds. Its desire for economy had tied it to a rigid defense strategy, but the Administration had not mastered the economic pressures exerted by the "military-industrial complex" (as Eisenhower was to call the alliance between the military procurers and the defense industries) for considerable increases in the level of the defense effort.

The broadest criticisms of this military-industrial complex have depicted it as a self-rewarding, self-perpetuating system that produces ever-increasing quantities of weapons to cope with what is perceived as an ever-increasing threat. Doubtless the pressures for expansion and for threat perception were there. But there were countervailing trends as well. The growth of central power in the Defense Department away from the immediate tie-in to industry matched the growth of the arms industry. Since 1949 the Secretary of Defense has rarely failed to identify with the President as budget cutter, rather than with the services, their suppliers, and their congressional allies as advocates of particular procurements. The arms race in the fifties was for weapons *quality*, not sheer quantities. Military expansion could have been much faster than it was in both the East and the West. On the American side the way expansion was held down—by indiscriminate economizing pressures —assured a provocative rigidity in strategic posture.

The military-industrial complex had also produced a new group of civilian experts in military matters. To help design weapons, make hardware choices, and fight each other in the bureaucratic politics of the Pentagon, the Armed Services had developed a group of institutions—some of them private firms, some within the government, some located in the universities—that did research not directly tied to military hardware development. These "think tanks" first had a major effect in the late fifties, persuading the government to recognize the reciprocal character of the military confrontation with Russia. The analysis of American force posture showed that it was in effect provocative because it could operate against a growing Soviet nuclear strength only on a hair trigger. The value of forces that could survive surprise attack grew until, in the late fifties, the bizarre notion of firing nuclear-tipped missiles from submerged submarines had become a central development requirement. Second, the defense intellectuals extended this insight about stability to disarmament negotiations. Eisenhower had anticipated them with his "open skies" proposal in 1955. In the late fifties, the defense intellectuals became increasingly concerned about the possibility of a surprise attack.

Again, Sputnik precipitated action. The wide use of independent scientists by the government had produced a scientific "constituency" within the government that had no spokesman at the White House level. In 1958, as part of an effort to emphasize research and development, Eisenhower appointed James R. Killian of M.I.T. as his science adviser and head of a President's Science Advisory Committee. PSAC would become, under Kennedy, an important force in the pursuit of the Test Ban Treaty.

THE MISSILE GAP

Spokesmen for the Army, Navy and Air Force complained that the limited capabilities they had been permitted to acquire would not enable them to perform the combat tasks assigned to them. Such complaints are indigenous to military establishments, as Eisenhower doubtless knew. Another complaint was new, however, and ominous: in the future, the Soviet Union would be far ahead of the United States in deployed strategic nuclear missiles.

The "missile gap" became a public issue with the publication in mid-January 1959 of an article in *The New York Times,* purportedly based on interviews with numerous authorities on the defense effort, forecasting that by 1960 Moscow would have three ICBM's for every American one and would increase to a peak of fifteen to one in 1964 before the Polaris and Minuteman missiles were scheduled to enter the American force in sizable numbers.[6]

The Secretary of Defense, Neil McElroy, confirmed the Administration's projection of a missile gap two weeks later when he stated that the United States did not intend to match the Soviet Union "missile for missile." His statement, coming the day after Premier Khrushchev had indicated that Soviet missiles were in assembly-line production, caused severe reactions. One widely read authority on military affairs termed it a "disastrous announcement that the United States has withdrawn from the missile race."[7]

The missile gap added to the anxieties that had been nurtured over the two preceding years and the way had been prepared to make national-security policy an issue in the 1960 election. Eisenhower had been challenged in the area in which his judgment was the most authoritative. But this was also an area in which challenges of the government's conduct of external relations could be the most rewarding politically. To pose the question of the adequacy of American defense, particularly after the spectacular demonstration of Soviet technical prowess, was to address the element of external relations most salient to broad public opinion.

NATO AFTER SPUTNIK

The United States had prodded Western Europe toward economic integration with the Marshall Plan and through the Organization of European Economic Cooperation. It had encouraged Western European military integration through NATO planning and the United States military-assistance program. Western Europe had followed this impetus toward integration by setting up a common market in coal and steel in 1954 (the European Coal and Steel Community), and a common nuclear-power research and development effort (the European Atomic Energy Commission, or EURATOM) in 1957. The more ambitious idea of a customs union,

---

[6] Arnold L. Horelick and Myron Rush, *Strategic Power and Soviet Foreign Policy* (Chicago: Univ. of Chicago Press, 1966), p. 78.

[7] Hanson Baldwin in *The New York Times*, reprinted in *Congressional Record* (February 5, 1959).

or a general common market, highlighted the split in Europe that the Coal and Steel Community and EURATOM had foreshadowed. The "inner six"—West Germany, France, Italy, Belgium, Holland and Luxembourg—proceeded with the market. Great Britain, having refused to join, organized an "outer seven" in a feeble effort to offset the disadvantages of her self-exclusion. The first internal tariff reductions were scheduled for January 1, 1959.

But long before, in anticipation of these tariff reductions, economic activity expanded among the inner six. With the Japanese economy also expanding rapidly, American exports shrank, producing an international payments deficit for the United States of more than $3 billion in 1958—the first substantial deficit in the postwar era. The imbalance was to persist through the sixties, despite the efforts of three administrations to cope with it.

These events form the background for the remarkable development of French national assertiveness in the late fifties and its impact on the North Atlantic military alliance. France, before General Charles de Gaulle took power in 1958, interposed no special obstacles to the achievement of American objectives in NATO. Like other members of the alliance, she had certain national interests that conflicted with the needs of NATO, and she had fallen short in military contributions. Under De Gaulle, however, France became a formidable and unique obstruction to United States policy in NATO.

The French National Assembly turned to De Gaulle in 1958 when it became desperate to maintain legal authority in the face of extreme political pressures from the French Army, which had ominously independent goals. He extricated France from Algeria, suppressed the unruly army, established his dominant position in French politics, expanded the nuclear-weapons program (kept alive by the Fourth Republic throughout the mid-fifties), and recast France's diplomatic posture so as to raise the country's international prestige. The stability of the French political system now ceased to be a major problem.

After 1958, in foreign relations De Gaulle was France. No ruler of a Western power since the Second World War dominated the external relations of his country as much as De Gaulle did. He used his power to pursue two closely related objectives: to stabilize France internally and to acquire major world-power status for

France. The close personal identity of De Gaulle with these objectives was misleading, for it led his foreign and domestic critics to condemn his behavior as personal pique and idiosyncrasy. In fact, his behavior amounted to far more than that. He adopted an aggressive diplomatic posture that improved France's international standing, helped consolidate his position as ruler of the French Fifth Republic, and, therefore, stabilized the new French regime. At the same time, he used his extraordinary domestic position to pursue external objectives. He could stare down Bonn or freeze out London. He could veto and boycott, where others did not. Until 1968 his government was relatively secure at home and he was constitutionally able to act arbitrarily whereas the British, German, and other Western governments were not. Above all, he was willing to run the risks entailed in his methods, such as jeopardizing European integration. For other European political leaders, European integration served to reconcile the demands of domestic politics with the requirements of foreign relations. But De Gaulle was not dependent on political integration for this purpose, and as a result he demonstrated that integration was vulnerable to the veto of any political leader able to do without it.

As part of its NATO policy throughout the fifties, the United States sought to discourage the acquisition of nuclear weapons by other members of the alliance. The British, who had already acquired nuclear status by detonating their first device in 1952, were an exception.

After the Suez fiasco, Harold Macmillan, the new Prime Minister and a wartime friend of Eisenhower, had set about restoring relations with Washington and reestablishing Britain's lost military prestige by substantially revamping her military posture along the lines of the American New Look. Since the British government was in severe financial difficulty after Suez, Macmillan economized by sharply reducing British military manpower and increasing British reliance on nuclear weapons.

To help, the United States immediately sold Britain sixty intercontinental ballistics missiles—the Thors—and agreed to cooperate with a British program for developing a missile that could carry nuclear warheads from Britain to Russia (and thus give credence to Britain's claim that it was a major nuclear power). Officials in

Washington were discomforted by the extent to which the British government was capitalizing politically on what were modest and highly qualified American commitments for help with the new missiles. Nonetheless, Washington went along with the Macmillan government's efforts to score quick points in its domestic political confrontation.

When De Gaulle came to power, the British were already on their way to achieving a second-generation strategic nuclear-weapon system. But rising costs forced the cancellation of this effort, and Britain then arranged to purchase the Skybolt, a new American missile still in early stages of development. Our technical aid was expanded further through the United States Atomic Energy Act amendments in 1958, which increased the President's discretion in the handling of nuclear-technology secrets.

It is important to note that sympathy for British aspirations for world-power status and independence from continental Europe ran counter to another major American objective in Western Europe—an increase in the size of conventional military forces there and the encouragement of military, political, and economic integration. It is thus likely that our aid to the British effectively damaged the prospects for NATO rearmament and European integration.

But our cooperation with the British did not alter the two dominant tenets of American nuclear policy: (1) the United States would not give up custody of its weapons or permit others to decide when to fire them—in practice, the United States would maintain a veto over those of its weapons assigned to allied forces, and (2) the United States would not give aid in nuclear technology to a "non-nuclear" power.

Our second tenet had originally been based on the view that the ability to produce nuclear bombs or warheads per se made one a full member of the nuclear club. (According to this interpretation, only Britain qualified for aid at the time.) Gradually, however, American officials came to appreciate the value of a stategic nuclear force that could survive a surprise attack, and the United States came to understand the technical difficulties of building and maintaining such a force. Nuclear-warhead development was only part of this formidable problem. Thus, by the time France sought entrance to the nuclear club the basis upon which we had granted technical aid to Britain a few years earlier no longer seemed valid. In effect, our definition of "nuclear power" had stiffened, and we were reluctant to share our secrets with a country that was a long way from being a full member of the club.[8]

The American reaction to French nuclear aspirations, then, reflected a growing conviction that assistance had to stop somewhere. It also reflected doubts about the stability of the French government and its ability to keep secrets. Paris, however, inevitably concluded that the shift in American policy represented a form of discrimination against France.

Barely five weeks after taking office, De Gaulle told Dulles of his determination to develop nuclear weapons, with or without the assistance of the United States.[9] He also quickly made clear his desire to modify NATO substantially by establishing a tripartite directorate—France, Great Britain, and the United States—to replace what he called the Anglo-American directorate. The new directorate would then coordinate global strategy among the three countries. He refused to allow American missiles not directly under his control to be stationed on French soil. Six months later, in June 1959, he forced the removal of more than 200 NATO fighter bombers from French bases because they carried nuclear weapons the French did not control. The French Foreign Office made clear that these acts were related to the failure of Britain and the United States to treat France as their equal in the alliance and that it resented in particular the American failure to assist France in its nuclear-weapons program.[10]

De Gaulle's was a voice for national independence in a Western Europe that, after Sputnik, had diminished confidence in the United States nuclear umbrella. The root of Western European skepticism about American nuclear power was an odd combination of nationalism and pacifism, born of the growing prosperity and the terrible prospects of nuclear war in Europe. On one hand, Euro-

---

[8] This changed attitude was reflected in the fact that M. Alphand, the French Ambassador to the United States, was informed that detonating a few nominal bombs would not qualify France to receive American secrets. See Leonard Beaton and John Maddox, *The Spread of Nuclear Weapons* (New York: Praeger, 1962), p. 88.

[9] *The New York Times*, July 6, 1958.

[10] *The New York Times*, June 14, 1959; *Manchester Guardian*, June 9, 1959.

pean critics of the United States feared that we would start a nuclear war needlessly, but on the other hand, they wanted to rely on our nuclear-deterrent capability rather than raise the level of their own defense efforts. But even before De Gaulle, France began to raise a new question: would the United States *fail* to strike even if Europe were threatened? This new concern, however, did not eliminate the older one.

In 1958 NATO adopted plans to use tactical nuclear weapons supplied by the United States as ground-force equipment—and this deployment of nuclear weapons made further German rearmament look even grimmer to the many Europeans who were already worried about Germany. Yet the same considerations that made speeding up the deployment of tactical nuclear weapons necessary —principally the persistent failure to meet NATO's force requirements—made it necessary to rely on German divisions along NATO's crucial central front.

The NATO Council meeting at the end of 1959 reached a new low in NATO relations. A month earlier, De Gaulle had announced that he was opposed to any form of Allied military integration for the French army, associating with this move a particularly strong statement of French independence from NATO. Just as the military sessions preliminary to the NATO Council meeting got under way, a French government spokesman announced that France still refused to participate in the integration of the air defenses of Western Europe, a step widely recognized as urgent. General Nathan F. Twining, the Chairman of the U. S. Joint Chiefs of Staff, charged in a secret meeting of the NATO military committee that France was responsible for the failure of NATO to reach its planned military strength. The accusation leaked to the press, to the relief of the NATO Secretary General, Paul-Henri Spaak, who was " 'happy' it had emerged in public."[11]

France evidently faced unanimous opposition to its refusal to integrate air-defense forces. In the ensuing months it yielded on this point, an indication that it was oblivious neither to the rationale of military analysis nor to international political realities. The United States, in turn, began to show signs of modifying its nuclear-sharing policies.

The first signs of change in Washington were reports that the

11 *The New York Times,* December 15, 1959.

powerful Congressional Joint Committee on Atomic Energy was conducting secret hearings, reportedly on a plan to supply some allies with nuclear weapons. Asked about this at his news conference on February 3, President Eisenhower responded by strongly supporting amendment of atomic-energy legislation to permit giving nuclear weapons to some allies.

Ten days later the French exploded a plutonium bomb—their first nuclear detonation. Changing the statutory limitations on nuclear sharing now became urgent business if the United States hoped to head off De Gaulle's establishing an independent French nuclear force. In its earliest versions, in February and March 1960, the sharing proposal evidently included another objective: the reduction of American military expenditures abroad in order to aid the American balance of payments problem.

From the outset the Joint Committee made plain that it intended to maintain the major constraints already written into the statute. Furthermore, the White House agreed with Congress that the United States should keep its veto. The main difference sharing would make, then, would be to give our allies a veto too. Proposals to share control of some nuclear weapons would assure Europeans that their governments could prevent the use of the nuclear weapons assigned to the shared forces.

But they still could not prevent the United States from the unilateral use of its own nuclear forces, which were considerably larger. Nor could Europeans ensure that the United States would be *willing* to use nuclear weapons when *Europeans* wanted to use them. The United States would continue to exercise a veto over the use of the shared nuclear weapons. In preliminary soundings, De Gaulle rejected the proposal for a shared force out of hand.[12]

General Norstad suggested that the shared weapons be under NATO control, with unanimous approval required in order to use the common nuclear force. It would mean fifteen "fingers" on the "safety catch," as British critics later put it. He also proposed that the shared weapons be in an integrated force composed of national military forces.[13]

---

12 See, for example, Joseph Alsop, *New York Herald Tribune*, May 27, 1960.
13 Norstad's suggestion is reported in *The New York Times*, March 3, 1960. His assurance to the Joint Committee that the United States would keep control was reported in *The New York Times*, March 11, 1960.

By the time the NATO Council convened again in December 1960, a proposal for a strategic nuclear force under NATO command had been much scrutinized. The proposal to share strategic nuclear forces, however, exacerbated fears about giving German troops more nuclear weapons (particularly among the left wing of the British Labour party) that had first arisen when the Germans, along with the other NATO forces, had acquired tactical nuclear weapons through bilateral arrangements with the United States.

France had already withdrawn most of her ground forces from NATO in order to fight the war in Algeria. In 1960 De Gaulle also withdrew French naval forces from the Mediterranean Command of NATO. Britain had trimmed the Army of the Rhine to four small divisions. NATO had only twenty-one divisions of mixed weight and readiness. Of these, seven were German, and there would soon be twelve.

One way to modify anti-German reactions was to emphasize the multilateral character of a shared strategic nuclear force as proposed by General Norstad. Addressing a business group in Coventry, England, in October 1960, Norstad declared that NATO should become "the fourth atomic power" with nuclear weapons of all types supplied by the United States under a guarantee that they would not be withdrawn during the life of the alliance. The objectives, Norstad made clear, were to halt the trend now led by France toward national nuclear forces and to reassure those Europeans who feared the withdrawal of American forces from Europe.[14] Two weeks later the French National Assembly adopted De Gaulle's bill to develop an independent French nuclear striking force. At the NATO Council meeting in December, Secretary of State Herter, now representing a lame-duck administration, proposed the establishment of a multilateral but fully integrated nuclear force under NATO command using Polaris missiles on land-based mobile carriers. His action assured that the subject would be carried to the agenda of the Kennedy Administration.

By the time Eisenhower left office, the general import of Gaullist France's foreign policy for NATO had become quite clear. France's determination to become a nuclear power and De Gaulle's insistence that France have equal standing with Britain and the United States in NATO affairs had already proved disruptive. For

[14] *The New York Times,* October 16, 1960.

the time being, De Gaulle tacitly accepted the integration of French forces in a mobile nuclear task force, but French opposition to integrated forces delayed for a year the establishment of an integrated air-defense system for Europe.

As the predominant French leader through the sixties, De Gaulle would continue to pose an alternative to the vision of one supranational Western European state: namely, a Europe of strong national states no longer divided between East and West. De Gaulle thus directly challenged American policy, which since 1947 had strongly favored the political and economic integration of Western Europe. The proposal for an integrated NATO nuclear force, which had acquired the official mantles of both Washington and SHAPE headquarters by the end of 1960, would be laid aside quietly five years later, partly because of De Gaulle's opposition. But the impact of the French government's stand against integration was greatly increased by the inconsistencies of the American policy in NATO and the weak expediencies upon which many of NATO's most impressive achievements had been built.

De Gaulle's challenge, in short, exposed other basic weaknesses of the movement for European integration. First, De Gaulle was correct in perceiving that our leadership in NATO tended to favor Great Britain, the NATO member that had traditionally been least amenable to European integration. Furthermore, though the United States talked of integration within NATO, we were actually moving toward greater independence from the Alliance by promoting a division of labor between us and the rest of its members. And most fundamentally, De Gaulle challenged European political integration because it seemed to suggest that national political leaders of democratic states could avoid dealing with troublesome national issues they must otherwise face by turning these issues over to military and economic technocrats in supranational agencies such as the European Coal and Steel Community and NATO.

De Gaulle's challenge of Western policy, like the man himself, was of classic dimensions. His own vision of a Europe of nation states may have been tattered, but he demonstrated that the vision of an integrated Europe was no more heroic, for it was based largely on hopes of escaping from, rather than solving, the problems that inevitably arise within *democratic* national politics.

THE POLITICAL COMPLICATIONS
OF SAYING "NO"

The lesson for Eisenhower from the charges against Truman about the fall of China and the stalemate in Korea was clear enough: do not allow American forces to become bogged down in a shooting war that must inevitably take casualties and do not become identified with negative choices—that is, decisions *not* to act.

In deciding whether to become involved in an international problem a President faces two special considerations. Because this country is the preeminent Western power, all our allies as well as any other state that might expect the United States to take an interest in it often look to Washington for help. And normally, of course, these countries seek American aid in solving their problems only on their own terms. The fact that the American President is mainly responsible for decisions about resource priorities in the United States government means that he confronts the allocative costs of taking action in a way that no one in Congress or out of office does. His critics can condemn the President for failing to deal with a particular foreign problem, but they need not face the question of where the resources would have to come from to deal with it.

The problem of which foreign-policy areas should take priority persisted for Eisenhower throughout his eight years, but they were particularly troublesome with respect to two areas: the Middle East after the Suez crisis and the Formosa Strait. By contrast, the best examples of the Eisenhower Administration's handling of the resource-allocation problem by deciding against involvement were its self-restraint in Africa and Latin America. This section will examine the efficacy of the Eisenhower Administration's policies in these four major areas.

For the Eisenhower Administration, the Anglo-French attack on Egypt posed a direct challenge to its leadership of the Atlantic alliance. The attack could not succeed without American cooperation, yet the United States had not been consulted about it in advance. Eisenhower's refusal to go along with London and Paris was in effect an act to enforce discipline within the Western alliance structure and assert American dominance over it. The dominance of the United States was partly an outgrowth of the Truman Administration's programs, supplemented by Dulles' black-and-white concept of the world as divided between freedom and Communism and by his determination to take the initiative. It was also, of course, a reflection of the disparities in strength among the Western powers.

The disparity in power between the United States and its allies and the problems of discipline and dominance that it produced were comparable in certain respects to those in the Soviet bloc. In their power aspirations, Moscow and Washington were not easily distinguishable, though Washington displayed less discomfort with pluralism internally and externally, reflecting the more competitive political systems of the United States and its principal allies in Western Europe. In general, the United States dealt with its allies and clients in a distinctly less authoritarian manner than did Moscow.

The British and French had acted on their own in attacking Egypt because they had concluded that they could not otherwise get the United States to act with sufficient resolve to be helpful to them. The Eisenhower Administration, beginning before Egypt's seizure of the Canal, had attempted to minimize American involvement in the Middle East, and, from beginning to end, it avoided committing resources or accepting obligations in this area. Yet it remained saddled with the rhetoric of action—particularly of active anti-Communism. As we attempted to pick up the pieces of our own policy in the Middle East, we used our anti-Communist rhetoric to extricate ourselves. In doing so, however, the Eisenhower Administration produced a situation much like one it had inherited in Asia from the partisan politics of Truman's Presidency: a predisposition to become heavily involved in a distant local situation in the name of anti-Communism. The Lebanon and Formosa Strait crises both posed sobering questions for the Eisenhower Administration concerning the potential of small powers—especially its client states—to draw the United States into solving *their* problems *their* way, regardless of American interests, and in doing so, to tie down U.S. forces and risk committing the United States still further. Both situations involved American interests only indirectly;

in both the United States acted in haste and to its eventual embarrassment.

THE EISENHOWER DOCTRINE

Our intervention to halt the British-French-Israeli invasion of Egypt in the fall of 1956 had ultimately proved quite embarrassing to the United States with both sides in the Suez fiasco, as discussed in Chapter 4. Not only were we traditionally associated with Britain and France, but the credibility of our nuclear protection for European nations was shaken by the Soviet nuclear threat leveled against Britain and France to stem their intervention in the Middle East and by our own severe treatment of our two allies.

In an effort to disassociate ourselves from Nasser without abandoning the other Arab states to his leadership, we turned to the rhetoric of active anti-Communism in that part of the world. Accordingly, in January 1957 Eisenhower asked Congress for a joint resolution that would "authorize" the President to use American armed forces "as he deems necessary" to defend the Middle East nations "requesting such aid against overt armed aggression from any nation controlled by international Communism." This resolution was to become known as the Eisenhower Doctrine.

Neither the SEATO treaty nor the Baghdad Pact had been as exclusively directed against international Communism as was this resolution. It also provided for economic and military assistance to the area, with special provisions for prompt implementation of assistance programs. Eisenhower and Dulles concentrated on the anti-Communist orientation of the resolution. Dulles, appearing before the Senate Foreign Relations Committee, attributed the economic stress generated by the Suez crisis to the loss of revenues from an oil embargo and from the closing of the Suez Canal. These events, he concluded, would encourage the Soviet leaders to commit aggression.

The President's request for congressional action was a way to share political responsibility with a reluctant Congress. Critics charged that Congress was being asked to sign a "blank check" that would authorize unspecified future actions. Besides, they argued, the Eisenhower Doctrine had missed the point of the Suez crisis—that the pressing threats to American interests in the Middle East were not those of overt Communist military conquest. After much delay, and some revision—principally to avoid using the word "authorizing"—Congress passed the resolution.

The method of securing approval for the draft resolution, however, partially frustrated its purposes. Like so many of the Eisenhower Administration's efforts, it had floundered in the paradoxes of governing. With so much controversy surrounding its passage, the resolution hardly demonstrated the solid backing in Washington that the White House had sought, nor did it discourage later recriminations from Congress over the fate of American interests in the Middle East. Eisenhower's appeal for advanced congressional support, furthermore, reflected a deference to congressional authority that was not much appreciated by either Democratic or Republican legislators, who were unwilling to take responsibility for Eisenhower's foreign policy.

The Eisenhower Doctrine did, however, serve a more immediate purpose: it helped Washington abandon Nasser and construct a pro-American, anti-Communist, and anti-Nasser bloc, forcing the states in the Middle East to choose between Cairo and Moscow on one hand, and Washington on the other. Regional members of the Baghdad Pact—Turkey, Iran, Iraq, and Pakistan—had expressed early support for the Eisenhower Doctrine. Lebanon, Jordan, Saudi Arabia and Libya also came out in favor of it. Egypt and Syria drew closer together as a somewhat isolated leftist-nationalist faction.

In Jordan, King Hussein put down his left-leaning Army opposition in a dramatic encounter in April 1957. Washington sealed his victory by sending the Sixth Fleet into the Eastern Mediterranean and adding $30 million in economic assistance to Jordan.

Washington was able to use the Eisenhower Doctrine to shift the key political issue in the Middle East from Western colonialism and imperialism (the Anglo-French effort to retake the Suez Canal) to Soviet imperialism, but only at the cost of severely limiting ourselves in the Middle East.

In May 1958, rioting broke out in Lebanon. The Lebanese government accused the new United Arab Republic (a federation formed in 1958 by Egypt and Syria) of causing the conflict. Iraq, facing similar difficulties, also blamed the U.A.R. The United Nations Security Council sent an observation team to Lebanon, but it failed to confirm the Lebanese charges. In July, a bloody army coup in Iraq liquidated the royal house and the government before the Sixth Fleet could act, throwing the Lebanese government, and the surviving Hashimi monarch, Hussein in Jordan, into panic. A day after the Iraqi coup, U.S. Marines were dispatched to Lebanon and British troops were sent to Jordan to forestall further trouble.

But when the Iraqi troubles did not spread, Washington and London soon found themselves under attack from domestic critics who charged that military intervention was unnecessary. Soviet and pro-Nasser propaganda made the most of Western discomfort, and Moscow called for a summit conference. United Nations spokesmen wanted to get the troops out. India, the leading neutralist, protested the military intrusions. By August, when the United Nations General Assembly met, the danger of violence had abated, and Washington faced the real prospect of a U.N. censure. The General Assembly, however, neither censured nor supported the Anglo-American action.

On the other hand, once in Lebanon, the United States found itself caught between a sagging government and its leftist opponents who, though aided by Syria, were an integral part of the national Lebanese political scene. Before the United States could withdraw, it had to deal with both groups. Robert Murphy, a senior American diplomat, united the two factions behind a candidate of national conciliation for the impending national election. With this compromise arranged, the United States withdrawal began in October, leaving the Lebanon crisis a matter of partisan debate in the November congressional election in the United States, but not a matter of widespread public anxiety.

Nowhere were the disadvantages of the Eisenhower Administration's inclination to view complex international issues as a simple struggle between freedom and Communism more evident than in the Middle East crisis of 1958. Leftist Arab nationalists found themselves courted by Moscow and pushed toward the Soviet Union by the polarity underlying the Eisenhower Doctrine. The polarized political climate in the Middle East in 1958, for example, ultimately turned Iraq, Saudi Arabia, and Lebanon away from the United States. But these countries had by no means ignored the domestic threat of Communism. According to a well-informed judgment, Syria had joined with Egypt in order to counter the growing influence of the Communist party in Syria.[15] Similarly, Nasser, though willing to exploit the link between Communism and Arab nationalism in other states, suppressed Communist-party activity in Egypt.

Initially, the Eisenhower Doctrine, coupled with American military and economic assistance, had produced an impressive line-up of Middle East states allied with the United States. Yet within a year leftist Arab nationalists had isolated Jordan, overthrown Iraq, and reduced to the vanishing point the utility of Lebanon and Saudi Arabia as American allies.

THE INTERVENTION IN QUEMOY

The Eisenhower Doctrine had served to translate American goals in the Middle East as anti-Soviet Communism at a time when Arab nationalism was mixing with left-wing radicalism to produce a rich spectrum of political ideology and factionalism. On the island of Formosa, however, which had been the seat of government for Nationalist China since the Communist conquest of the Chinese mainland in the late forties, the Communist/anti-Communist line had been clearly drawn for American policy well before Eisenhower's inauguration.

As an early gesture of change in our Asian policy, Eisenhower had "unleashed" the Nationalist Chinese armed forces by withdrawing the Seventh Fleet from acting as a "shield against the mainland." With this shield removed, the tiny island groups of Quemoy and Matsu, offshore from the Chinese mainland in the Formosa Strait, and under Nationalist control, came under persistent mainland attack in late 1954. At Eisenhower's insistence, Congress authorized the President to "employ" the armed forces "as he deems necessary" to protect "Formosa and the Pescadores against armed attack." The crisis abated by April 1955, though it remained unresolved.

In August 1958 the mainland batteries opened fire again. Dulles and Eisenhower quickly made two points in response: (1) there would not be an American retreat in the face of Communist aggression and (2) the shelling was "an ambitious plan of armed

[15] Philip E. Mosely, *The Kremlin and World Politics* (New York: Vintage, 1960), p. 554.

conquest," as Eisenhower charged in a national television address, that "would liquidate all of the free-world positions in the Western Pacific area and bring them under captive governments. . . ."

The initial American position, then, was tough and rigid. But within the month much happened to encourage a more flexible position. Public reactions to the tough line laid out by Dulles and Eisenhower in the midst of the congressional campaign were important. The Administration expected some partisan criticism and got it. But the public itself showed wide opposition to a showdown over the Formosa Straits. Adding to the Administration's embarrassment, the State Department announced that 80 percent of the letters received were critical or fearful about the Administration's stand.

Events in Asia also encouraged reconsideration of our initial stand. The mainland shelling was intense enough to prevent re-supplying the islands without full-scale U.S. military support. Yet Washington had decided that the Navy would escort island-bound Nationalist ships no closer than the 3-mile limit. The prospect that ammunition would soon be exhausted brought Dulles under heavy pressure to go further.

The aging Chiang Kai-shek had every reason to involve the United States in an invasion of mainland China. The main acknowledged objective of his regime was to return to the mainland and defeat the Communist government there, and the Eisenhower Administration's critics had said as much when they were not busy attacking the regime on Formosa for its internal failures.

Finally, on the diplomatic level, the Administration got little support for its original stand. Dulles intimated that Asian statesmen had privately encouraged Washington to be firm. But European allies expressed their misgivings publicly. Washington's attempt to negotiate with Peking by resuming contact with its representative in Warsaw only showed the cleavage between the United States and China.

In short, by the end of August there were few incentives for continuing a rigid policy. At a news conference on November 30, after affirming that the United States had not changed its position, Dulles proceeded in effect to do exactly that. He denied that the United States had any obligation to defend the offshore islands or to help the Nationalists return to the mainland. A week later

Peking announced a temporary ceasefire, which it later extended. In effect, Peking acknowledged its inability to take the islands by force at that time. Dulles' statement, on the other hand, meant that the United States would not support the Nationalist government if it maintained the military buildup on the offshore islands because a buildup might be interpreted by Peking as preparation for an invasion of the mainland. Dulles denied having demanded that the Nationalists reduce the garrisons on the offshore islands, but in a joint communiqué from Taiwan in late October, he and Chiang had renounced the use of force to recover the mainland.

The Eisenhower Administration's policy toward Nationalist China had now come full circle since 1953. One of Eisenhower's first acts as President was to "unleash" the Nationalist government by removing the Seventh Fleet shield that Truman had stationed in the Formosa Strait. The fleet had stalemated the China conflict for the duration of the Korean War by guaranteeing the Chinese Communist government that the Nationalists would not invade the mainland and vice versa. Now, six years later, in what was to be one of Dulles' last major acts, he had once again "leashed" Chiang Kai-shek.

THE ELECTIONS OF 1958

The results of the 1958 congressional elections showed that the Administration's vulnerabilities in responding to crises both at home and abroad could be exploited for partisan purposes. Domestic issues doubtless contributed much more than foreign affairs to the election results—the economy was just recovering from a recession, and a scandal had forced Eisenhower's key assistant, Sherman Adams, to resign. But foreign crises did have some impact on the election: the external threats implicit in Sputnik, the Formosa Strait crisis of late summer and fall (which contributed to the militancy of the campaigns), the intervention in Lebanon, and the hostile reception given to Nixon in Caracas affected the public and were reflected in the criticisms of opinion leaders in Washington.

While Eisenhower played a partisan role in the campaign, repeatedly charging Democratic irresponsibility in spending, the leading spokesman for the Administration was Vice-President

Nixon. Neither Eisenhower's role as foreign-policy leader nor his role as party leader gave the public the impression of an active and concerned President supported by broad consensus among national public-opinion leaders.

The Democrats returned the heaviest majority to Congress since 1936: 263 to 174 in the House and 64 to 36 in the Senate. Most important in explaining these results was the fact that Eisenhower himself was not a candidate. The 1958 election confirmed what had become apparent in 1956—that Eisenhower's great personal popularity did not help Republican congressional candidates very much. The lesson for Democratic and Republican Congressmen alike was that grappling with the President in the next two years would not be as important as grappling with the other party in Congress. These factors moderated the partisan behavior between President and Congress from 1959 through 1960, but they did not prevent an increase in partisanship on Capitol Hill.

LATIN AMERICA AND AFRICA: SELF-RESTRAINT OR NEGLECT?

As we have noted, a primary concern of the Eisenhower Administration was the question of how best to allocate limited financial, military, and economic resources in order to further American interests through our foreign policy without overextending ourselves in the long run. The Administration's basic answer to the question was to concentrate its resources and attention on the geographic areas in which confrontation with Soviet expansion seemed the most urgent. The implications of this decision for Latin America and Africa was a hands-off policy—a policy best reflected in the disproportionately small outlays we made to Latin America and Africa in government economic and military assistance. During the first five years of the Eisenhower Administration we spent $12.6 billion on military and economic assistance (in grants and long-term loans) to Asia and the Middle East, while we spent only $1.9 billion in Latin America and only $350 million in Africa.

The Administration's determination to minimize its involvement in Latin America throughout the fifties was expressed in its major premise that, more than anything else, Latin America needed investment capital and that sufficient capital could be provided only by private American (and other) investors. This argument represented a justification for (1) not attempting to encourage political, social, and structural economic changes in Latin America and (2) not making heavy commitments for economic assistance to these countries.

In 1953 Eisenhower sent his brother, a well-known college president, on a tour of Latin America. Milton Eisenhower reported that these countries needed more stable economic conditions and more capital. He recommended substantial increases in U.S. Government grants and loans but emphasized that primary reliance must be on private investment.

The Administration delayed in deciding what its response to the report would be because it did not want to divert the attention of Latin American diplomacy from the pressing issue of Communist interference in Guatemala. (Squabbling within our government over how to administer loans for Latin American economic development also contributed to the delay.) In 1954 the United States intervened covertly to stop a Communist-supported takeover in Guatemala. At the Tenth Inter-American Conference that year the United States had won some support for its preparations to deal with the developing problem in Guatemala, but it had failed to establish a clear policy concerning economic and military assistance. By then, however, the budget ceilings for external affairs were weighing heavily on the State and Defense Departments. The Administration decided to rely primarily on private trade rather than on economic and military assistance. It encouraged private investments in Latin America through investment guarantees and other incentives and by encouraging Latin American governments to change legislation that discouraged foreign investments.

Latin American governments wanted more U.S. government loans and U.S. subsidies to stabilize their export-market prices. Because their economies depended heavily on the export of a few primary products, such as coffee or tin, they were highly vulnerable to price fluctuations. In 1957, at the Inter-American Economic Conference in Buenos Aires, the United States delegation encountered strong pressure for an additional commitment of resources. The Secretary of the Treasury, Robert B. Anderson, countered with the argument that foreign capital would be insufficient and that the Latin American governments would have to finance much of their economic development from domestic sources.

Grantors and recipients of economic assistance have no commonly accepted standards about sharing the burdens of economic development. Anderson's statement raised a serious point about the financing of economic development. Typically, capitalists in underdeveloped states invest their accumulated wealth in other countries. When their governments seek development assistance from the United States, therefore, they are asking for the United States to invest where their own investors will not. This phenomenon suggests that economies needing development usually have some features that make them unattractive to foreign investors, public and private, as well as to their own investors. Washington could (and did) find ample reasons not to commit much public capital to Latin American development throughout the mid-fifties.

After Sputnik, however, U.S. policy in Latin America attempted to redress the neglect of previous years. But to the extent that our change in posture was noticed at home or abroad, it reinforced the public impression that our foreign policy was reactive rather than innovative.

In 1958 Vice-President Nixon toured Latin America on a goodwill mission, but hostile crowds in Caracas and Lima threatened him with physical harm. Officials in Washington knew about the volatile protest movements in Latin America, and the Vice-President had been briefed to deal with student demonstrations, but not with violence. The Nixon riots shocked Washington into action by suggesting strongly that the low priorities we had accorded to Latin America during the fifties could be truly dangerous to American interests.

The riot in Caracas could be attributed to dissatisfaction with the American identification with the dictatorial Jimenez regime, deposed in early 1958. United States policy now shifted to avoid identification with dictatorial regimes, to the benefit of a young left-wing political entrepreneur in Cuba, Fidel Castro, whose revolutionary group would overthrow the harsh authoritarian regime of Fulgencia Batista the next January. Our foreign policy also shifted to permit the establishment of an Inter-American Development

Bank, a proposal that Washington had long resisted because of the Bank's expected call upon the U.S. Treasury for operating capital.

The Batista military dictatorship in Cuba fell at the beginning of 1959. After taking power, Castro turned increasingly to the Soviet Union for help and announced his ideological identification with Communism. He expropriated American property in Cuba, imprisoned and expelled American citizens, and proceeded with a far-reaching social and economic revolution that bore no resemblance to the typical palace revolutions of Latin America. By the election season in 1960 it appeared that Eisenhower had permitted the establishment of a Communist dictatorship on the U.S. doorstep. (Secretly, however, the Eisenhower Administration had begun CIA preparations for an invasion of Cuba by Cuban exiles.)

As the sense of urgency about Latin America grew during the late 1950's, the presence of colonial powers receded in Africa, leading to the argument that greater American involvement was necessary on that continent as well. Our avoidance of involvement in Africa, however, had stemmed from factors different from those underlying our Latin American policy.

To begin with, our African policy lacked even the rudimentary rationale that had been developed for the low priorities given Latin America. Before 1955, when the Eisenhower Administration still had under consideration the main patterns and postures of its external relations, European colonial powers still governed Africa south of the Sahara. Through the mid- and late fifties, however, the African nations rapidly became decolonized. Except for the white-settler states (principally the British colonies of the Rhodesias and Kenya), Britain and France were less reluctant to let go of their African colonial interests than their Middle East interests. No pan-African movement united against the colonial powers, which remained influential in the area and on fairly good terms with their former colonies. Soviet influence, with one exception, did not pose threats to which Washington had to respond, and we were happy to leave Africa mainly to others. In 1960, the Belgian government abandoned the Belgian Congo to independence, and chaos and violence soon broke out. The Soviet Union promptly intervened to support local challengers of central authority and the United Nations took up peacekeeping operations supported by the United States.

SUMMITRY AND DISARMAMENT

In all other major foreign-policy areas the Eisenhower Administration quickly settled down after 1952 to a static position: holding the line of American authority in NATO and with its allies in the Middle East; holding the line against Soviet expansion in the Middle East and Asia; holding the line of opposition to Communist China; and maintaining a military posture that would be viable over the long haul.

To make fundamental changes in international conditions, the Eisenhower Administration had three choices. First, it could intervene directly in regions and countries to effect changes. But the Administration was inhibited from such broad activism by budgetary constraints and by doubts about its ability to change social and political conditions abroad (as well as at home).

Second, the Administration could assume a more aggressive military and psychological posture. But this choice was foreclosed when the rhetoric of "rolling back the captive nations" was surrendered during the early months of Eisenhower's tenure.

Third, the Administration could try to change its relationship with the Soviet Union—a choice to which Stevenson devoted much attention in his 1956 campaign. And it is plain from the way Eisenhower nurtured disarmament proposals in the White House office that this option had a special place in his thinking as well. In fact our efforts in summitry and disarmament represented the only important impetus for foreign-policy innovation during Eisenhower's second term that were more than a direct reaction to external events or to public alarm about our ability to cope with them.

Despite our sporadic attempts at disarmament negotiations during Eisenhower's first term in office, it was not until the beginning of 1957 that the American delegation was seriously prepared to pursue with the Soviet Union a disarmament policy that had been launched by Eisenhower back in December 1953.[16] Harold Stassen, who had succeeded Rockefeller as Eisenhower's special assistant for disarmament, inherited the task of trying to keep alive the "open

[16] For an authoritative account of this extraordinary series of events see Bernhard G. Bechhoefer, *Postwar Negotiations for Arms Control* (Washington: Brookings Institution, 1961), pp. 245–249, 256–259, 326–349, and 398–429.

skies" proposal presented by Eisenhower at Geneva in 1955. Stassen was made the chief United States negotiator at the five-power conference for disarmament negotiations held in London in the spring of 1957. As such, he was responsible for preparing position papers for negotiations and for conducting the negotiations themselves.

By spring of 1957 it became apparent that the Russians had also been reappraising their disarmament policy and seemed amenable to fruitful negotiations. Pressing for the agreement that now seemed possible, Stassen undertook to negotiate directly with the Russians in private in London. But in doing so he overstepped his mandate and caused consternation among our allies, particularly West Germany. The Adenauer government was in the midst of an election campaign in which the opposition party, the Social Democrats, had been advocating direct negotiations with the Soviet Union on German reunification. Stassen's direct negotiations embarrassed Adenauer, and fissures appeared in the NATO alliance. Dulles seized on the complaint from Bonn to thrust Stassen aside and take over negotiations himself. He hammered out a comprehensive disarmament plan that won the agreement of all our NATO allies, thus healing the breach caused by Stassen. But the package, composed mainly of proposals already rejected by the Russians, effectively ended negotiations with Moscow.

Dulles now appealed to the General Assembly in an effort to score against the Russians with a resounding vote there. The appeal had special meaning to experienced negotiators on both sides, for they had learned to assess the seriousness of the other side's proposals by its self-restraint in using the proposals for propaganda appeals. In no negotiation had propaganda been absent on either side. Yet never before had a delegation appealed from the negotiating table to the General Assembly.[17] The result "was virtually to destroy years of painstaking efforts within the United Nations," and "to create a shadow over Western sincerity that will take years to dissipate."[18]

Sputniks I and II orbited while the General Assembly was in session. Their worldwide impact enhanced Soviet truculence over Dulles' appeal to the General Assembly. Khrushchev, after the space triumphs of late 1957, called for a summit meeting. It was a rec-

[17] *Ibid.*, p. 435.
[18] *Ibid.*, p. 432–433.

ognized way of putting Washington on the defensive. A year later, with the West's high estimates of Soviet strategic capabilities amply evident, the American congressional elections out of the way, and the Formosa Strait crisis cooled off, Khrushchev opened the Berlin issue again by fixing a six-month deadline on starting negotiations over Berlin. He was prodding Eisenhower toward the summit. As the Berlin deadline approached, however, Khrushchev postponed the time limit, thus turning Berlin into a rolling crisis.

The atmosphere in Washington was flaccid. Eisenhower's public statements about nuclear war gave the impression that American military policy was adrift. In March 1959, he stated flatly that there could be no "ground war" in Europe, and that nuclear war was "self-defeating."[19] "What good would it do," he said "to send a few more thousands or even a few divisions of troops to Europe?"[20]

Eisenhower's successor was to do precisely that—but as a symbolic and political gesture, rather than to stop a massive Soviet attack. Eisenhower hardly needed to be told about the political role of NATO's military force. His reactions in this situation, however, suggest an overconcentration on the military purposes of NATO—to the detriment of the American negotiating position.

Dulles' attitude toward negotiating with the Russians changed to reflect the new mood. In January 1959 he suggested that a settlement of European problems with Moscow that placed Russia at a political or military disadvantage could not be realistic and that the Soviet Union would have to be treated with greater consideration than it had been before.[21] Had Dulles lived, this late softening of his own attitudes about a general settlement with Moscow might have been clarified.

In 1958 the three nuclear powers stopped testing unilaterally. Khrushchev, at the conclusion of a series of Soviet nuclear-weapons tests in the spring of 1958, declared that Russia would stop testing nuclear weapons in the atmosphere, providing the West followed suit. It was a brilliant gesture, partly because it caught Britain and America out of phase—both countries were planning tests later in the year. They demurred, tested again in August, and announced a voluntary suspension for one year, effective November 1. The

---

19 *The New York Times,* March 12, 1959.
20 *Ibid.*
21 *Department of State Bulletin* (February 2, 1959), pp. 157–159.

Soviet Union resumed tests again in October, but quit on November 3, and the test ban went into effect.

A year later Eisenhower announced that he would not renew the ban, but he did not authorize new testing. The reciprocal test suspension remained intact until after Kennedy became President.

The Soviet announcement of a test suspension served to change the direction of the Soviet diplomatic drive. Khrushchev now dropped his demands for a summit meeting (although, at the end of the year, he issued a six-month ultimatum for a summit meeting on Berlin). The prospect of a Soviet-American summit affected the interests of different states differently. British participation at the "high table" has been an attractive prospect to every British government since Churchill first proposed a heads-of-state meeting in 1951. In the early fifties, the summit offered West Germany the brief hope of unification, but beginning in 1955 the prospect of Soviet-American agreement appeared threatening to Bonn because it might entail abandonment of German unification as a goal. For Khrushchev, a successful summit conference could help with hardline cold warriors in his own government. But since Soviet bloc expectations could never be wholly realized by a Soviet-American settlement, the prospect of a summit also posed risks for Russia. Similarly, the United States government could lose a great deal both as a bloc leader and as a partisan administration at home if the summit negotiations ended in dashed expectations.

By the end of 1958 Dulles was seriously ill with cancer. With a national election pending in Great Britain, Prime Minister Macmillan took the initiative for a summit meeting. He visited Moscow in February 1959 just as Dulles went on medical leave. Eisenhower moved slowly: he resented the pressure from London. Only after Macmillan's electoral victory in October did he agree to a meeting, and then conditionally. He insisted that thorough groundwork first be laid by preliminary negotiations at the working level and that no negotiating could occur under a Russian threat over Berlin. De Gaulle was in even less hurry. Before going to the summit he wanted to visit Moscow and to detonate a nuclear weapon.

In the meantime Khrushchev, on Eisenhower's invitation, visited the United States for twelve days in September 1959. He addressed the U.N. General Assembly, toured the country, and conferred privately with Eisenhower at Camp David, the presidential retreat. Camp David hardly met Eisenhower's prerequisites for the summit meeting, but it eliminated his chief objection to the conference, for Khrushchev now dropped a fixed deadline for negotiations on Berlin. But the main achievement at Camp David was symbolic—a demonstration that the two heads of state could talk in confidence, or at least in secret. The "spirit of Camp David" became a reference point in Soviet negotiations. It had no specific content but connoted better things to come. It also encouraged Eisenhower's propensity to turn to personal diplomacy—to undertake state visits aimed at modifying broad public attitudes in other countries in favor of the United States.

In September 1959 Eisenhower undertook a series of foreign trips "to assure," as he has put it,

> *all the people I could reach of the sincerity of our search for peace and our desire to be helpful. I wanted to try to raise the morale of struggling and underprivileged peoples, to enhance confidence in the value of friendship with the United States, and to give them assurance of their own security and chances for progress.*[22]

In August he went to West Germany, Great Britain, and France. A second trip included eleven countries looping from Italy across the Middle East to India and back through Greece, France, and Spain. Together, these trips served to help unite the NATO countries in preparation for the summit, as well as to display Eisenhower's personal popularity in a series of triumphal visits.

A third trip took place at the end of February 1960. After visiting Puerto Rico, Eisenhower went on to spend nine days visiting Brazil, Chile, Argentina, and Uruguay. Returning from Paris in May, he stopped in Portugal, and in June spent two weeks visiting Korea, Taiwan, and the Philippines.

Although these trips may have had some intangible value, they reflected the aimlessness of foreign relations during the Eisenhower Administration's last eighteen months. The final trip had been scheduled around a visit to Japan to celebrate Japanese ratification of a security treaty with the United States. The Japanese government canceled the visit because of anti-American riots. The episode

---

[22] Eisenhower, *The White House Years*, Vol. II, p. 486.

was a substantial setback to the public-relations objectives of the whole trip.

After Camp David, a summit meeting was scheduled for mid-May 1960. On May 1, a Soviet rocket brought down a secret, high-flying American photo-reconnaisance aircraft, a U-2—complete with uninjured pilot—on a planned intrusion into Soviet air space from Pakistan. These aircraft had been overflying Soviet territory from secret bases in Pakistan and Turkey for many months, operating under an elaborate cover as a weather-research project. There is some evidence that the Russians had known about them and could have shot a U-2 down over its territory before but waited until this moment to do so. Having shot the aircraft down, moreover, it would have been easy to postpone disclosure of the incident. Instead, Khrushchev chose to publicize the incident dramatically four days after it occurred. Washington had already issued the prearranged official lie to cover the operation—a lost aircraft on a weather-observation flight. But the details released by Moscow quickly discredited the lie, aggravating our government's embarrassment. Eisenhower now decided on a policy of full disclosure. In addition, however, he stated that he took personal responsibility for the flight.

Barely a week later, in Paris, the summit conference aborted at the opening session. Khrushchev demanded that Eisenhower apologize for the U-2 flights and punish the wrongdoers responsible for them. Since Eisenhower had accepted personal responsibility for the flights, he could hardly comply. On the other hand, our government's failure to maintain the official lie may have begun to put Khrushchev in a difficult position with the more militant factions within his own government that did not want him negotiating with Eisenhower, thus making it necessary for Khrushchev to demand the humiliating apology.

Critics considered Eisenhower's acceptance of personal responsibility unnecessary, the result of inappropriate personal compunctions. He has stated more expedient reasons: how could he negotiate effectively in Paris if he would not take responsibility for activities which were the subject of negotiation?[23]

According to one interpretation, Khrushchev seized on the U-2 incident to cancel the conference, having learned from information

[23] *Ibid.*, pp. 550–553.

obtained from the spy plane that the United States would have been able to collect sufficient intelligence data during such missions to know that the Russians did not have the ICBM's they claimed to have.[24] While that would be an overriding cause for calling off the meeting, both sides had taken deliberate actions that had made the meeting less acceptable to the other. Each side, concerned with its own competitive position, had boxed the other in.

Moscow exploited the U-2 incident, stridently condemning American duplicity and imputing that Washington did not want a summit meeting. For the American public, approaching the summer presidential nominating conventions, the Eisenhower Administration appeared again on the defensive, responding to the initiatives of Soviet diplomacy. Even to the American public, the cancelled summit seemed in part the consequence of fumbling in Washington.

The desire for major changes in international affairs—such as disarmament or some other step to moderate the Cold War—had produced few results by the last year of the Eisenhower Administration, despite Eisenhower's personal interest. Indeed, his own concern with moderating the Cold War—his willingness to meet with Khrushchev and his moderation in pursuing the arms race—only contributed to the impression that his administration was on the defensive.

CONCLUSION

It seems clear that the Eisenhower years were a period of political and governmental consolidation. But it is difficult to judge the Eisenhower Administration's handling of foreign policy because of the disparity between its foreign-policy pronouncements and its actions. This disparity permeated all Eisenhower's foreign policies. The rhetoric of policy was active, even aggressive; but the actual policy was usually constrained. Confronted with the Administration's rhetoric, one has difficulty evaluating how discriminating this Administration was in choosing when and where to act.

The expansion of the military-alliance network through the Middle East and Asia was hardly discriminating. Yet, after the

24 Horelick and Rush, *op. cit.,* pp. 122–123.

formalities were over, as the Administration began to face the annual costs for military and economic support for the Baghdad Pact and SEATO members in 1955 and 1956, it silently cut back such support. In the course of building the military-alliance network, it had embroiled itself in several intractable regional conflicts —between Pakistan and India in the Asian subcontinent and among the Arab nationalists (complicated by the Arab-Israeli conflict) in the Middle East. In Western Europe, seeking a more effective military capability by NATO, the Administration had become more closely identified with West Germany—to the discomfort of its other allies—and had provoked a parochial nationalism in France by its favors to London and its preference for Bonn. In all these cases, it had been highly selective. The question is whether the Administration's choices were wise or necessary.

Our rhetoric of anti-Communism helped draw the Administration into rigid support for loudly anti-Communist regimes while initially neglecting important non-Communist states such as India. The rhetoric of activism, similarly, was too general to commit the Eisenhower Administration in any one situation, but it sometimes predisposed the Eisenhower Administrators to act in haste, as in Lebanon and the Formosa Strait.

The New Look began as a serious effort to take advantage of technological developments in order to cope with the problem of having only limited resources that could ultimately be deployed for military capabilities. But this strategy went astray in two respects: in the inadequacy of our defense budgeting and planning and in the facile and imprecise spinning out of strategic concepts.

The largest disappointment in the Eisenhower Administration's foreign relations record is its performance in handling the domestic political elements that influence foreign policy. Despite all the assets his Administration held at the beginning for reconciling public opinion to foreign relations, and despite all its efforts to do so, Eisenhower, like his predecessor, came to suffer a loss of public confidence in foreign policy.

It is true of course that the Eisenhower Administration suffered from popular alienation much less than did the Truman Administration. The widely perceived threats that it had to meet in external affairs were hardly comparable to the impact of the Korean War on American public opinion. Eisenhower started from a stronger political base than did Truman, and his popularity never drifted as low. Yet, the similarities between the Administrations, given these vital differences, are striking. In the end the Eisenhower Administration suffered from a growing chorus of criticisms from the interested and active public, and from quiet, unarticulated anxiety among the less attentive public. Both Truman's and Eisenhower's difficulties marked a significant gap between the governed and their governors—though the gap had been much wider in 1952.

In Eisenhower's second term, however, he failed to adapt his leadership to accommodate the heavy Democratic majorities in Congress and became increasingly partisan, evidently reflecting the alienation of the men around him from the Democratic congressional leadership. As for the broad public, their anxiety had been triggered by Sputnik and nurtured by critics of the Administration who were themselves responding to less widely known events—the mishaps in American alliance policies associated with the Suez crisis, the unrest in Latin America and Japan, and the Lebanon and Formosa crises. The public at large was not willing to grapple with these details, but it did assess the general posture of the government according to its perception of external conditions. The Administration's critics were able to reduce public confidence in the Eisenhower Administration because its posture seemed, even from a great distance, unduly complacent.

The appearance of complacency—some of which was real—derived principally from two sources. One was Eisenhower's self-imposed inhibitions in governing—his restrained executive leadership and deference to Congress and his belief in limiting the level and scope of government action. The other was his attitude toward competition with the Soviet Union, never fully articulated. This attitude was reflected in Eisenhower's strong commitment to disarmament and summitry, his skepticism about pushing the arms race ahead full tilt, and, finally, his acceptance of a potential missile gap. These decisions cannot be laid simply to his fascination with budget balancing. He played a cool game with the Russians—cooler than he could articulate or even make explicit. In the end, this game contributed to the growing uneasiness in broad public opinion over Eisenhower's handling of external affairs.

We will never know how much Eisenhower would have eased

the way for his successors in their dealings with the Chinese and Russians had he made plainer this propensity to hedge in the direction of détente. We do know that the years of good feeling he provided, though they soured somewhat at the end, built a mood of trust in public life that was to be drawn upon in the late sixties. Had he articulated and publicized his inclination to moderate the arms race and be conciliatory to the Russians, he would probably have paid a significant political price in domestic popularity, effectiveness, and public trust.

APPENDIX TO CHAPTER 5

A survey in Washington and Chicago a few weeks after Sputnik reported 43 percent agreeing and 46 percent disagreeing that the Russian satellite was a "serious blow to U.S. prestige."[24] As an indication of some disturbance in public attitudes, we can judge the percentage agreeing to be high. A more satisfactory indicator would be a survey run repeatedly, over time, to trace secular changes. One poll that is taken several times a year deals with public perceptions about how well the President is doing. The percentage of the national sample who approved of the way Eisenhower was "handling his job as President" had been sliding in 1957, but it actually showed a dip in the first poll taken after Sputnik. (See Table 5-1.)

At the same time, in November 1957, 53 percent of a national sample wanted to "take a new look at our defense policies," and only 26 percent were satisfied with them. (See Table 5-2.) We have no numbers to compare these with unless we compare answers to roughly similar questions. In March 1959 49 percent of a national sample agreed that the United States was either keeping ahead of the Soviet Union in military power, or staying even, while 34 percent agreed that the United States was dropping behind.[25] By comparison, these results indicate a considerable rise in confidence sixteen months after the November 1957 poll. A national sample in January 1958 on whether the Russians could wipe out most Ameri-

[24] American Institute of Public Opinion, October 27, 1957.
[25] *Ibid.*, March 6, 1959.

Table 5-1

"Do you approve or disapprove of the way Eisenhower is handling his job as President?"

	Approve (*percent*)	Disapprove (*percent*)	No opinion (*percent*)
1957			
January (high point)	79	11	10
March	72	18	10
May	67	21	12
June	62	23	15
July	63	23	14
November (after Sputnik)	57	27	16
1958			
January	60	30	10
February	58	27	15
March (period of business recession)	52	33	15
April (low point)	49	35	16
May (Pentagon reorganization)	54	31	15
June (Adams–Goldfine case)	53	32	15
July (Marines to Lebanon)	52	32	16
August	58	27	15
September	56	28	16
October	57	26	17
November	52	30	18

SOURCE: Figures from American Institute of Public Opinion releases of months listed. Compiled in *Public Opinion Quarterly*, **25** (Spring 1961), p. 136. Reprinted by permission of the American Institute of Public Opinion, Princeton, N.J.

can cities with their new rockets yields similar percentages: 51 percent agreeing, 35 percent disagreeing, with 14 percent of no opinion.[26] Other polls show considerable initial resistance in the United States to the idea that the Russian satellite was a serious blow to American prestige. By comparison, these numbers indicate considerably shaken confidence.

[26] *Ibid.*, January 29, 1958.

Table 5-2

"Are you satisfied with the present defense policies of the United States—or do you think there is a need to take a new look at our defense policies?"

	Satisfied *(percent)*	Take new look *(percent)*	No opinion *(percent)*
National total	26	53	21
By political affiliation:			
Republicans	35	42	23
Democrats	20	59	21
Independents	27	55	18

SOURCE: American Institute of Public Opinion, November 24, 1957. Reprinted by permission of the American Institute of Public Opinion, Princeton, N.J.

Many factors affect the public's confidence in the government. A recession began in late 1957, undoubtedly decreasing the government's popularity, though possibly the reaction was not felt until 1958. Furthermore, Eisenhower's popularity had been diminishing before the turndown in the economy, as table 5-1 shows. There had also been some upward shifts of important magnitude in perceptions about Soviet capabilities before Sputnik.[27]

Survey data also reveals a reduction in public confidence in our responses to external threats toward the end of Eisenhower's tenure. That his personal diplomacy during his last few years in office helped to offset this trend is suggested by the fact that in October 1959 only 18 percent of the respondents answered "yes" to the question, "Do you think we are likely to get into another world war in the next five years?" (This figure had been as high as 48 percent twice during Eisenhower's first term.)

Nonetheless, by June of 1960, after the active spring primary campaigns and the attention given to national and international issues, 34 percent of the national sample said it expected war in the next five years. By December 1960, after the election, the percentage expecting war had climbed to 50 percent.

27 "Do you think Russia has the edge on the U.S. in atom bombs and hydrogen bombs?" National total: 9 percent yes, 77 percent no, 14 percent no opinion. *Ibid.*, April 2, 1955. "Do you think Russia has gone farther than or not as far as the United States in developing H-bombs?" National total: Russia farther, 19 percent, United States farther, 33 percent; both same, 20 percent; don't know, 28 percent. *Ibid.*, May 19, 1957.

chapter 6

The New Frontier:
Innovation and Crisis

THE 1960 PRESIDENTIAL CAMPAIGN

John F. Kennedy was a rare political entrepreneur who gained his political seasoning during the Eisenhower Administration. In his political career he had never settled down to maintain a safe majority in a local or statewide constituency, and in 1956, as the junior United States Senator from Massachusetts, he set about becoming President before very many people thought he was ready. To do so, he turned his attention from the Senate to the task of building a national constituency, and in 1960 he went to the Democratic nominating convention with an impressive record in the state presidential primaries, winning the presidential nomination on the first ballot.

Running against Richard Nixon, the incumbent Vice-President, Kennedy won the 1960 election by a tiny plurality—less than .2 percent. But his electoral victory, though narrow, left him with some political assets for conducting foreign policy. The campaign had fostered a mood of expected change without producing sharp partisan issues in foreign relations. Both candidates had confined themselves instead to general talk about the need for new initiatives. For Nixon this approach represented a way to dodge criticisms of the Eisenhower Administration without repudiating it. For Kennedy, the promise of general action represented the kind of campaign commitment that was unlikely to prove embarrassing later and thus reflected his inclination to keep his future options open if he gained office.

In keeping with this approach, Kennedy was more of a hard-liner on foreign policy than Stevenson had been in his 1952 and 1956 campaigns. Kennedy did not, for example, attack Eisenhower's failure to negotiate with the Russians. Instead, he exploited the stagnation of the post-Sputnik doldrums—the "missile gap," the slow-down in the economy, the evident drop in American prestige abroad, and the Eisenhower Administration's seeming reluctance to act. During his campaign, Kennedy gradually settled on a simple message of arousal and optimism: to get the country moving again. "I have premised my campaign," he said,

> on the single assumption that the American people are uneasy at the present drift in our national course, that they are disturbed by the relative decline in our vitality and prestige, and that they have the will and the strength to start the United States moving again.[1]

Getting things moving again was a young man's appeal—the young candidate telling a young electorate and a new prosperous and optimistic middle class that controversial issues could be resolved and problems mastered. This theme would soon be adopted by other candidates in state and local campaigns and even in other countries—a tribute to Kennedy as a politician. Kennedy used his theme to link foreign and domestic affairs: Wilson, Roosevelt, and Truman, he said, were "successful around the world because they were successful here, because they moved this country ahead, because only in this way could America show a watching world. . . ."[2]

KENNEDY'S PRESIDENTIAL STYLE

"The Chief Executive," Kennedy told the National Press Club after his election, "must be the vital center of action in our whole

---

1 Arthur M. Schlesinger, Jr., *A Thousand Days* (Boston: Houghton Mifflin, 1965), p. 68.
2 *Ibid.*, p. 68.

scheme of government."[3] Probably no one has entered the White House more self-conscious about his role of leadership than did Kennedy. Roosevelt's chaotic administrative methods had been given new respectability by two studies of his leadership.[4] Thus Kennedy came to office with new respect for what had been too quickly dismissed as Roosevelt's "administrative chaos" and for the need to avoid being cut off from independent sources of information. "I can't afford to confine myself to one set of advisers," he told Richard Neustadt during the campaign. "If I did that, I would be on their lead strings."[5] Reacting against the methods of the Eisenhower Administration, Kennedy promptly dismantled much of the White House staff organization, although he later rebuilt part of it as needed for orderly procedures.

Kennedy's preferences for keeping his policy options open, maintaining diverse channels of communication, and developing maximum flexibility in policy making were elements of his presidential style, and they directly affected his conduct of foreign policy. Whereas Dulles had come to depend increasingly on his own capacity to manipulate other governments in order to maintain flexibility in foreign relations, Kennedy's flexibility and initiative began with his manipulation of men, ideas, and resources at home.

Advised that Eisenhower had lost the political initiative in 1953 because of the difficulties of taking over the government, Kennedy got a running start on the Presidency after the election, quickly making key appointments, searching for additional talent to fill the appointive posts of the executive branch, and preparing for legislative proposals (and aiding the talent search) by establishing a series of task forces to report to him on major areas of public policy.

Kennedy, like Eisenhower, took over from a predecessor whose foreign policy had lost momentum, and like Dulles (for Eisenhower), Kennedy came to power determined to take the initiative. Truman's foreign policy had become paralyzed over the loss of domestic political support and the resulting internal demoralization

---

[3] *Ibid.*, p. 120.

[4] Richard E. Neustadt, *Presidential Power: the Politics of Leadership* (New York: Wiley, 1960); Arthur M. Schlesinger, Jr., *The Age of Roosevelt*, Vol. II: *The Coming of the New Deal* (Boston: Houghton Mifflin, 1959), Chaps. 32–34.

[5] Schlesinger, *A Thousand Days*, p. 123.

associated with the Korean War. Eisenhower's foreign policy had become static under Dulles' autocratic hand, and when Dulles died, it remained quiescent in the post-Sputnik malaise.

Kennedy reinforced his drive to find departures in foreign policy by taking a broader view of the presidential role than Eisenhower had done. Eisenhower's foreign policy cannot be explained without taking account of Secretary of State Dulles' relationship with the President, but Dean Rusk, Kennedy's Secretary of State, did not play a comparable role. If we were to explain Kennedy's foreign policy in terms of the men around him and their influence, our list would be much longer: it would be drawn from Democrats in exile and in office who were associated with the National Advisory Committee of the Democratic party, divided into Truman and Stevenson factions. It would include the development economists, principally from Harvard and MIT, and others from Harvard, principally McGeorge Bundy, Arthur Schlesinger, Jr., and J. K. Galbraith. Kennedy had stayed aloof from the factional fights within the National Advisory Committee between the hard liners (headed by Acheson), who wanted to reemphasize Europe, rebuild the NATO alliance, and reestablish American superiority in nuclear strategic power, and the Stevensonians, who wanted to give new emphasis to economic and political development in the underdeveloped areas and take steps to reach a détente with the Soviet Union.[6]

Kennedy drew these men into association with his Administration, neutralizing and restructuring these two factions by adding other people as well. Rusk was the President of the Rockefeller Foundation, and although he had been an assistant secretary of state under Truman, he too had remained aloof from the Democrats in exile. Kennedy made Chester Bowles Undersecretary of State and appointed Acheson as a special adviser. To Adlai Stevenson he gave the prestigious ambassadorship to the United Nations. At the head of his White House staff for foreign affairs he placed McGeorge Bundy, a Republican who had written foreign-policy speeches for Dewey in 1948. Walt W. Rostow, an MIT economist and a hard liner on foreign policy, joined Bundy's staff and later went to the State Department to head its policy planners.

Eisenhower had been a nonpartisan leader with a partisan

[6] *Ibid.*, p. 200.

Cabinet. Kennedy was a vigorous partisan leader who, like Roosevelt, sought Republicans for his Cabinet. He appointed as his Secretary of the Treasury a former sub-Cabinet officer under Eisenhower, Douglas Dillon, a New York Investment broker. Kennedy also tried to bring Republican Wall Streeters Robert A. Lovett and John J. McCloy into his Administration, but when he failed, he appointed Robert S. McNamara, the new president of the Ford Motor Company, as Secretary of Defense.[7]

KENNEDY'S OPTIMISTIC ECONOMIC PROGRAM

Kennedy's inaugural address on January 20 was a sermon on public duty and national peril. Ten days later he began to unfold his program. Not since Truman's legislative message after V-J Day had a President with such enthusiasm for public action laid before Congress the outlines of a general effort. Truman's program had recommended the maintenance of wartime price and wage controls over the economy, the reactivation of public works (highways, hospitals) that had been discontinued during the war, and the extension of welfare benefits. Kennedy's program was very different.

"The present state of our economy is disturbing," he said. "We take office in the wake of 7 months of recession, $3\frac{1}{2}$ years of slack, 7 years of diminished economic growth, and 9 years of falling farm income." He concluded, "In short, the American economy is in trouble. The most resourceful industrialized country on earth ranks among the last in the rate of economic growth." He prescribed an expansionist economic policy: "We must show the world what a free economy can do—to reduce unemployment, to put unused capacity to work, to spur new productivity, and to foster higher economic growth within a range of sound fiscal policies and relative price stability."[8]

"Efficient expansion at home" was to be the linchpin of do-

---

[7] Theodore C. Sorensen, *Kennedy* (New York: Harper & Row, 1966), p. 255.

[8] The State of the Union: Message of President Kennedy delivered to the Congress, January 30, 1961, 87th Congress, 1st Session; Council on Foreign Relations, *Documents on American Foreign Relations, 1961* (New York: Harper & Row, 1961), pp. 16 f.

mestic and foreign programs alike. More than anything, moving ahead that first year meant getting the economy going. If the slack in our economy could be taken up and if expansion could proceed at an adequate rate, domestic problems would be alleviated, the balance of payments would be improved, the international prestige of the United States and of free institutions would be reestablished, and the government in Washington would be in a better financial position to deal with domestic and external problems.

Truman's legislative message in 1945 had laid out an ambitious program of continued direct economic controls and social-welfare proposals. Kennedy's legislative program included some additional social-welfare spending proposals. But the core of his domestic program was a strategy of induced economic expansion. In the next four years increased federal spending totaled $20 billion, while taxes were cut about $20 billion and the supply of money and credit increased more than 10 percent per year. Kennedy's objective —to manage the economy for maximum utilization and growth— reflected a profound shift of attitudes about economic policy.

Nowhere did Kennedy's strategy of induced expansion mark a sharper contrast with the fiscal and economic policies of the Eisenhower Administration than in dealing with the balance-of-payments problem that had plagued this country since 1958. For ten years after World War II the world demand for American products had greatly exceeded the domestic demand for foreign products, providing a comfortable margin between American dollars earned abroad and dollars spent. The Marshall Plan, the military- and economic-assistance programs of the fifties, the Korean War, and the costs of stationing American forces abroad all helped to deplete our dollar credits. But the persistently favorable balance of payments firmly established the dollar as the preeminent reserve currency, and dollar creditors throughout the world remained confident that the dollar was the currency least likely to be devalued.

Many economists claimed that to maintain an adequate rate of growth in the American economy it would be necessary to permit a gradual price inflation, but the Eisenhower Administration, which had a premonition that a trade-balance problem would develop, rejected this upward drift of prices. Instead it sought to secure a "sound dollar"—that is, a completely stable price level— partly because it feared that the persistent (if moderate) inflation of

American prices would reduce the foreign demand for American products and accentuate the trade-balance problem. The Eisenhower Administration did manage to stop the historic upward drift of prices while maintaining a rate of economic growth that many economists had considered impossible. But meanwhile, competitive foreign production grew even faster.

When the balance of trade turned against the United States in 1958, the Eisenhower Administration attempted to use the federal budget as an instrument for reducing the dollar drain. With the West Germany economy booming, Eisenhower brought pressure on Bonn to assume more of the costs of American troops stationed in Germany and to assume a greater share of the economic assistance to underdeveloped countries. But when the Eisenhower Administration took further steps late in 1960 to stem an increasing drain of dollars by ordering American dependents home from Europe, Europeans read this action to mean that the United States was going to solve its trade-balance problems at the expense of its commitments to the defense of Europe.

Kennedy's approach to the balance-of-trade problem was quite different, and he signaled this change in our policies by cancelling Eisenhower's order to bring back the dependents of American troops in Europe, demonstrating our long-term commitment to the defense of Europe.[9] Instead, Kennedy's solution was to link the defense of the American dollar directly to the need for an expanded economy. This new linkage was reflected in the major programs for domestic and foreign policy laid down by Kennedy in a series of messages to Congress during his first four months in the White House. His State of the Union message, for example, outlined needed improvements in military, economic, and diplomatic "tools." Barely a week later, Kennedy specified a series of executive actions he was taking to reduce the unfavorable outflow of dollars and asked the Senate to approve United States membership in the Organization for Economic Cooperation and Development, a group of NATO countries concerned with economic development and

[9] At the same time, however, we indicated a deliberate shift away from European interests on the colonial issue by recording a vote at the United Nations siding with the anticolonial bloc. This demonstration is reminiscent of some of Dulles' efforts at the beginning of the Eisenhower Administration to win friends among the new states.

finance. He continued Eisenhower's efforts to get prosperous West Germany—which now had the third largest gross national product in the world—to carry more of the burden of subsidizing American forces in Europe and to assume greater responsibility for foreign economic aid.

At the end of March Kennedy elaborated on the economic tools referred to in his State of the Union message. After the spectacular successes of the Marshall Plan, American economic assistance had resulted in a mixture of success, failure, and frustration. The opponents of foreign aid argued either that one could not do with economic assistance what the American government seemed to be trying to do, or that we were going about it the wrong way. Kennedy did not doubt that aid could be useful. By the beginning of his Administration, the friendly critics of foreign aid consisted of those who wanted stricter economic criteria used and those who saw economic assistance as a political tool with which to reward friends and friendly acts of other countries. The second position was basically pessimistic: it assumed that, all claims to the contrary, the objective of American aid was not to work an economic miracle that would in turn transform the politics and society of the recipient states, but merely to prod and cajol other governments in limited ways. Kennedy clearly adopted the first position in principle, but his Administration still used aid as a political tool. With a similar optimism about achieving a higher rate of steady economic growth in the domestic economy, Kennedy based his foreign-aid program on the premise that economic assistance could carry underdeveloped countries into self-sustaining growth. "There exists, in the 1960's," he told Congress,

> a historic opportunity for a major economic assistance effort by the free industrialized nations to move more than half the people of the less developed nations into self-sustained economic growth, while the rest move substantially closer to the day when they, too, will no longer have to depend on outside assistance.[10]

Reacting against the Eisenhower Administration's propensity to reward client states with economic assistance, the Kennedy Administration held that economic aid should go to states that met certain

10 *Documents on American Foreign Relations, 1961*, p. 38.

objective standards of performance specified by the United States. This system, the Administration hoped, would serve as a major incentive for national economic development without entangling the United States in the internal politics of foreign-aid recipients. The core of the Kennedy aid program was the provision for five-year low-interest economic-development loans, so that recipient countries could then make long-term plans with confidence that they would receive American aid during that period.

Five-year loans, however, would not permit the United States to use its grants as a bargaining tool from year to year in order to prod the recipient country into carrying its economic-development plans forward. As it turned out, Congress would not approve the five-year provision, and nothing more was done about this idea until 1966.

MCNAMARA'S DEFENSE PROGRAM AND THE ATLANTIC ALLIANCE

When President Kennedy took office he immediately began to reconstitute the Atlantic alliance by making strong diplomatic appointments, devoting much attention to NATO affairs, receiving official visits from the British Prime Minister Macmillan and German Premier Adenauer and visiting De Gaulle in Paris. Surprisingly, the Bay of Pigs disaster in April (see Chapter 8) marred only temporarily the favorable image of the new President that had been developing in foreign capitals.

What proved to be the most important development of the Kennedy Administration's relationship to our allies was not the strengthened diplomatic team but the shift in policy initiatives from the State Department to the Defense Department under the strong, often brilliant, and sometimes insensitive leadership of its new Secretary, Robert S. McNamara. The initiatives of our Pentagon, together with De Gaulle's growing resistance to military and economic integration in Europe, became the hallmarks of American relations with Western Europe in the early sixties.

When McNamara assumed office he found the tools for a major revolution in military affairs at hand: (1) his statutory authority as Secretary of Defense (dating from 1953 to 1958), which had never been used to its full potential; (2) a staff inherited from his predecessor, carefully trained to show him how to use the full reach of his authority; and (3) experts with methods called (with exaggerated specificity) "systems analysis" who were prepared to launch new strategic doctrines and a management revolution through new program-budgeting techniques.

Under Eisenhower, the Defense Department staff had focused on developing the New Look in an effort to achieve economies that would make our defense burden tenable over the long haul. Under the Kennedy Administration, with its different conception of what would help our economy and its different methods for generating new defense policies, the Department concentrated instead on increasing the stability of the nuclear "balance of terror."

Propelled by the urgency of the Berlin crisis in early 1961, McNamara had already directed the expansion of both our strategic missile program and our airlift capacity—two moves designed to provide immediate improvements in our defenses. At the end of February President Kennedy laid before Congress the result of McNamara's far-ranging reappraisal of the defense establishment.

Kennedy recommended additional steps to strengthen our deterrent and conventional forces, to limit the danger of accidents, and to increase the flexibility of American forces. He recommended a quicker phasing-in of the less vulnerable, solid-fueled, intercontinental missile forces—the submarine-launched Polaris and the land-based Minuteman—and the more rapid phasing-out of the vulnerable, liquid-fueled Titan missiles and B-47 bombers. Speeding up the production of Polaris and Minuteman would give us an expanded force by the mid-sixties. For immediate strengthening of our strategic nuclear force, Kennedy proposed steps to reduce the vulnerability to surprise attack—more aircraft on airborn alert, more planes kept on ground alert, and improvement of our detection and warning systems for incoming intercontinental missiles.

To improve our conventional forces and thus widen our range of possible military responses, Kennedy recommended spending more funds on developing new non-nuclear weapons. To reduce the danger of accidental war and the vulnerability of American forces, nuclear forces would be brought under tighter control through more secure channels of command and communication.

The net increase in defense expenditures for the following fiscal year was modest. Thereafter, McNamara's defense budgets increased sharply from the Eisenhower ceilings. The change reflected the fiscal optimism in the White House. Kennedy had instructed McNamara to "Develop the force structure necessary to our military requirements without regard to arbitrary or predetermined budget ceilings."[11] Our increased spending also reflected our more immediate desire to face the Berlin crisis by offering the Russians concrete evidence of the Administration's resolution on this issue.

The McNamara program sharply distinguished, however, between resolution and provocation. A strategic nuclear force that could survive attack would be under *less* pressure to act in haste than one that would be wiped out by a first strike from the enemy. A force that could survive to deliver a retaliatory strike would give the government more time to consider its actions in a crisis. Underlining the new approach to stabilizing the "balance of terror," Kennedy declared in a speech on March 26, 1961: "Our arms will never be used to strike the first blow in any attack."

The "missile gap" quickly dropped from sight. The issue had rested on projected future disparities in missile strength predicted by Congress in 1959, and the Kennedy Administration had found these projections quite outdated by early 1961. Soviet strength had been considerably overestimated. In addition, McNamara was impressed by Eisenhower's reasons for not responding to the warnings of the air-power enthusiasts. Kennedy, like Eisenhower, wanted to make discriminating choices in his defense policies, and luckily, unlike Eisenhower, he had a Secretary of Defense who could offer him such choices.

In October 1961, long after it had become apparent that the "missile gap" issue was dead, Deputy Secretary of Defense Roswell L. Gilpatric buried it. "We have a second-strike capability," he said in a major public speech, "which is at least as extensive as what the Soviets can deliver by striking first."[12]

The new defense policies were part of a complicated negotiat-

---

[11] House Armed Services Committee, *Hearings on Military Posture,* 87th Congress, 2nd Session (1962), p. 3162.
[12] *The New York Times,* October 22, 1961.

ing posture Kennedy was constructing. This posture was intended to be not only tough, with increased military capabilities, but also flexible and conciliatory, with more choices available in military, economic, and diplomatic moves. The efforts at conciliation took two forms. First, Kennedy elevated the status of formulating disarmament agreements by assembling the staff responsible for this task in a new Arms Control and Disarmament Agency. Kennedy linked ACDA to the State Department and instructed it to get the test-ban negotiations out of the doldrums. Second, he would seek to establish a better working relationship with the Soviet Government. Kennedy's effort to pursue agreement with the Soviet Union on arms-control measures required the active support of the Defense Department, which McNamara's strong leadership assured.

Our new defense posture immediately aroused the suspicions of our European allies. McNamara's object was to increase the stability of our strategic balance with the Soviet Union by reducing the vulnerability of our strategic forces—and hence, the need for an American first strike or a hair-trigger response, and by developing a wider range of conventional choices in order to avoid using nuclear weapons if possible. Washington saw this flexibility as making it more likely that the United States could use its military capabilities in behalf of its allies. But Europeans saw our flexibility instead as giving the United States the option not to defend her NATO allies.

Nowhere was the difference in perspective between the United States and Europe more striking than with respect to nuclear "locks." When Kennedy became President he found on his desk a proposal for installing electromechanical devices on nuclear weapons located in Western Europe that would prevent their being fired without authorization. This idea was consonant with McNamara's efforts, and Kennedy seized upon it, ordering all U.S. nuclear weapons in Europe "locked up." He wanted to be sure that in a military crisis the President would be able to act with the absolute assurance that no American-made nuclear weapons would be set off by us or our allies until authorized by the President to do so.

The practical effect of these new controls, however, was to eliminate the prospect anticipated in Europe that the Supreme Allied Commander would use American nuclear forces in Europe to meet a Soviet attack even without clear authorization from the President. With one stroke, the Supreme Commander's role had been radically reduced.

In May 1962, in a secret speech to NATO ministers assembled in Athens, Greece, McNamara stated our strategic axiom for nuclear weapons that had evolved by 1961 in the decision to lock up nuclear forces: all nuclear forces on "our" side must be controlled from one source in the interest of controlling and terminating nuclear war, should it occur. He repeated the substance of this message in a commencement speech at Ann Arbor a month later, driving home the import of his axiom for the British and French: ". . . limited nuclear capabilities, operating independently, are dangerous, expensive, prone to obsolescence, and lacking in credibility as a deterrent."

In McNamara's attempt to formulate the strategic doctrines that would constitute American military policy, perhaps the most difficult considerations to subject to formal analysis were the political functions of NATO and the American role in NATO, partly because the success of these functions depended on their remaining somewhat implicit. The uncertainties about the custody and command arrangements for nuclear weapons in Europe before the force was locked up had assured the American nuclear commitment to our allies by entrusting the Supreme Commander with a nuclear trigger. The fiction of equality among the NATO members served another function as well: to mask the dependence of our European allies on American forces and strategy and thus to reduce the criticism of these governments from their domestic political opposition. And finally, by not articulating our nuclear strategy explicitly after 1955 the Eisenhower Administration prevented attention from being called to those unique interests of the United States that conflicted with NATO interests. But McNamara's revamping of our force postures and strategy destroyed these protective ambiguities and raised new uncertainties among Europeans about the American nuclear commitment to them.

The Kennedy Administration's enthusiasm for a build-up of conventional forces in Europe was particularly troublesome. This buildup began in preparation for the Berlin crisis in early 1961, but it took new impetus from the Cuban missile crisis of October 1962. With nerves still strained from the Cuban crisis, Rusk and McNamara argued at the NATO Council meeting in December 1962 for increased contributions of conventional forces by the NATO allies.

McNamara had just undercut Britain's claim to an independent nuclear force by cancelling the development of the American air-to-ground missile Skybolt, which was designed to extend the life of bombers into an era when the Soviet Union would have strong air defenses around its major urban centers. For Washington, future status as a nuclear power depended on ballistics missiles. Skybolt was thus of only secondary importance to us, though it could provide an additional element of flexibility.

Britain, however, could not afford ballistics missiles and had staked its future status as a nuclear power on the U.S. Air Force's plans to develop Skybolt. Cancellation of these plans threatened deep political trouble for Macmillan's Conservative government.

Kennedy wanted to repair the damage the Skybolt cancellation caused Macmillan, much as Eisenhower had done when Britain had given up development of the intermediate-range missile Bluestreak in 1957. But the Cuban missile crisis occupied his attention until he was enroute to a meeting with Macmillan at Nassau in December 1962. Improvising, Kennedy agreed to supply the British with Polaris missiles without warheads. The British would arm them and fire them from British submarines yet to be built. The two statesmen also agreed, however, that these missiles would be assigned to a "NATO nuclear force" if one were to be established, where they would be "targeted in accordance with NATO plans." Britain could use them independently only where "supreme national interests" were at stake.

These nuclear arrangements satisfied none of the foreign-policy factions in Washington. The Nassau agreement displeased Anglophiles because it reduced the value of the Anglo-American "special relationship" in nuclear matters, disappointed European integrationists because it did not enhance European solidarity, and only partly satisfied those who objected to independent nuclear forces, such as McNamara in his speeches at Athens and Ann Arbor. The reaction in Washington showed the strains of an alliance policy that had to cope with the diverse political goals of its allies while it was coming to terms with the logic of nuclear strategy.

FRANCE AND EUROPEAN INTEGRATION

French President De Gaulle had reacted to McNamara's Athens attack on independent national nuclear forces with such a strongly nationalistic pronouncement that five of his ministers resigned. Offered the same arrangements on Polaris missiles that the British accepted, De Gaulle rejected them. France remained committed to the development of her own delivery systems—first nuclear weapon-carrying bombers and later nuclear-tipped missiles.

At Nassau Kennedy revived the hope for a so-called multilateral nuclear force (MLF), which Secretary Herter had proposed at ·the end of 1960. The idea lay dormant through the first two years of the Kennedy Administration, nursed along by a small group of enthusiasts in the State Department. The MLF would be a nuclear force in Europe at the disposal of Europeans jointly but not unilaterally by one country. It was supposed to renew the credibility of our nuclear commitment to Western Europe by offering American participation in an integrated force based in Europe. Yet Washington would continue to control an American "safety catch" against the nuclear trigger. The MLF was supposed to channel anticipated German aspirations for nuclear weapons while taking the steam out of the French program, but it may well have further stimulated the Germans and goaded the French on instead.

Both the Germans and the British favored the MLF as an acceptable second choice to having a special nuclear military relationship with Washington. France never did support the MLF: De Gaulle was not ready to settle for second choices. He had proceeded with nuclear tests despite the voluntary test moratorium after 1958. He continued to demand that France be treated on the same nuclear footing as Britain and accordingly requested nuclear assistance from the United States.[13] Finally, he refused to allow the placement on French soil of any nuclear weapons he could not fully control.

[13] See, for example, the press conference remarks of President Kennedy reportedly in response to a French offer "to purchase from the United States several hundred million dollars worth of military equipment, mostly of an atomic nature." *The New York Times*, April 18, 1962.

Kennedy attempted to cut through the preoccupation of Europe with these secondary questions in order to follow Marshall's example of 1948: to present the challenge to Europeans without presuming to tell them how to conduct their own business. He chose July 4, 1962, in a speech emphasizing the themes of independence and federation, to tell the Europeans that the question of their nuclear independence lay in their own hands. If they could establish the political superstructure to act as a unitary nuclear power, the discord with the United States about military command, weapons custody, and safety catches would all fall by the way.

Later, with his international reputation soaring after the missile crisis, Kennedy visited Western Europe in June 1963 and used the trip to press for this larger view of Europe's relations with the United States. But the approach was stopped by De Gaulle's skillful and intransigent opposition to European political and economic integration. De Gaulle wanted the chance to establish France's national claim to nuclear-power status and rejected the terms that Washington now offered Europe—equality only as a region, not for each country. De Gaulle had met Kennedy's challenge, but not on Kennedy's terms.

CONCLUSION

The Kennedy Administration shared with its predecessor a concern that Europe would become too inward looking. A customs union called the Common Market had been set up in 1956 consisting of France, Italy, West Germany, and the Benelux countries. This union provided a climate for economic expansion for these countries during the late fifties, adding to the great success of the Marshall Plan in the late forties. In the decade from 1948 to 1958 Western Europe had recovered from the war and gone on to unprecedented prosperity. But as customs barriers went up for outsiders and down within the Common Market, the British economy suffered and the United States began to import more than it exported, creating our balance-of-trade problem. We thus had a direct interest in resisting Europe's inclination to turn inward and enjoy the fruits of its success: we not only wished to relieve our balance-of-payments problem but we wanted Europe to carry a greater share of the costs of supporting economic development in the underdeveloped countries. Kennedy had spoken pointedly of both goals in his early presidential speeches, and both issues persisted through the eight years that followed. Kennedy invoked the vision of an Atlantic community in order to conduct negotiations with Europe that would lower trade barriers throughout the world, with Europe bargaining from a position of strength for reduced barriers to the United States and other markets. This liberalizing phase in trade negotiations came to be called the "Kennedy Round." Like the Berlin crisis, the "Kennedy Round" was a specific name for what was in fact an extended period of negotiations that would stretch through 1967.

The attention the Kennedy Administration gave to adjusting and reconstructing our relationship with Western Europe offered considerable promise to the Atlantic Alliance, yet the Alliance quickly turned sour. The Kennedy Administration was intentionally flexible about its relations with Western Europe but was also intent upon reasserting American leadership in the Alliance. The direction this leadership took, moreover, was set by the logic of nuclear strategy as viewed from Washington, and this logic required an exclusive nuclear strategic role for the United States coupled with only nominal British and French nuclear forces as a palliative for our hegemony. The effect of this assertion of American leadership was a degree of dominance in the Alliance that Washington had not asserted since the Suez crisis.

Kennedy and Western Europe never agreed on goals for the Atlantic Alliance. Western European states pursued their own divergent goals for their relationship to the United States. All of them—though none as much as De Gaulle's France—wanted greater independence from Washington in military policy. At the same time all of them, including France, were troubled by the more flexible strategy that the Kennedy Administration adopted because it put more of the burden of their defense on their own conventional forces. The internal difficulties of the Alliance, then, could be attributed to the persistent question about apportioning burdens of military defense.

chapter 7

The Problems of Great Power Status: Moscow, Congress, and the Underdeveloped Nations

THE TURBULENT SOVIET–AMERICAN RELATIONSHIP

Kennedy came to office intent on changing the Soviet-American relationship. The Stevenson Democrats—among them, Averill Harriman, G. Mennan Williams, Chester Bowles, Senator J. William Fulbright, and Stevenson himself—claimed that the military threat to Western Europe had diminished, that the American position in the underdeveloped areas of the world was far too dependent upon military instruments, and that a shift from military to economic and political weapons in foreign policy would open up prospects for a détente with the Soviet Union. They saw the ideological conflict with Russia as an impediment to practical understanding and the source of unnecessary rigidities in American policy in the underdeveloped countries. The Truman Democrats on the other hand—such as Dean Acheson and Paul Nitze—saw Europe as the main strategic prize and considered "situations of strength," in Acheson's phrase, the main asset in coping with the Russians. Others, such as George Ball and George Kennan, shared Acheson's concentration on Europe but held out Stevenson's hope for a change in the Cold War. And in fact the two viewpoints were not incompatible. The main difference lay in the expectations they held for negotiating with the Soviet Union. Acheson wanted to improve our bargaining position; Stevenson wanted to bargain.

Kennedy soon combined the two viewpoints, using his optimism about our national capacities as the bridge. We would build up our military strength, but we would stress flexibility, not massive retaliation, and we would expand our economic-assistance programs as well. The NATO alliance should be strengthened, as the Truman Democrats wished. But the United States would not permit its European allies to keep it from negotiating directly with the Russians at the summit. Khrushchev had successfully played on European fears about Soviet-American negotiations and on the Eisenhower Administration's fears about summit meetings. Kennedy's combination of hard-line and conciliatory policies toward Russia deflated summitry as a Soviet diplomatic weapon.

THE BAY OF PIGS DEBACLE

In the last weeks of the Eisenhower Administration the United States had broken diplomatic relations with Cuba, and Kennedy had been briefed about plans for a secretly sponsored invasion of Cuba by Cuban exiles to overturn the Castro regime and establish a government more acceptable to Washington. The invasion plan had evolved from President Eisenhower's decision the preceding March to train Cuban exiles for guerrilla operations in Cuba. By the time Kennedy first learned of the project, it had become more an invasion than a guerrilla infiltration. In the next few weeks it became wholly an invasion, but it remained a clandestine operation. Kennedy refused to allow direct American involvement, though unmarked U.S. Navy carrier jets did offer clandestine air cover for rebel bomber strikes.

Flying in from Guatemala, B-26's supplied by the CIA and piloted by Cuban exiles tried to knock out Cuban air power on April 15. Some of the pilots landed in Florida and claimed they were Cuban defectors using Castro's own aircraft, but American reporters had found out about the pending operations and quickly stripped away this disguise. A second air strike occurred two days later as an invasion force of 1400 Cuban rebels approached the Bay of Pigs. The strike failed to destroy Castro's air power, however, and his planes helped the Cuban Army to pin the invaders down. Isolated, with ammunition exhausted, they surrendered.

It was a humiliating defeat, and American prestige inevitably suffered. The U.S. effort to avoid direct involvement had largely succeeded, but the effort to keep our behind-the-scenes role secret had failed badly. Kennedy's prestige as an international and domestic leader suffered temporarily, then rebounded. In his inaugural address he had spoken of grave threats and setbacks, but as he pressed on for the summit meeting with Khrushchev, the failure at the Bay of Pigs left little permanent impression. Public-opinion polls indicate that domestic opinion rapidly rallied to him, and the reaction of many governments abroad was one of respect for the self-restraint shown by the American government.[1]

The euphoria of Kennedy's first weeks disappeared at the Bay of Pigs, for the disaster shattered confidence within the government as well as outside it. A bitter row developed over the errors of the Central Intelligence Agency, whose clandestine-operations division had conceived and executed the invasion plan. The plan depended on either a successful military conquest or a successful uprising triggered by the invasion. But our government's best experts on military invasions had not been consulted on the practical difficulties of the operation itself, and the best estimates of the intelligence division of the CIA about an uprising were that a general Cuban uprising would not occur.

The President's lack of accurate information on the prospective invasion was aggravated by his lack of control over the Cuban exiles, whose interests diverged somewhat from those of the United States. Cuban exile leaders, intent on their goal, did not care if they involved the United States more than the President wanted us to be involved. Since these exiles were trained and advised by American officials who developed a similar attitude, there were ample reasons why the participants did not want the President to know what he ought to have known. Sorensen has summarized the result:

> With hindsight it is clear that what in fact Kennedy had approved was . . . militarily doomed from the outset. What he thought he was approving appeared at the time to have diplomatic acceptability and little chance of outright failure. That so great a gap between concept and actuality should exist at so high a level on so dangerous a matter

[1] Arthur M. Schlesinger, Jr., *A Thousand Days* (Boston: Houghton Mifflin, 1965), p. 512.

reflected a shocking number of errors in the whole decision-making
process—errors which permitted bureaucratic momentum to govern
instead of policy leadership.[2]

Out of the Bay of Pigs debacle, however, came an Administration determined to probe and to doubt and a President disrespect-
ful of expert judgments and unwilling to take the assurance of
subordinates that they had thought of every contingency. These
attitudes were to serve Kennedy well in the Cuban missile crisis
eighteen months later.

THE CONFERENCE AT VIENNA

At the height of the Cuban Bay of Pigs crisis in April 1961
Khrushchev threatened Soviet involvement if the United States did
not end its "aggression." Kennedy reposted firmly, but neither
statesman carried the matter further. On the contrary, they proceeded with arrangements for private talks at their embassies in
Vienna in early June.

The accounts we have of the Vienna conference indicate that
Kennedy wanted to establish ground rules for Soviet-American coexistence in order to cope with political change in the uncommitted
areas of the world. He assumed that any attempt by one great
power to change the status quo in these areas would be countered
by the other. Perhaps thinking of Laos and the Congo, Kennedy
argued that both great powers should avoid becoming involved in
political changes in areas in which neither the Soviet Union nor
the United States was already involved and where the balance of
power would not be affected. Both countries would expect to become involved, however, in political changes that affected the
balance of power or involved the other party.

Kennedy's thesis was in effect a diplomatic supplement to
McNamara's efforts to stabilize the "balance of terror" through
changes in military strategy. McNamara's "flexible options" doctrine held that it was extremely dangerous and unnecessary for the
United States to be faced with a stark choice between capitulating
to Russia and escalating to massive nuclear attacks. Similarly,
Kennedy talked at Vienna about the dangers of getting "cornered."

[2] Theodore C. Sorensen, *Kennedy* (New York: Harper & Row, 1965), pp. 301–302.

Evidently he hoped that an agreement to maintain the status quo would avoid putting either side into a situation in which it would be forced to act out of desperation.

Khrushchev would not accept Kennedy's thesis. For him the "status quo" included the maintenance of political trends that (according to Communist dogma) would ultimately favor Russia, and to interrupt these trends—even by failing to cultivate them— was to upset the status quo as perceived in Moscow. Disagreement about defining the status quo, then, was only symptomatic of much more profound disagreements between the United States and Russia.

Kennedy's effort to reach agreement on these matters reflected his association with the Stevenson Democrats rather than the cold warriors led by Acheson. Kennedy came away chastened by the effort and more receptive to Acheson's position, though still temperamentally closer to Bowles and the other Stevensonians.[3]

BERLIN POKER: KENNEDY'S ROUND

On no issue had Kennedy's attempt at Vienna to establish a general understanding with Khrushchev about the status quo been more futile than on the status of Berlin. The American position in Europe rested in part on its backing of the West German regime, which depended in turn on affirming German reunification as a national objective. Reunification was more than an aspiration: no West German government could repudiate or undermine this goal and hope to survive. Berlin played an important role in keeping the issue of reunification open, for its vulnerable location inside East Germany offered the promise of future change.

The Soviet Union, on the other side, was committed to a shabby regime in East Germany that suffered from a seemingly fatal manpower hemorrhage into West Germany. The Soviet Union could not maintain a status quo that promised only a dying client with her lifeblood of young workers pouring out through West Berlin.

The quarrels over Berlin centered around Soviet demands to

3 The above has drawn heavily from Arthur M. Schlesinger, Jr. Though he has been properly classed as a Stevensonian, Schlesinger has written with admirable detachment about these factions in *A Thousand Days.* See especially pp. 299–301.

change what the United States considered the status quo (the independence of West Berlin from the East German government, with assured access routes to the West), in order to preserve what the Russians considered the status quo (the continued existence of East Germany). Kennedy might well have expected to be frustrated in discussing with Khrushchev a status quo that the two statesmen perceived so differently.

This difference between Soviet and American perspectives had already helped to produce a series of crises over the Berlin enclave in the late fifties. In 1960, Khrushchev had threatened that unless the West agreed to a settlement to unify Germany in East Germany's favor, Russia would grant East Germany the right to control the access routes into Berlin (thus effectively allowing East Germany to seal off Berlin from the West). But tension over this impending action abated after Eisenhower's summit meeting with Khrushchev that year when the Russian leader failed to carry out his threat. At the General Assembly meeting in New York that October, however, Khrushchev had demanded a summit meeting on Berlin shortly after the inauguration of the new President.

During Kennedy's first month in office the central crisis he faced was that of Berlin's status. He had come to office assuming that a summit meeting with Khrushchev was unavoidable; but he was able to delay the meeting, and he also quickly took steps to change the impression that had developed in the late fifties that a summit meeting was a concession to the Russians. Finally, to signal our resolve to defend Berlin, Kennedy made a second State of the Union Message on May 25, just before the Vienna conference, to request an additional $225 million for the American Army and Marine Corps.

After Vienna, Khrushchev set the end of 1961 as the deadline by which Russia would sign a formal peace treaty with East Germany that would include turning over to the East Germans control of the access routes to Berlin. This step would effectively ensure a blockade of Berlin by the East Germans and isolate the city from the West. Khrushchev underlined his resolve to keep this deadline by announcing an increase in Soviet military expenditures equivalent to $3.5 billion. In response Kennedy asked Congress for an additional $3.2 billion in defense expenditures and for the authority to increase our conventional military strength immediately.

Washington expected the next stage of the crisis in October. In the meantime, the United States busied itself with highly visible preparations, calling up the National Guard, establishing a political-military Berlin-crisis operations center in the Pentagon, and clarifying its own objectives for the impending confrontation. In mid-August, while these preparations were under way, Soviet authorities sealed East Berlin off from West Berlin, cutting its manpower losses to a trickle. The Soviets began cautiously, giving Washington time to react if it chose. First simple traffic barriers were thrown up, then these were replaced with barbed wire. Finally, the barrier was completed with deliberate thoroughness by using brick and mortar. The Berlin Wall was now a fact.

Washington's failure to respond to the Soviet efforts to seal off West Berlin has been attributed to indecision, inattention, inability to coordinate quickly enough, overly centralized (hence ponderously slow) military command and control arrangements, and finally, simple caution. Rarely do governments decide important issues for a single reason. It is possible that Kennedy decided not to respond to the erection of the Berlin barriers because he felt they would stabilize the East German situation and thus reduce the pressure on Moscow to change the status of West Berlin. That, at any rate, is what building the Wall actually accomplished.

The immediate repercussions of the Berlin Wall were adverse. West Berlin was stunned by it and by American acceptance of it. Having permitted the Wall, President Kennedy sent Vice-President Johnson to Berlin to encourage the West Berliners, and he sent a battle group of 1500 U.S. troops driving up the Autobahn from West Germany to Berlin to reassert the West's right of access and reinforce the American garrison in Berlin.

It is important to note, however, that despite the demonstrations to the contrary on both sides, the Berlin Wall provided the basis for a tacit agreement between the United States and the Soviet Union. The settlement over Berlin remained unspoken because neither Moscow nor Washington wished to articulate the reasons for it. The Soviet Union could not admit that stopping the manpower drain on East Germany made it unnecessary for Russia to ignite the Berlin powder-keg, for such an admission would undermine the legitimacy of the East German government. Similarly, the Kennedy Administration did not wish its failure to stop the sealing off of East Berlin to be viewed as an intentional concession to the Russians, for we could not make such a concession explicit without substantially damaging our relationship with the West German government or provoking strong domestic criticism in the United States.

For the next year tension over Berlin still remained serious. In October Khrushchev, as he had done in 1960, withdrew the deadline on Berlin. But new deadlines could always be set, and the prospect remained to complicate the Cuban missile crisis a year later. Meanwhile the Berlin Wall taxed the patience and morale of West Berlin and compelled the United States to demonstrate its support of the free Berliners, all of which in turn irritated the Soviet and East German officials.

The existence of the Soviet-American tacit understanding on Berlin would not be verified until after the Cuban missile crisis in November 1962, discussed below. During the crisis itself, the prospects for further trouble with the Soviet Union over Berlin seemed all too real, and, in fact, just after the crisis Russia triggered unnerving incidents in the access corridors and along the Berlin Wall. But the underlying status quo was never really disturbed: Russia did not try to create a serious Berlin crisis in order to cover her failure in Cuba, nor did she take advantage of our preoccupation with Cuba to make real gains in Berlin.

Since neither side could admit (and since neither side even knew at first) that the Wall had provided an accommodation, the Berlin crisis did not abate immediately. It intensified in September when the Soviet Union resumed nuclear testing with a detonation estimated at an unprecedented 57 megatons by the West. Early in November Kennedy announced that the United States would resume testing in order to preserve our nuclear superiority. The tardiness of the American resumption of testing—more than seven months after the Soviet resumption—indicated that the United States had not been prepared for the Soviet initiative.

Moreover, the American position on Berlin was by no means in order. The Western allies could not agree on a common negotiating position if serious negotiations were to get under way on the status of Germany (hence, Berlin) before the end of the year. Also, the Kennedy Administration lacked congressional support for anything but a weak response to Poland's and Yugoslavia's appeals for economic assistance to give them greater independence from Moscow—assistance that would have provided an opportunity for us to drive a wedge into the Soviet bloc. On the other hand, the Administration made it distinctly clear that we had definite strategic nuclear superiority over the Soviet Union and intended to maintain it.[4]

Thus, by the end of the year Kennedy's foreign policy was hardly keeping pace with the vaunted expectations about it at the beginning of 1961. Like the Eisenhower Administration, Kennedy and his associates found foreign affairs less tractable to unilateral change than they had anticipated. The new year, however, would provide another chance to respond to a Soviet initiative and to improvise a brilliant response that would give the Administration new momentum in foreign relations.

THE CUBAN MISSILE CRISIS

The Cuban missile crisis was the starkest confrontation of Soviet and American nuclear might since the first-detected Russian nuclear bomb was detonated in 1949.

After our Bay of Pigs fiasco Cuba moved increasingly closer to the Soviet Union. Castro had immediately declared Cuba a Socialist state, and Moscow began shipping its new client military equipment. Castro then turned his talents to the business of exporting revolution. (Like so much else about his regime, these efforts ranged from the comic to the sinister.)

The United States government, responding more than it cared to admit to the threat of social revolution raised by Castro and other elements in Latin America, expanded its economic assistance to this region. In October 1962, at a conference of American foreign ministers in Washington, United States officials also began to build a diplomatic wall around Castro. Campaigning for Democratic congressional candidates that month, Kennedy declared that his Administration was "taking a lot of steps to try to isolate Castro. . . ." The Cuban missile crisis erupted while the Inter-American Economic and Social Council met in Mexico City in October.

4 See particularly Roswell Gilpatric's speech, *The New York Times,* October 22, 1961.

In September 1962 the Soviet government had once again postponed the negotiation of a separate peace treaty with East Germany —this time until after our congressional elections in November. The purpose of the postponement became evident in Washington only a few weeks before the elections: American aerial reconnaissance detected that the Russians were secretly attempting to deploy nuclear-tipped ballistic missiles to Cuba by rapidly constructing offensive missile and bomber bases. Khrushchev evidently intended to reveal their presence at the U.N. General Assembly meeting in New York scheduled for after the election.

If the Russians succeeded in establishing bases in Cuba, vital targets in the United States and Latin America would lie within their missile range. More important, missiles launched from Cuba could not be detected by the elaborate electronic warning screens the United States had aimed northward against Soviet missiles in Europe and Asia. Cuban bases would make it possible for Moscow to strike the United States virtually without warning. And most important, the Cuban missile bases posed a critical test of American resolve. Kennedy had repeatedly made clear during his year and a half in office that he intended to stabilize the Washington-Moscow relationship by maintaining the status quo. The installation of Soviet nuclear missile bases in the Western Hemisphere would be a radical intrusion into a traditional sphere of American influence and security. To permit this intrusion would reduce the credibility of American commitments in Europe, the Middle East, and Asia as well.

For the next week the Kennedy Administration secretly worked at a furious pace to arrange and implement our responses to this Soviet provocation. Troops were moved to Florida, air and naval forces were deployed toward the Caribbean, and strategic nuclear forces were put on the alert.

The possibility of dealing with the Russians privately over the missiles in Cuba was eliminated by Russian efforts to mislead Kennedy through private messages—including, as it became clear when the ground-to-ground missiles were detected, an outright lie.[5] Furthermore, it would have been politically difficult at home and abroad for Kennedy to have responded satisfactorily to such a blatant Russian provocation without including some *public* demon-

[5] E.g., Sorensen, *op. cit.,* p. 668.

stration of our intentions. Nor could a private response have been accompanied by the type of concrete actions the Administration was preparing for without these actions quickly becoming known to the public. Finally, a public disclosure was a demonstration of Kennedy's unwillingness to play out the crisis on the terms Moscow was trying to set.

Rejecting an invasion for the time being, Kennedy chose a naval blockade or "quarantine" to stop the Russian buildup. Congressional leaders were briefed; presidential envoys were dispatched to explain the American action to foreign governments; speeches and proposals for the United Nations and the Organization of American States were drafted, all with remarkable secrecy.

On October 22, a week after seeing the photographs of Russian missile installations, Kennedy addressed the nation in a television broadcast publicly revealing for the first time both the Soviet actions and our responses to them. Kennedy called the Soviet action "a deliberately provocative and unjustified change in the status quo which cannot be accepted by this country, if our courage and our commitments are ever to be trusted again by either friend or foe." He announced what he termed "initial" steps in response, particularly our quarantine on all offensive military equipment under shipment to Cuba, and declared that the United States would hold Moscow responsible for any missile attack launched on the United States from Cuba and would respond in full retaliation against the Soviet Union.

Kennedy's appeal brought no significant dissents from American leaders. In the short run, at least, most Americans were behind their President. The Organization of American States (OAS) promptly (and somewhat surprisingly) approved the quarantine, and even Mexico and Brazil, which had opposed previous U.S. efforts to isolate Cuba diplomatically, supported our action in the crisis. At the United Nations, Stevenson dramatized the American position with blown-up reconnaissance photographs of the missile sites. Some European leaders, however, reacted skeptically to Kennedy's initial claims. The British, for example, showed surprising suspicion about the adventurism of Washington. Even five days after Kennedy's first broadcast the usually pro-American *Economist* deplored "forcing a showdown over the shipment of Russian arms to Cuba."

Privately, however, Kennedy's envoy, Acheson, had convinced Britain's Prime Minister Macmillan. De Gaulle, perhaps gratified that Washington was demonstrating the vital role of independent national behavior in a real nuclear crisis, stood behind us like a rock—after pointing out to Acheson that Kennedy had handled his allies the way De Gaulle would have, by informing but not consulting them. Little discord appeared within the United States or among its allies for Moscow to exploit in the crisis. Quite the contrary, the cohesion demonstrated in the face of the Soviet threat became a major asset for Washington.

After a tense week, the Soviet Union turned its ships back from the quarantine area. Khrushchev first acknowledged that Russians controlled the missiles and then agreed to stop work on the missile sites and withdraw the missiles. The United States agreed not to invade Cuba and worked out face-saving procedures for American inspection of the Russian missile withdrawal.

There was a flutter of doubt in Washington, but it was not sustained. Some, such as the eminent military strategist Bernard Brodie, argued that we could successfully have pushed even further because of known Soviet willingness to take calculated risks but to back off if they misfired.[6] Others worried about the practical difficulties of enforcing the pull-back of Soviet missiles. Since Castro had refused to allow the United States or the United Nations access to the Soviet sites in Cuba, Republican critics of the Administration voiced the fear that the missiles would be hidden in caves for the time being and that sites would eventually be constructed with more ingenious camouflages. But the White House maintained its position, evidently confident that our aerial reconnaissance flights could effectively monitor the removal of all missiles. (The potential problem of cheating was in fact not serious so long as the United States remained alert to the possibility of a secret Soviet missile build-up in Cuba. In effect the Cuban crisis could always be reenacted, and if so it was likely that the Russians would back down once again.) It should be noted that despite their criticism of the Cuban settlement, the Republicans were unwilling to blame what they considered a potential threat to our security on disloyalty within the government. Without the stark issue of subversion to con-

[6] Letter to the editor, *The New York Times*, November 13, 1962.

tend with and without a continuing crisis such as the Korean War, the Administration remained relatively invulnerable to partisan criticism.

Some aspects of the missile crisis still lack satisfactory explanations. One unanswered question is why the Russians thought they would succeed with their venture. Their record of caution elsewhere does not support the theory that they are indiscriminate risk-takers. It is more likely that the Russians thought they could get the missiles into place before the United States detected them. The timing of Khrushchev's missile deployment and his message to Kennedy in early September[7] suggests that the Russian leader would have come to the General Assembly meeting in New York prepared to exploit a radical change in the nuclear strategic balance.

If the Russians had succeeded in emplacing the missiles there would still have been the grueling game of mutual deterrence to be played out. The United States had missiles and manned aircraft targeted on the Soviet Union. The immediate effect of the Soviet disclosure would probably have been a breathtaking drop in American prestige in Europe and the underdeveloped areas, and perhaps a failure of nerve in Europe and Washington as well. But this new situation would also invite new dangers for the Russians —particularly the danger that the United States would launch a preemptive nuclear strike when it discovered its new vulnerability.

Another puzzle, then, is why the Russians were willing to run such risks. One explanation is that internal pressures within the Soviet state provided the impetus for the Cuban venture. Contrary to common American beliefs at that time, Soviet foreign policy had not been going well. Moscow's success in winning support and influence in the underdeveloped world had fallen short of expectations, and the Communist-bloc claims of rapidly catching up with the West were proving to be exaggerations. Khrushchev had identified himself publicly with the Soviet goal of closing the nuclear gap with the United States. But, as was then becoming apparent in the West, Moscow had chosen not to pay the high resource costs for closing this gap. Instead the Soviet Union had decided in the late fifties, much as the United States had, to forego large-scale ICBM deployment and await the development of the next generation of

7 Sorensen, *op. cit.*, p. 667.

missiles, which would be cheaper and less prone to obsolescence.

Finally, the Chinese Communists were now in open political conflict with Moscow, and this rift with Peking increasingly forced Moscow to compete for leadership in the bloc. Peking had experimented with post-Stalin ideological liberalization in 1956 but had repressed the movement in 1957. Thereafter, the divergent domestic practices in Russia and China fueled reciprocal suspicion and reproaches. The two governments quarreled secretly over China's ambition to acquire nuclear weapons, and Moscow withdrew its technicians from China and discontinued all technical and economic help in 1960. Publicly, the quarrel was restricted at first to oblique criticisms on both sides, but the rift became quite visible when the Chinese delegation walked out of the Moscow Party Conference in October 1961.

Once the breach began to widen, Peking could attack Moscow's de-Stalinization campaign on two grounds. First, it was a departure from the orthodoxies Moscow had earlier laid down. Second, like so much that came from Moscow, the de-Stalinization program was in fact a distinct product of the leadership struggle within the Soviet Union in the mid-fifties. Similarly, the more flexible and conciliatory aspects of Russian foreign policy from that time on (including, as it became clearer in 1961, the failure to exploit fully the Soviet missile technology in order to achieve nuclear strategic superiority over the United States) resulted largely from the same domestic forces. Khrushchev, for example, had won a leadership struggle with the soft-line Moscow faction by posing as a hard liner; but he shifted ground and adopted a doctrine of "peaceful coexistence" once he had gathered up the reins of domestic power. As De Gaulle challenged American leadership of the Atlantic bloc on the grounds that the policies advocated by Washington served American interests rather than European interests, Peking challenged Moscow on the grounds that its new domestic and foreign policies ran against the interests of the Communist bloc. The Chinese claimed that a more belligerent leadership would be far better for the common cause of revolutionary Communism. Success with the missiles in Cuba could have helped the Soviet Union solidify its bloc leadership.

Still another explanation for Russian adventurism in Cuba was Kennedy's handling of the Bay of Pigs a year earlier. Khrushchev had chided Kennedy at Vienna for lacking resolution in dealing with the first Cuban invasion, and the Russian leader may have interpreted Kennedy's weakness as an invitation for the Soviet Union to venture into the Western Hemisphere.

After the missile crisis, Khrushchev, attempting to save face, claimed that the missiles were placed in Cuba merely to defend the island against U.S. attack. The explanation is interesting because it appears to reflect Kennedy's claims about the need for Soviet-American agreements to maintain the status quo.

KENNEDY'S FUMBLING WITH CONGRESS

More than any modern President in peacetime, Kennedy built his domestic popularity on his foreign policy. The firm manner in which he took charge of the Presidency made his popularity soar to a peak of 83 percent by late April 1961, measured by the opinion surveys—probably a rally-'round-the-flag reaction after the Bay of Pigs. His popularity declined unsteadily over the next eighteen months to 61 percent just before the Cuban missile crisis, then jumped to 74 percent immediately afterward and remained there into 1963, when it began drifting downward again to a low of 57 percent shortly before his death.

From the beginning Kennedy found it difficult to translate his popularity into legislative support. As had been the case since the late forties, Congress readily increased defense and security-related expenditures, but defense economies, foreign-assistance programs, trade liberalization, increased contacts with the Soviet bloc, and a more flexible policy toward Moscow all encountered opposition. The ineffectual management of White House relations with the legislative branch seemed to be one difficulty. Another was the wide gap in Democratic congressional leadership created by Lyndon Johnson's leaving the Senate to become Vice-President and by the death of the venerable House Speaker Sam Rayburn.

Domestic issues unquestionably limited Kennedy's legislative success more than did foreign policy—rarely is it otherwise. His successful appeals for public support over Berlin in his early months in the White House and his dramatic nuclear-missile diplomacy in 1962 were acts of Cold War leadership with potentially high popularity. But Kennedy could not capitalize further on a policy of Cold War militancy because many of his other objectives in foreign relations required a restrained posture abroad.

Facing the same problems, though with a vastly stronger popular base, the Eisenhower Administration had popularized foreign aid by making it a weapon for fighting the Cold War. Dulles and Radford had made military posture more appealing by giving it a more militant and economical face. Dulles had also avoided negotiations with Communists whenever he could in order to avoid the domestic public suspicion that our Administration was too conciliatory with the Communists. The Kennedy Administration, however, wanted a flexible and expensive defense posture; a "secularized" foreign-aid program (that is, one that did not stress anti-Communism or Cold War utilities); and a program of active and conciliatory diplomacy with the Soviet Union. The political costs of these policies could be considerable.

Kennedy campaigned strenuously for a Democratic Congress in 1962 until the missile crisis took him out of the campaign for the crucial last two weeks. The President's party usually loses congressional seats in the nonpresidential election years. Kennedy's election in 1960, however, had helped few of the Democratic congressional candidates who won their seats that year. Since the presence of Kennedy on the ticket in 1960 had helped congressional candidates so little, the Administration hoped that his absence in the off-year 1962 election would hurt equally little and that the Democrats could hold their majorities in 1962. Furthermore, if Kennedy could actually help the Democratic candidates in 1962, he could demonstrate that his narrow margin of electoral support in 1960 had widened and this new popularity could be translated into electoral success. He had much to gain and little to lose by campaigning for Democrats in 1962.

Kennedy campaigned almost exclusively on domestic issues. A Democratic gain of one or two Senate seats and five or more House seats would make it possible to enact bills dealing with medical care, public works, and urban affairs.

Instead, the Democrats lost four seats in each house of Congress —a better record than average for an off-year congressional election but nonetheless short of Kennedy's expectations. The Cuban missile crisis appears to have helped the Democrats in the 1962 elections, partly because the irritations of the Soviet postcrisis involvement in Cuba did not become apparent until after the elections were over.

THE NUCLEAR TEST BAN TREATY

The new Congress dealt slowly and not very enthusiastically with Kennedy's program in 1963. Most of the annual appropriations bills for the fiscal year beginning in July were not enacted until December, and of the major items in the President's legislative program only the Test Ban Treaty had been approved by Thanksgiving.

The idea of a nuclear test ban had arisen inside the government during the early fifties. Stevenson had made it an issue in the presidential campaign of 1956 against firm Republican opposition. Not until the early sixties, however, did the prerequisites for a treaty fall into place.

Kennedy inherited from the Eisenhower years a voluntary moratorium on atmospheric tests that the United States and the Soviet Union had observed since November 1958. But his legacy also included test-ban treaty negotiations that had been bogged down on technical inspection problems and complicated by mutual suspicion between Russia and the United States. Kennedy came to office intent on proceeding with the test-ban dialogue, but the Soviet generals, it now seems, were then demanding tests for the new weapons developed during the moratorium. Russia broke the moratorium in September 1961, setting disarmament negotiations back temporarily, but increased the pressure from the non-nuclear powers on both Moscow and Washington for a clear agreement to stop atmospheric tests.

At the same time the prospects for working out the problems of independent enforcement and inspection required in a test-ban treaty had receded. The role the U.N. Secretary General played in the Congo crisis of 1960–61, thwarting Soviet aspirations to establish its influence in the Congo, reinforced Soviet suspicion (already strong) about the true neutrality of international agencies that would be necessary to carry out inspection provisions in a disarmament treaty. The Cuban missile crisis made it even more difficult for Moscow to make further concessions to the United States without compromising its position within its own bloc. Peking had reacted with lurid contempt to Khrushchev's backdown in Cuba. Yet, as the Moscow-Peking differences grew, Russia found it more attractive to reduce its differences with the United States.

Kennedy joined Macmillan in a special appeal to Khrushchev in April 1963 to break the deadlocked treaty negotiations by abandoning an interminable argument over the precise number of on-site inspections that would be allowed. Washington now proposed instead to limit the three-power negotiations to nuclear tests that contaminated the atmosphere, since these explosions required no on-site inspections. Within ten days the delegates had actually initialed a draft treaty. The three states were to agree to refrain from testing in outer space, in the atmosphere, or under water, and from abetting such tests by others.

The Senate, after hearing the considerable misgivings of American nuclear-weapons designers about the deleterious effects of a test ban on their work and listening to the fears of the U.S. military that the treaty would give the strategic advantage to Moscow, nonetheless ratified the Test Ban Treaty by an 80 to 19 vote on September 24. More than a hundred other nations also acceded to the treaty. At last Washington and Moscow had reached an agreement that could slow the arms race. In the euphoric aftermath, the Kennedy Administration negotiated the sale of wheat to Russia, and at the end of 1963 the Soviet government announced cuts in its military budget. President Johnson followed by announcing cutbacks in our military expenditures and production of nuclear materials in January 1964.

We should note, however, that the Test Ban Treaty had not been popular with Congress, despite the huge vote for ratification. Relations with the Soviet Union since the Cuban missile crisis had followed an uneven course, with the Russians at once tough and friendly. Moscow had intermittently heated up and cooled down the Berlin crisis, used the disarmament negotiations to propagandize, and intimidated the U.N. Secretary General; yet it had worked out the test ban with rare dispatch and by mid-1963 American fears about Soviet cheating in the removal of its missiles from Cuba had abated. Some observers saw Soviet behavior as clever toughness, others as a result of the rift with Peking. Just prior to the three-power test-ban meetings in Moscow in July 1962, a Chinese Communist delegation had also met there in last-ditch talks to heal Sino-Soviet wounds. They failed, and the Soviet government published a full statement of its grievances against Peking. Regardless of Russia's underlying motives, however, it was difficult for the Kennedy Administration to make headway with Congress in approving conciliatory and flexible policies toward a nation that displayed such contradictory behavior toward us.

DEALING WITH THE UNDERDEVELOPED NATIONS

Although Kennedy had come to the Presidency appealing to the public as a mover and shaker, much of his foreign policy lacked popular appeal. The two previous Administrations had chosen to win public support by relying on Cold War rhetoric, thus narrowing the policy choices open to them and increasing the already formidable difficulties of exploring possible settlements with the Soviet Union. Even an aroused public leaves an Administration with considerable latitude in the conduct of external relations, but the public's concern with the Cold War set limits that Kennedy found particularly confining in developing policies for the underdeveloped areas of the world. Kennedy did not reject the premise of Russia as a great-power rival, but he perceived the Soviet challenge as more flexible and the issues in the underdeveloped areas as more complex than the Eisenhower Administration had been willing to depict them. Soviet-American rivalry made it important to deny Moscow hegemony in the underdeveloped areas. Yet this rivalry itself was largely irrelevant to the concerns of the new states, which needed to be addressed on their own terms.

THE MIDDLE EAST

The fate of the Middle East is a sensitive issue in American politics because of U.S. investments in oil there and the interest of American Jews in the well-being of Israel. After the Suez crisis the Eisenhower Administration had emphasized the Communist threat in the Middle East as a way to reconstruct the American position there. But the dimensions of the struggle for political power in the Middle East were in fact much broader than just conflict between East and West. By the time Eisenhower retired, American policy in this area had begun to reflect these complexities and Egypt's Nasser had proved to be a relatively competent independent nationalist leader who was not at all inclined to become a tool of either Soviet or American policies.

After 1958 the new regime in Iraq, whose political complexion was closer to the Soviet Union than Egypt's was, opposed Nasser's leadership of the Arabs. In 1962, leftist-nationalist revolutionaries overthrew the traditional government in Yemen. Saudi Arabia and Jordan quickly came to the support of the deposed regime. The next year, Arab nationalist (Baathist) coups occurred in Iraq and then Syria, leaving Jordan and Saudi Arabia the only traditionalist regimes in the Arab world and heightening their isolation in Arab politics.

In the face of these changes the Kennedy Administration limited its role in the Middle East. It quickly recognized the new government in Yemen, evidently under the mistaken impression that the traditionalists would not sustain an effective opposition. But when the conflict continued, we drew the United Nations into negotiating a withdrawal of foreign support from both sides of the conflict in Yemen. Nasser's forces lingered on in violation of the agreement until the Arab-Israeli war in 1967.

Egypt's failure to comply with the U.N. withdrawal arrangements, coupled with its unremitting hostility toward Israel, led to a display of congressional pique with Egypt. A congressional amendment to the Foreign Assistance Act of 1963, passed over the protest of President Kennedy, denied aid to Egypt if she engaged in or prepared for "aggressive military efforts" against other recipients of American aid.

This amendment, only one of several congressional stipulations designed to limit the President's discretion in administering the foreign-aid program, illustrates well the domestic political price Kennedy paid for resisting the temptation to label all forces for change in the Middle East as Communist and thus to cast our own choices in the area into a narrow Communist-anti-Communist framework. By focusing on the specter of direct and indirect Communist aggression in the Middle East the Eisenhower Administration had loosened domestic constraints on presidential discretion. The Kennedy Administration, by emphasizing instead the realities of nationalist rivalries in Middle East politics, aroused congressional sensitivities about the Arab-Israeli conflict and reduced congressional support for the President's policies. Seeking broader choices in the Middle East, Kennedy's choices were in fact reduced by Congress and the new constraints ultimately proved embarrassing to the Administration in its Middle East relations.

AFRICA

Most of Africa's new states had gained their independence from colonial rule only in the late 1950's. As Britain had done in India in 1947, Britain and France relinquished their colonial power quite abruptly in their African colonies. In India, however, a competent professional government bureaucracy and army remained, while Black Africa in the late fifties had much less of this human "infrastructure" of government. It lacked trained native government functionaries of every kind, from clerks to diplomats.

Moreover, the new African states suffered from a strong propensity to balkanize themselves: to divide into ethnic groupings within each nation. Without the capacity to police their nations effectively, the central governments had as much difficulty coping with secessionist groups as they in maintaining law and order.

Our change of presidential administration in 1961 increased our rate of diplomatic adaptation to the needs of Africa. Kennedy appointed former Michigan Governor G. Mennan Williams as Assistant Secretary of State for Africa; the new Administration gave more attention than its predecessor to appointments for the new American embassies in Africa; and we increased our economic assistance to Africa. Williams, after an awkward beginning, settled down to dealing with the new national leaders of Black Africa as he found them: generally tough politicians who were addicted to strong, broadly ecletic ideological programs that were part of their efforts to improvise new methods and ideas for coping with the turbulent politics of their new states.

The fate of the Belgian Congo in 1960–61 amply illustrates both the problems faced by new African nations and the Kennedy response to the crises posed. In July 1960 Belgium abruptly abandoned its vast African colony to independence, and the Congo quickly split into three centers of power. The nominal central government of the Congo, unable to control or administer the country, called in a United Nations military force to establish law and order. The United States supported the U.N. intervention in order to forestall Soviet support for a rebel faction based in the province of Katanga, which had seceded from the central Brazzaville government.

By January 1961 three governments coexisted in the Congo: the central government in Leopoldville, a rebel government in Elizabethville in Katanga, headed by Moise Tshombe and backed by Belgian mining interests, and another rebel force at Stanleyville, headed by Antoine Gizenga and supported from North Africa and Moscow by an anticolonialist bloc. In February Moscow seized upon published reports of the political assassination of Patrice Lumumba, Gizenga's predecessor, to demand the withdrawal of the U.N. force in the Congo and the dismissal of Secretary General Hammarskjold as an "accomplice" of the murder. Kennedy defended the U.N. role against "any attempt by any government to intervene unilaterally in the Congo." Debate in the Security Council indicated that most non-Communist governments were anxious to maintain the United Nations force in the Congo. The United States continued to back the United Nations peacekeepers with materiel and logistic support on the grounds that the Congo needed to be held together and, more broadly, that it was important to avoid the balkanization of Africa. But the Katanga secession dragged on. The rebel faction was finally put down with American airlift and U.N. support at the end of 1961, and when it was all over, Tshombe –the rebel leader–emerged as Prime Minister of the central government!

CONFLICT AND DEVELOPMENT IN ASIA

Pakistani-Indian Rivalry

Before 1958 Washington had been inclined to treat Pakistan as an appendage of the Middle East (even though its East Wing bordered on Calcutta and Burma). But as American interest in India grew, we came to view Pakistan as part of South Asia, locked into this region partly because of its bitter territorial dispute with India over control of Kashmir. The Pakistani government had been taken over in 1958 by its British-trained Army Chief, Mohammed Ayub Khan, who promptly instituted économic and political reforms. By 1961 Pakistan's new regime boasted impressive economic-growth rates, had demonstrated considerable administrative competence, and was moving methodically toward broader political participation with indirect parliamentary elections based on an oligopoly of village electors called "basic democrats."

Since its independence India had been ruled by the Congress party, headed by its preindependence leader, Jawaharlal Nehru. The party consisted of a broad variety of state parties, and the locus of its power reflected the considerable strength of the state governments. From its beginning, India achieved a remarkable degree of democratic participation, thus attracting the special sympathy of the Stevensonian Democrats in the late fifties and the support of Senator John F. Kennedy.

The Stevenson Democrats could win support from the Truman Democrats with the argument that India was large, competently governed, and relatively stable—hence, a potentially important ally for us. On the other hand, India's decentralized political system made economic development difficult, because the powerful state governments and party organizations controlled public action in the production and distribution of food.

Pakistan, on the other hand, with a moderate constitutional autocracy, could implement economic development plans more expeditiously. As part of his effort to consolidate the new regime, Ayub Khan decided to emphasize the development of the private sector. Pakistan achieved a considerably higher rate of economic growth than India did, and for a cost that was compatible with the structure of the Pakistani regime: a growing disparity in income distribution, which in turn helped to consolidate the military-business-civil service oligarchy.

Kennedy's inclinations were to favor India over Pakistan, as he demonstrated by appointing the Harvard economist and braintruster of his campaign, J. K. Galbraith, as Ambassador to New Delhi. Nonetheless, economic assistance to Pakistan increased proportionately more than our aid to India under Kennedy.[8]

8 The annual average of Pakistan's total economic assistance for the three fiscal years of the Kennedy Administration, 1962–64, was 47 percent higher than the annual average for the four years preceding, 1958–61. The equivalent figure for

Ayub Khan, worried about Kennedy's known sympathy for India, arranged to pay a state visit to Washington in 1961, just when the Administration found itself in trouble getting its first foreign-aid bill through Congress. The White House arranged, in turn, to have Ayub address a joint session of Congress. His performance helped pass the bill and deterred the Administration's efforts to shift its support to India.

The balance of our support did ultimately shift toward India, however, as a result of Chinese attacks against the Indian border outposts in Ladach and Assam in 1962. India was able to contain the Ladach attack, but Chinese forces in Assam carried their incursion down the slopes of the Himalayas to isolate the North East Frontier Agency and threaten all of Assam, inflicting a humiliating defeat against the Indian forces there and greatly alarming the Indian government with the prospect of a major Chinese invasion. Washington and London promptly responded with military aid. To Pakistan, however, the generous U.S. military aid to India not only appeared to indicate U.S. sympathies, but it tipped the Indian-Pakistani balance in military power against Pakistan. Ayub promptly set about negotiating with the Chinese over disputed borders and improving trade relations with the Soviet Union.

The Kennedy Administration's policies toward Pakistan and India did not produce immediate difficulties for it with Congress or with the public, for helping India to stave off a Chinese attack was a popular step. But our military aid to India was ultimately to open the door to future trouble: when India and Pakistan renewed their old quarrel over Kashmir, American weaponry was used by both sides to fight one another! The Johnson Administration was to pay for Kennedy's policies in this area in lost popularity with Congress and the public when India and Pakistan renewed fighting in September 1965.

The Island Nations

In Indonesia the Kennedy Administration was able to maintain a policy of friendly aloofness, partly because the Sukarno regime

---

India was 42 percent. Computed from Agency for International Development, *U.S. Overseas Loans and Grants and Assistance from International Organizations, 1945–66* (1967), pp. 11 and 28.

faced no direct challenge from within. We refused to meet the demands of Sukarno's government for increased U.S. aid; we bore with patience the wild fluctuations of policy from Sukarno's increasingly ineffective regime as the Indonesian economy drifted into stagnation; and we declined to become visibly involved with any effort to find an alternative to Sukarno.

In Japan, as in Indonesia, the Kennedy Administration's main impact was exerted through diplomacy. The Japanese economy had boomed in the fifties and continued to do so with only minor faltering in the early sixties. The boom brought Americanization and modernization to Japanese culture and business methods, new confidence in domestic politics and external relations, and the rise of strong left-wing political sentiment based on the alienation resulting from the country's rapid social and economic change coupled with the pacifism that was a legacy of the Japanese defeat, the atom-bomb attacks, and the American occupation. Japan had been pacified and Americanized only to find that the United States was not pacific; it had been neutralized by the American occupation under MacArthur only to be used by the United States as a military base and then encouraged by Washington to carry some of the military burdens of defending the Far East.

Anti-American attitudes throughout Japan had erupted in civil disorders that forced the cancellation of Eisenhower's state visit in 1960. In 1961 Kennedy appointed Edwin O. Reischauer as ambassador to stem this tide. A distinguished scholar of Japan, with a Japanese wife and a thorough fluency in Japanese, Reischauer set about restoring the "broken dialogue" with the United States, bringing Japan into a more realistic orientation to American culture, politics, and foreign policy.

Indochina: Limited Commitment in a Peripheral Area

American involvement in Southeast Asia was to remain a minor aspect of our foreign policy until the years of the Johnson Administration, but the roots of this involvement can be traced back to the end of World War II. At that time the United States helped the European colonial powers—Britain, France, and the Netherlands—to reclaim their colonial territories in Southeast Asia from the defeated Japanese, who had seized these areas during the war. We supported our European allies at first because no alternative American policy had been developed and because no other provision had been made for governing the liberated territories. Later, however, even when the full extent of nationalist opposition to colonial rule in Asia became evident, the United States continued to side with the colonial powers in Asia. "Primarily because of our disinterest in Asia and our concern over the sensitivities and political problems of the colonial powers in Europe," Reischauer has written, "we chose to ignore Asian nationalism, except in our own domain of the Philippines."[9]

When the Kennedy Administration came into office, it cautiously attempted to reduce American commitments in Indochina in the face of growing difficulties with our position there. Kennedy did not want to exacerbate the situation in Indochina nor did he want to modify our policies substantially because he evidently feared that either course would kill the prospect for a test-ban treaty with Russia.

Kennedy's attention to Indochina began in Laos, which posed the most urgent problem in Southeast Asia at the outset of his Administration. Laos was one of the three states created at the Geneva Convention of 1954 when the French gave up colonial Indochina. According to the Geneva settlement, Laos was to be a neutral state, but since 1954 the Eisenhower Administration had attempted to support an anti-Communist regime there. By 1961 Eisenhower's efforts to "de-neutralize" Laos had so antagonized the strong neutralist-nationalist faction in that country that it was driven first into diplomatic alliance with Moscow, and then into active military cooperation with the Pathet Lao, a Communist faction organized and supported first from North Vietnam and then from Moscow itself. A few days before Kennedy's inauguration the United States had openly violated the Geneva accord by sending its Laotian client, Phoumi Nosavan (a right-wing military figure) six fighter bombers and a military advisory team for each of his battalions; by doing so we lent further legitimacy to Soviet military support of the Pathet Lao. By the time of the inauguration the United States was

9 Edwin O. Reischauer, *Beyond Vietnam: The United States and Asia* (New York: Vintage, 1967), p. 21. The historical summary given above depends in part on Reischauer's account, pp. 20–27.

isolated in its sponsorship of the Phoumi faction, joined only by Thailand and South Vietnam, from which clandestine American material support came by airlift.

After rejecting direct military intervention the Kennedy Administration strengthened the Phoumi faction, moved Marines to Thailand, alerted troops on Okinawa, and deployed the Seventh Fleet into the South China Sea. These actions were intended to demonstrate that we wanted nothing less than the neutralization of Laos. Meanwhile, Kennedy assured the Russians publicly and privately that we wanted both nothing less and nothing *more* than neutralization. Khrushchev agreed to reconstitute the Commission and indicated that he had no desire to "take risks over Laos" when "it will fall into our laps like a ripe apple"; the crisis subsided.

At the Vienna conference in June Kennedy obtained Khrushchev's commitment to reneutralize Laos, and a coalition government was gradually put together in this small country after lengthy negotiations at Geneva. The government was established in June 1962 and heralded by simultaneous announcements from Khrushchev and Kennedy. Thirteen states, including the United States, the U.S.S.R., Communist China, the Vietnams, and India, signed the Declaration of Geneva in July.

But the coalition government soon lost the support of the Pathet Lao. As a result, the Geneva negotiations had the effect of shifting the support of the neutralist faction in Laos away from the Pathet Lao and toward Phoumi in order to defend Laotian independence against a Communist faction supported from Hanoi. The neutralist faction gradually gained ascendency over Phoumi's faction in the coalition government, winning indigenous support for its manifest independence, while the Pathet Lao continued to operate in the mountains. Laos was now a divided but more stabilized state.

The problems Kennedy faced in determining the appropriate degree of American involvement in Vietnam were similar to those presented by Laos, and in both areas the Administration suffered the frustrations of dealing with an area it was willing to treat only as peripheral to our interests. In both areas Kennedy's goal was to hold down American involvement and expenditures in order to concentrate on other areas deemed more important to our interests, such as India, Africa, and Latin America. In Laos, Kennedy's policies succeeded, but in Vietnam they laid the foundation for substantially increased American involvement.

When the French returned to Vietnam after World War II they found Ho Chi Minh's Communist movement established in the North and receiving de facto recognition from Chiang Kai-shek's Nationalist government in China. At first Ho's regime took an uneasy role within the French Indochinese Federation, but the two were at war by 1946. In 1949 the United States began to support the French effort against Ho's Vietminh as Chiang's government lost control of the mainland China to the Communists.

The war in Indochina reached a climax in 1954 when the French enclave at Dien Bien Phu in the North came under siege. The French government asked the United States to break the siege with air strikes. By then the United States was paying for 80 percent of the French effort. President Eisenhower decided against committing American forces to break the siege, and Dien Bien Phu fell to the Vietminh that spring. It was a major defeat for the French that proved to be politically, though not militarily, decisive. They concluded they could not go on because of the unpopularity of the war in France. At the Geneva Convention that summer France and the Vietminh agreed to divide Vietnam along the 17th parallel and set up an international control commission. A separate agreement provided for elections in 1956 to reunify Vietnam. The Geneva agreements represented a face-saving package for the French.

Britain, Communist China, and the Soviet Union—but not the United States—assented to the proposed 1956 elections in Vietnam. Whether this assent meant that they expected South Vietnam to fall to Hanoi in two years is unclear. It *is* clear, however, that the Eisenhower Administration had no such expectation; in fact Dulles organized SEATO in part to give South Vietnam the protection of a regional security pact. The United States also installed a new ruler in Saigon, anti-French mandarin Ngo Dingh Diem, and undertook to strengthen his regime through subsidy. Clandestine American operations by the CIA evidently helped Diem to weaken the rival political groups in a somewhat feudal power structure.

Our actions were based primarily upon political rather than moral criteria; our objective was to stop the takeover of South Vietnam by the Vietminh. Since the Eisenhower Administration perceived the Communist world as monolithic, it viewed a Vietminh victory as a clear gain for the Soviet-led Communist enemy (a view that also gave strength to our moral criteria for supporting South Vietnam). All forms of our intervention in Vietnam—economic assistance, military training and equipment, and sub rosa operations by the CIA—were being used elsewhere by us as well. Military and economic aid were common forms of American intervention, and during 1954 the CIA arranged the overturn of the left-wing government in Guatemala. Moreover, the Administration's level of intervention in the new state of South Vietnam was actually lower than what we had contemplated to save the French at Dien Bien Phu a few months earlier. But moral issues were to become more important later on. As the inhumane side effects of the war on both sides grew and became more visible, our moral position became questionable. As the French had discovered earlier, however, our participation in the war's inhumanities might have received less notice had we been winning.

Measured by the standards of advanced democracies, the new Diem regime was not particularly attractive. Washington expected it to be more honest, efficient, and democratic than the French colonial regime. The expectation was unfulfilled. Yet Diem's regime was not conspicuously less appealing than the other alternatives in Vietnam or than other American clients—in Taipei, Seoul, Baghdad, Lisbon, and Havana, for instance. Given our earlier support for the French effort to hold Indochina, Diem seemed to offer a distinct improvement in our moral position.

The American-sponsored government in Saigon was only partially successful in consolidating its power over South Vietnam. Many hardcore Vietminh had stayed in the South after 1954. Dubbed by Diem as the "Viet Cong," these Southern forces became the heart of the resistance, spreading their control over the rural population with a shrewd combination of service and terror that was often superior to the government's combination of coercion and authority. The Viet Cong organized themselves as the National Liberation Front (NLF), a rival government to Diem's.

By the time Kennedy was elected President Hanoi was supporting the insurgency in the South. In 1961 Ho's government began to infiltrate into South Vietnam some of the more than 100,000 Vietminh troops that had fled north from the South in 1954.

Kennedy became President at a time of growing demands from Diem for more American supplies and personnel in Vietnam to match the open support of the Viet Cong from Hanoi. His advisers had been aware of the deepening crisis in Vietnam. Diagnosing the problem as a preoccupation with traditional political and military methods, they undertook the development of American guerrilla-warfare capabilities. Upon taking office they found that career officials in both the State and Defense Departments had anticipated them by starting to prepare a counter-insurgency plan for Vietnam including extensive social and military reforms. In May Vice-President Johnson returned from a trip to Southeast Asia to advise Kennedy against American combat involvement in Vietnam, but he recommended changes in the military effort there coupled with more political and economic reforms. Johnson also spoke of a major economic-development program for the lower Mekong River basin.

Diem, however, successfully resisted American pressures for reform and change. With the situation still deteriorating, Kennedy sent a White House team to Saigon in October 1961, headed by General Maxwell D. Taylor. The Taylor team recommended sending 10,000 more U.S. troops to Vietnam—a virtual doubling of our forces there. The White House found Taylor's recommendations attractive in part because they offset the conciliatory position it had been taking in Laos and its failure at the Bay of Pigs. Kennedy, considering the United States overinvolved in Laos, was taking steps to reduce our commitments there. At the same time the Bay of Pigs debacle had left him vulnerable to charges that he was unwilling to stand up to the Communists. After some hesitation he ordered the proposed buildup in Vietnam and for the first time put the American advisers there into uniforms. He evidently expected these actions to solve the Vietnam problem.

Since the Americans in Vietnam had limited access to both government officials and populace, we depended largely on Diem's government for progress reports. Kennedy's State of the Union Message on January 14, 1963, reflected the optimism that prevailed more than a year after he had raised the American commitment there: "The spearpoint of aggression has been blunted in South Vietnam," he said. Earlier, McNamara, on his first visit to Vietnam, had matched this optimistic statement: "Every quantitative measurement we have shows we are winning the war."[10]

In fact, however, the war had not been going well. Our hopes for victory in 1962 had rested on the so-called strategic-hamlet program, conceived by a British officer with experience in Malaya but badly executed by Diem's brother, Ngo Dinh Nhu. American reporters covering Vietnam, resenting the official optimism and the prodding of the U.S. Embassy in Saigon to "get on the team," began to release news stories that belied the official accounts. By 1963 the American newspaper reader could discern a distinct "credibility gap" between official accounts and other news sources.

The gap continued to grow. The chief American military adviser in Saigon proclaimed a victory for us in January at Ap Bac, 50 miles south of Saigon, while American correspondents on the scene filed stories making clear that a victory had not been achieved. Rumblings of failure in the handling of the strategic-hamlet program also grew. The program was designed to use military means to increase the security of a spreading geographic area. Village life would be reorganized in the interests of security and in the process basic social, economic, and political change would be carried out. Instead the plan failed to provide security and merely disrupted village life, adding to the antagonisms generated earlier when Diem had abolished local selection of local officials.

The incongruity between press and official accounts of the progress in Vietnam had produced some restlessness among Washington officials by the spring of 1963. Senate Majority Leader Mike Mansfield, for instance, called for a reassessment of American policy in Vietnam. Yet official optimism persisted. In May Kennedy expressed the hope that the United States could begin to withdraw some of its forces by the end of the year. This hope rested on the assumptions that the scale of the Communist effort would not be significantly increased and that the counter-insurgency efforts of the Diem government would improve. Both assumptions proved incorrect.

In May a Buddhist uprising began. Though urban based, it reflected discontent from the countryside as well. In August Diem

10 Quoted in Schlesinger, *op. cit.*, p. 549.

loosed his special security forces against the Buddhist pagodas, seizing monks, nuns, and school children. Kennedy officials in Washington now began to think about letting Diem fall. In a television interview on September 2 Kennedy called the handling of the Buddhists "very unwise" and charged Diem's regime with having "gotten out of touch with the people." He even hinted that Diem's brother, who was in charge of the security forces, might have to be removed from office. We followed with selective and un-publicized suspension of assistance in October. These acts effectively provided the license for a military junta that toppled the regime and murdered Diem and his brother three weeks before Kennedy's own death.

As American involvement, American costs, and American atten-tion grew, the legitimacy of the Diem regime and its successors were soon to be widely questioned in the United States because of their corruption, repression and unpopularity. The American as-sociation with repressive means to keep the government in power would also be challenged, as would the morality—and the ex-pediency—of opposing the strongly based insurgent forces in South Vietnam. The Kennedy Administration's doctrines had concen-trated instead on engineering better methods of countering insur-gents (on the grounds that such methods would eliminate the need for political repression and might thus make it possible to get a morally acceptable non-Communist regime).

The Kennedy Administration's decision to let Diem fall re-flected its impatience with him, its optimism about the impact of nation building and counterinsurgency, and its anxiety about the political opposition and repressive measures in Vietnam. Diem lost support in Washington because he did not prove to be sufficiently concerned about the political and social roots of the insurgent prob-lem—a subject the Kennedy Administration took very seriously. In short, Diem did not appear to be a modern "nation builder."

Washington was also concerned about the growing visibility in the United States of the Vietnam difficulties. Kennedy himself had criticized Eisenhower for identifying the United States with undemocratic regimes in the late fifties. Evidently he believed that not only were these regimes ineffective but that the American public was antagonized by its government's support of regimes that offended democratic standards. The Kennedy Administration could not afford the public antagonism it anticipated if it continued to support the Diem regime.

The most visible aspect of South Vietnam's problems—a factor that added greatly to the Administration's growing doubts about supporting Diem—was the Diem regime's repressive activities to crush the Buddhist uprising begun in May. Diem's actions may in fact have been no different from the repression of other ethnic, religious, or political factions elsewhere in Asia, the Middle East, or Latin America. But in this case the growing American involvement made domestic Vietnamese politics newsworthy in the United States, giving Vietnam the very prominence the Kennedy Administration had wanted to avoid.

In August 1963 Kennedy recalled the American Ambassador in Saigon since 1961, Frederick E. Nolting, a man closely identified with Diem. Nolting has reported that when he sought an explanation for our official turn against Diem, Secretary of State Rusk told him: "We cannot stand any more burnings."[11] And indeed the Kennedy Administration could not, if it wished to prevent Vietnam from mobilizing the attention of the American public.

In general, letting Diem fall made matters worse in Vietnam. The coup that destroyed him swept aside the fragile political structure he had built and left politics in the hands of young military officers. During the next fifteen months three more military coups succeeded in Saigon and still more were attempted. Over the next three years there would be nine different governments. The succession of Army-backed civilian regimes and army rulers that followed were less traditionalist than the austere mandarin Diem and more tractable to the Americans, but they were hardly more progressive. In fact, the post-Diem regimes were no more capable of winning public support, no less corrupt, no more efficient, and no more responsive to the peasant or worker than Diem had been. Usually dominated by North Vietnamese émigrés who were insensitive to Southern ethnic, religious, and political groupings, these regimes hardly represented a gain in popular rule.

Once the military became the arbiters of the South Vietnamese political order, they repeated the same pattern of behavior that had

11 "The Origin and Development of United States Commitment in Vietnam," speech by Frederick E. Nolting, April 2, 1968, *Congressional Record* (May 14, 1968), pp. E 4186–4190.

sapped Washington's confidence in Diem: they remained preoccupied with carrying on a relatively sedate power struggle among themselves and with maintaining the American commitment to South Vietnam—at the expense of political and economic conditions that underlay the instability of the country's regimes. The Kennedy Administration had let Diem fall in order to give greater weight to improving political and economic conditions. Yet, as a consequence of Diem's fall, the Saigon government's neglect of these problems actually grew.

Two alternative courses of action, if pursued in the summer and fall of 1963, might have changed political conditions in South Vietnam. First, the Kennedy Administration might have negotiated a political settlement with Hanoi. But this alternative had been ruled out by Washington. In fact the precipitating cause of our letting Diem fall had evidently been the indications that his regime, through the efforts of his powerful brother, was turning toward a neutralist solution for South Vietnam.

Second, the Kennedy Administration might have tried to move into the vacuum left by Diem's removal by supporting a reform-minded regime ready with specific programs for improving political and economic conditions. In fact, we evidently made no such preparations for filling the Vietnamese political vacuum. The Nuclear Test Ban Treaty had been signed in Moscow on August 5, and when Kennedy withdrew support from Diem in early September the Treaty was before our Senate Foreign Relations Committee. The Senate ratified the treaty on September 24, more than six weeks before Diem's overthrow. Kennedy evidently decided at that time, however, that further involvement in Vietnam in order to secure a new and better regime would jeopardize the Test Ban Treaty. After assessing his priorities, Kennedy chose the treaty over Vietnam.

LATIN-AMERICA: THE ALLIANCE FOR PROGRESS

Before a glittering audience of Latin American diplomats assembled in the White House in March 1961, Kennedy announced "a vast new 10-year plan for the Americas, a plan to transform the 1960's into a historic decade of democratic progress," repeatedly intoning the plan's Spanish name, *Alianza para Progreso,* in his flat Boston accent.

Latin America was changing rapidly. Its birth rate was the highest for any continent, its rate of urban growth phenomenal. Yet economic stagnation persisted. The Alliance, like the rest of the Kennedy Administration's economic-aid programs, gave primary attention to economic objectives, though from the beginning the political obstacles to economic development in Latin America proved particularly difficult to overcome.

Most of the Latin American nations had gained their independence in the early nineteenth century, but they were still underdeveloped by the standards of the midtwentieth century. The U.S. government and American businessmen had had considerable experience with them, and a wide range of men in business and public affairs understood in detail the close relationship between their political and economic problems.

Through private investment the United States could provide only a small proportion of the additional capital needed for economic development, and through government grants and loans we could provide even less. The Latin American governments needed to take steps to induce saving for capital investment, to stop the flight of their own private capital toward foreign markets, and to make the investment climate for foreign capital more attractive. The necessary environment for inducing these savings and investments, according to this line of reasoning, could be established through the fiscal and economic policies and business legislation of the Latin American governments involved.

The Kennedy Administration did not deny the importance of private investment. But sole reliance on it, said Kennedy's economic advisers, would only continue the basic conditions of stagnation. The hostile business climate was itself part of the problem. National economic-development plans, meeting recognized economic criteria established and enforced by a regional organization (in the manner of the Marshall Plan) rather than by the United States, the advisers suggested, should produce the conditions needed to attract more private investment. The Kennedy Administration was prepared to use American public grants and loans to create those conditions where necessary, channeling funds through public enterprises in the recipient country.

At the same time, prior experience had made it plain that American aid channeled through the recipient government might well reinforce the status quo rather than change it, whereas sound economic-development plans were more likely to assure that the Alliance did not simply subsidize the status quo or reward those whom the status quo already favored. Past experience with development plans, however, suggested that merely enforcing economic performance criteria would not be enough to assure that the necessary social and economic revolution would occur.

The Alliance needed to be sold in every participating country, including the United States. In the Latin American countries it could succeed only if it served as a rallying point for the supporters of change against the defenders of the status quo. Public figures in Latin America—to say nothing of the American Congress—who were potential supporters of the Alliance needed the encouragement and reassurance provided by publicity and political promotion, so that if they ventured to change things they could do so as part of a large and popular undertaking. For these reasons, it is not surprising that both the United States and the potential Latin American beneficiaries surrounded the Alliance with strong rhetorical flourishes—with a mystique.

Economic aid for the first year would be covered by the $500 million left over from the Eisenhower Administration's Inter-American Fund for Social Progress. In his March 1962 foreign-aid message, Kennedy proposed $3 billion in development funds for the Alliance in the next four years, including $600 million for the fiscal year 1962–63. This proposed expansion of American appropriations occasioned the first annual stock-taking of the Alliance. Complaints came from all directions. Latin American countries criticized Washington for bureaucratic delays while their own economic and social reforms lagged. Critics in Congress charged that the Latin Americans had shown no clear intention to do their share. Congress cut Kennedy's fund proposals modestly and added the Hickenlooper amendment forbidding aid to countries that expropriated American-owned property without prompt and adequate compensation. Kennedy, to offset a mood of disappointment in Latin America, visited Venezuela and Colombia at the end of the year.

The exchange of recriminations was not the only indication of disagreement between Washington and its Alliance partners. An important divergence of views appeared over what seemed to be a central point of agreement reached in 1963: the need for stronger multilateral control over the Alliance. The idea had originated in a report by former Presidents Kubitschek of Brazil and Lleras of Colombia, approved at the annual meeting of the Alliance at São Paulo in November. For the Latin Americans, stronger multilateral control through an inter-American committee could help to reduce U.S. control over the disbursal of assistance funds. For the United States, the committee could set and enforce performance standards, relieving Washington of the uncomfortable roles of lawmaker, auditor, and policeman. Since the United States was the principal contributor, we could not otherwise avoid playing these roles, as we had learned in NATO throughout the fifties when we had supported the NATO military command in its call to meet the agreed national quotas. The multilateral form of the Alliance could also protect the United States from the charge that we were using economic aid as an instrument of political manipulation.

Since the United States and Latin America never fully agreed on Alliance objectives, however, bilateral aid remained a vital part of U.S. policy—and a persistent way to manipulate domestic politics in Latin America, as the experience with Brazil indicates. Brazil, the largest and most populous country in Latin America, had a federal form of government and relatively broad participation in its domestic politics. The defense of the status quo was maintained not merely by a narrow oligarchy but by a wide variety of political groups who benefited from the high rates of inflation under the status quo. In 1961 the United States discreetly supported the national assembly's successful effort to clip the powers of new Brazilian President Goulart when he seemed to be drifting to the left. Two years later, when Brazilian criticism of Goulart had declined and his constitutional powers had been restored, Washington provided $400 million in financial aid to help rescue the faltering financial structure of the Brazilian economy. Goulart, however, failed to cope with the mounting inflation—it climbed at the record pace of 100 percent in 1963—and the United States cancelled its assistance. The cancellation conformed to the Kennedy approach in economic assistance: setting and enforcing performance standards. But our action also amounted to using economic aid for political manipulation—the very thing the Kennedy economic-assistance program was supposed to avoid. In practice it was hard to avoid sliding from one policy to the other.

Had Washington been willing to risk Brazil's failure, it could have restricted its role to the enforcement of performance criteria. But "playing it cool" was as difficult for the Kennedy Administration as it had been for its predecessor. Concerned about political developments in Brazil, the Kennedy Administration had used economic aid first to discourage, then to encourage, and finally to penalize the Goulart government. With the fate of Brazil at stake, as it turned out, American officials could not be content merely with awaiting performance and enforcing standards.

The first years of the Alliance saw a noticeable drift toward the right in Latin American politics. The military intervened in the politics of Argentina, Ecuador, and Peru in 1962, and in Guatemala, the Dominican Republic, and Honduras in 1963. Military interventions did not necessarily lead to the establishment of dictatorships—in Latin America, as elsewhere, the military have often played a stabilizing role in national politics. But military intervention in each case did interrupt the development of popular participation in politics and thus hampered the Alliance objective of democratic development.

CONCLUSION

Kennedy, like Eisenhower, came to the Presidency determined to make major revisions in our foreign and domestic policies; but, unlike Eisenhower, he was prepared to use to the fullest the power and status of the Presidency to accomplish his goals. He increased our military flexibility (along with military expenditures) in an effort to get away from the stark choice between massive retaliation and surrender that he identified with the strategy of the Eisenhower Administration. He broke away from the established clichés of the Cold War by relying less heavily on the Communist threat to justify foreign programs and actions than either Eisenhower or Truman had and by taking a more positive approach to the underdeveloped nations. Finally, in dealing with nuclear strategy Kennedy talked with rare candor about the limits of American power. Because our strategic power could not be utterly superior, reasoned Kennedy, it would be to our advantage to stabilize the balance of terror by reaching accommodations with the Soviet Union about strategic forces and about geographically remote areas, such as Africa, where the interests of both great powers were peripheral. In both efforts Kennedy was reacting against the rigidities that he and other critics had attributed to the Eisenhower Administration. And in all Kennedy's attempts at change he demonstrated an unusual capacity to crystallize, articulate, and publicize public issues.

Eisenhower enjoyed massive public confidence in his conduct of foreign relations until 1958, and he and Dulles had invoked the clichés of the Cold War to supplement and sustain this public support. This broad base of public approval allowed them to conduct foreign policy with a large degree of unarticulated flexibility— though this flexibility was mostly tactical, as we saw in the Suez crisis. Ultimately, Dulles and Eisenhower could not escape the rigidities of their own Cold War rhetoric, but they were trapped as much by Eisenhower's belief in restricted presidential power as by their inclination to oversimplify foreign-policy issues in public statements.

Kennedy's inclination as President was to dramatize to the public the seriousness of the predicaments he was attempting to address. He treated the Berlin crisis this way throughout most of 1961, and during the following two years he made similar appeals. In effect, he appealed to the public to "rally 'round" the President and give him support without worrying about details—an appeal that was equivalent to Eisenhower's and Dulles' use of Cold War rhetoric to win general public support for foreign policy. But by diminishing the use of Cold War rhetoric Kennedy diminished the onus attached to negotiating with the Soviet Union, and the test-ban negotiations in turn demonstrated what British politicians had already discovered: that negotiating with the Russians could actually be converted into a political asset at home.

In appraising the Kennedy Administration's conduct of foreign policy, the main difficulty lies in the disparity between the extraordinary articulation of policy that preceded every change or attempted change and the Administration's actual performance. After all the doctrinal articulation and fanfare that preceded the Alliance for Progress, for example, this program came to look like a rather ordinary effort to deal with some very persistent problems of political and economic development in Latin America.

The disparity between policy explanations and actual performance would come to assume tragic dimensions in Vietnam. The Kennedy Administration, after energetic efforts to gain Soviet agreement on neutralizing Laos, remained aloof in Vietnam while the Diem regime fell, leaving Kennedy's successor the stark choice between propping up the shaky junta that succeeded Diem or letting the political situation in South Vietnam deteriorate into irredeemable chaos. Perhaps the Kennedy Administration took too seriously its strategy of regional aloofness and its new doctrines about counterinsurgency tactics; perhaps, as also seems likely, it had decided against increasing the American commitment in Vietnam for fear such a move would jeopardize ratification of the Test Ban Treaty. Either way, Vietnam casts a shadow across the foreign-policy achievements of the Kennedy Administration.

chapter 8

Johnson's Foreign Policies: Europe, Latin America, and the Shadow of China

Lyndon B. Johnson was fifty-five when he took the oath as President of the United States in his native Texas on November 22, 1963, following President Kennedy's assassination in Dallas. Johnson had been a Congressman for eleven years, a Senator for twelve years, and Vice-President for nearly three. He had risen to national prominence as a remarkably able Senate majority leader for seven years and had gone to the 1960 Democratic Convention as a major presidential contender. Johnson's search for delegate strength had been confined to the party regulars, while Kennedy had proceeded to demonstrate in several presidential state primaries that he had strong popular appeal. After Kennedy won the Democratic nomination on the first ballot he picked Johnson as his running mate. Johnson balanced the ticket, helped unite the party, and carried crucial Southern states in the election. When Kennedy's death made Johnson President, he had established an impressive record as legislative and sectional leader, but he had not yet become an important *national* figure.

When he took over the Presidency Johnson gave first priority to maintaining continuity with the Kennedy Administration. He kept Kennedy's major cabinet appointees, and even Kennedy's White House staff for the time being. He also made Kennedy's ambitious legislative program his own. Kennedy had laid the ground-work for the legislation's passage, but the program was stalled in Congress when he died. With a month left in the first session of the 88th Congress, Johnson pushed through the appropriations bills and a badly tattered foreign-aid bill. He failed to win approval of a civil-rights bill, but he demonstrated his interest in that objective.

In 1964, Johnson would go on to establish brilliant legislative record, and by mid-August he could declare:

> *This has been a year without precedent in the history of relations between the Executive and the Legislative branches of our govern-ment. This session has enacted more major legislation, met more national needs, disposed of more national issues than any other session of this century or the last.*[1]

During the next two years Congress was to approve new medical-aid programs, aid to education, voting-rights legislation, reform of our immigration laws, a higher-minimum-wage law, an extension of the War on Poverty, and a new program to counter urban blight.

In foreign affairs, as in domestic affairs, Johnson's main goal on taking office was to maintain continuity with the Kennedy policies. The prospects for success in the areas central to our inter-ests, however, appeared less encouraging than at home. The Alli-ance for Progress was lagging. Laos represented a well-publicized stabilization of Soviet-American affairs, but next door Vietnam was becoming a growing drain on American resources. The efforts to solve the malaise in NATO had become bogged down with the Multilateral Force (MLF) and its implications, and Western Europe was moving in step with De Gaulle's nationalism. Kennedy's pur-suit of a détente with the Soviet Union had produced a test-ban treaty, but it had also resulted in compensatory congressional re-strictions on trade with the Iron Curtain countries and on aid to them.

Vietnam would ultimately affect all these areas, dominating the entire horizon of Johnson's foreign policy. At the beginning of his Administration in 1963, however, most of them were—or ap-peared to be—more important than Vietnam. The Kennedy legacy in Western Europe and Latin America seemed particularly impor-tant.

---

[1] *Public Papers of Presidents of United States: Lyndon B. Johnson 1963–64,* **II** (Washington, D.C.: Government Printing Office, 1965), p. 987.

STANDING BY IN WESTERN EUROPE

The principal business pending with Europe in late 1963 consisted of the MLF and the so-called Kennedy round of trade negotiations. Trade relations had been in intermittent negotiation since the enactment of the Trade Expansion Act of 1962. The United States sought to gain better access for its exports to the Common Market in return for lowered trade barriers to American markets. More generally, it sought an "outward looking" European trading system—one that would enlarge the scope of the original Common Market to include Britain in particular. The 1962 Trade Act had rested on the assumption that the United States would negotiate mutual tariff reductions with a single trade area in Europe. However, in January 1963 France had broken off the negotiations of the six Common Market countries with Britain concerning her entrance into the market. For the next five years the British government continued trying to gain entrance to the Common Market, and France continued to exclude her.

Similarly, France opposed the development of the MLF. Johnson stayed the hands of the MLF enthusiasts when he became President but came out supporting it fully the next April (1964). By November Washington and Bonn could announce a new military accord that seemed to clinch the German commitment to the MLF and assure support from other West European governments, if only to prevent the formation of a German-American bilateral nuclear force. French participation would not be essential. De Gaulle, however, threatened to withdraw from the Common Market and to deny French cooperation toward the attainment of European unity if Bonn did not accede to France's agricultural trade demands and abandon the MLF. De Gaulle had touched raw nerves. In West German politics European unity meant German reunification, and taking France out of the Common Market would also hurt the German economy seriously. (Withdrawal would have hurt the French economy too, but it was in better order than Germany's. De Gaulle's threat was believed.) Bonn wavered. Johnson pulled back on the MLF in December 1964, leaving the burden of finding a solution to the Europeans.

At the same time McNamara supplied the opening for a solution. Europe could rely on American nuclear protection, he told the NATO Council. Forty percent of the American nuclear stockpile was either in West Germany or allocated to the defense of Europe. Their targeting, he claimed, would not permit the United States to do what Europeans feared—to defend the United States without defending Europe as well. In an earlier effort to reassure the other NATO members, the United States had already invited NATO observers to take up posts at SAC headquarters in Omaha, which they had done. Now McNamara proposed a select committee to participate in the operational planning for American strategic nuclear forces in NATO. The sharing of American information and offer of a staff role for other NATO members was intended to deflect allied demands for sharing in the command of nuclear forces toward support for an integrated, common nuclear force instead.

Arrangements for the select committee proceeded while De Gaulle withdrew French land and air forces from all NATO commands (as he had already done with French naval forces). When Bonn questioned the status of the French forces remaining in West Germany under national rather than NATO command De Gaulle coldly stared Bonn down: did Bonn want French forces there or not? The answer was yes. France was still a member of NATO but no longer a participant. In March 1966 France informed her allies that they had one year to remove themselves and their headquarters from French territory. During 1967 NATO headquarters moved to a suburb of Brussels.

Both the MLF and the new information-sharing and planning procedures were marginal to the main course of American foreign policy. Neither one required much change in Washington's cooperation with other countries in deploying and controlling nuclear weapons or in generating strategic plans and doctrines. American alliance policy remained dominated by the inner logic of American strategic doctrine, which stressed the unitary control (which meant in practice unilateral American control) of all nuclear capabilities in NATO.

Johnson's withdrawal of support for the MLF could be taken as a blow to supranationalism in Europe. But the MLF was not a sound building block for European integration in the mid-sixties.

With the declining sense of military threat, military integration in Western Europe hardly carried the value that it had during the Korean War. Moderating the pressure for military integration and encouraging commercial and political links with Eastern Europe, by contrast, would have allowed Johnson to attenuate the division of Europe between the North Atlantic and Warsaw Pacts and thus to outflank De Gaulle in his appeal for a Europe "from the Atlantic to the Urals." Johnson had raised that prospect in his State of the Union Message in January 1965, and he made some preparations to pursue the linking of Eastern and Western Europe as an important aspect of American policy. Yet, as his attention increasingly riveted on Southeast Asia, these efforts became a silent casualty of the war.

In 1965 De Gaulle extended his boycott of the Common Market to the other machinery of European economic cooperation, blocking the further development of supranational institutions in Europe. (He forestalled, for example, the consolidation under a single executive office of the Coal and Steel Community, EURATOM, and the Common Market.) Challenging the trend toward European integration meant challenging objectives that Washington had supported for twenty years. De Gaulle also challenged the American presence in Europe and American policies elsewhere, particularly in Vietnam. In January 1964 France recognized Communist China, enhancing Peking's prestige at a time of increasing American involvement in Vietnam.

In 1956 France had tried to challenge the world interests of the United States by colluding with Britain and Israel to take the Suez Canal and shatter the Nasser regime in Egypt. Eisenhower had disciplined her and ignored French nuclear aspirations. But France's behavior in the sixties brought quite different responses. De Gaulle now served as the main explanation of the fissile tendencies evident in NATO. In fact, however, other factors contributed to these tendencies as well: the national aspirations of the other European Nato members were becoming increasingly independent, as De Gaulle sensed, and after 1963 the United States turned its attention increasingly to Vietnam. De Gaulle was thus a significant symptom of Western Europe's malaise.

Some accommodations with De Gaulle did get worked out nonetheless. For example, early in 1966 the French boycott of the economic community stopped when the machinery of the community was changed to meet De Gaulle's criticism. The new arrangements permitted economic integration to proceed on the basis of a confederal, not a federal, scheme. It was also possible to gain agreement on other difficult issues once the effort to win De Gaulle's consent was abandoned. For example, in December 1967 the NATO ministers (without the presence of a French delegation) ratified the American strategy of a flexible military response.

Few initiatives were being taken in European affairs in 1966 and 1967 and De Gaulle's behavior was not the only reason for the malaise. The war in Vietnam distracted the United States from its interest in changing the political structure of Europe and strained America's relations both with her European allies and with Russia, thus making attempts at political change more difficult for either the East or the West.

Any distraction of American interests from Europe is likely to cause difficulties with our European allies, if only because their interests receive less attention from us. But Vietnam in fact caused less antagonism from European governments than had the Korean War, although the intensely hostile public demonstrations against Vietnam from certain opinion groups may well have exceeded those occurring during the Korean War. Official patience in Europe over Vietnam reflected the changed world conditions since the Korean War. Russia seemed less of a threat in the early sixties than in the early fifties; almost no one feared that Russia would escalate the Vietnam War, while in 1950 many Europeans had shared Washington's view that Korea marked a new phase of Soviet belligerence. Europe, moreover, was stronger and less dependent on the United States than it had been in the fifties, and the Soviet bloc more divided than in 1950.

There were advantages to this situation for the United States. For example, the carping criticism of nervous European allies during the Korean War was largely absent in the mid-sixties (if one ignored De Gaulle), though its absence was not evidence of European support for the Vietnam War. The criticism of the early fifties was the behavior of dependents trying to influence a sponsor whose patronage was indispensable. In the mid-sixties the silence of Europeans indicated their interest in getting along with the United States while not being highly dependent upon us.

THE ALLIANCE FOR PROGRESS
AFTER KENNEDY

Kennedy's Alliance, as we saw, had already lost some luster by the time he died. Many of its difficulties were inherent in the politics of development. The slow pace of appropriations bills in Congress during 1963 had added to Latin American anxieties. Sharp congressional reductions in foreign-aid funds had not spared the Alliance in either 1962 or 1963. The $850 million Kennedy requested in January 1963 had diminished to $590 million in the final version of the bill Johnson pressed through Congress after the assassination.

Under Johnson a definite shift in tone occurred in the Alliance. Johnson appointed Thomas C. Mann as Assistant Secretary of State for Inter-American Affairs and put in his hands responsibility for economic aid as well as diplomatic tasks. Kennedy had promoted a program of economic assistance by surrounding it with a mystique of social and political development in Latin America along democratic lines. Mann neglected the mystique, turning instead to an older theme: nonintervention by the United States in Latin American domestic affairs. The change of tone upset both United States and Latin American liberals. They had become disillusioned with the nonintervention doctrine, seeing it as a defense of the status quo.

In March 1964, just as a dispute over these changes began to sharpen, Brazil's President Goulart fell to a military coup. The Brazilian Army abandoned long-observed standards of constitutional restraint to pull down Goulart and establish what it proclaimed to be a reformist caretaker government under General Castello Branco. It initiated a program of social, economic, administrative, and political reform and it stopped Brazil's galloping inflation, but to do so it deliberately suppressed democracy in Brazil. The coup was as much designed to wipe out chaos as Communism, though Washington found it convenient to emphasize the fact that the military takeover had forestalled Brazil's drift toward Communism.

The United States became a strong sponsor of the new regime, expecting that Castello Branco would carry out major economic and political reforms that had eluded regimes based more on popular support. And to some extent Castello Branco did. Alas, however, our stake in the success of his regime made it difficult for us to withhold economic assistance in order to induce satisfactory economic performance, as we had done with Goulart. Our strong support of Castello Branco made the democratic development issue more muddled than before: Kennedy had held out the prospect of economic *and* democratic development; Mann under Johnson insisted that economic development might require the sacrifice of democratic development. In fact, however, this position was not novel: the Eisenhower Administration had supported General Mohammed Ayub Khan when he took over the government of Pakistan in 1958. Ayub Khan instituted a military suppression of political factions in Pakistan, but he also produced a more stable and expanding economy.

Our policy in Brazil in 1964 was a clear departure from Kennedy's original standard of refraining from political manipulation in Latin America, but its intent was consistent with Kennedy's emphasis on foreign aid for economic development: our intervention did help to suppress democracy in Brazil but it encouraged more rational economic and fiscal policies. The chaotic instability of Brazil had prevented concerted political and economic development quite as much as powerful oligarchs prevented economic and political reforms in more stable political systems.

Social unrest, including insurrection, persisted in Latin America, representing a driving force sometimes for reform and sometimes against it. In September 1964 Chile elected Eduardo Frei President by a large majority. A Christian Democrat, Frei pledged "a profound revolution within liberty and law." He quickly emerged as a leading spokesman for democratic change in Latin America, without posing the value conflicts between democratic politics and economic change Castello Branco represented in Brazil.

Latin American reformers, as well as oligarchs, continued to be plagued by Castroism. The United States led the effort to isolate Cuba diplomatically and economically, often with grudging cooperation or public noncooperation from regimes eager to avoid antagonizing their own left-wing political groups. The Caribbean, however, provided Johnson with another and even less auspicious occasion to seek Latin American cooperation when the Administration needed to be extricated from its intervention in the internal politics of the Dominican Republic. A left-wing military group seized control in April 1965, deposing the Cabral regime, which had ruled in Santo Domingo since its military coup in 1963. The new regime had ties with Juan Bosch, the constitutionally elected president who was then in exile, and they proposed to restore his Presidency. A counter coup moved against the pro-Bosch group, led not by the moderate Cabral but by a general of narrower perspective, Wessin-y-Wessin. The pro-Bosch group was now in jeopardy. They asked for American assistance but were denied help on the grounds that the United States ought not to intervene in an internal matter. Within hours, however, the tide had turned. The Wessin-y-Wessin faction now asked in writing for the aid of U.S. troops. Washington denied the request by specifying that the United States would intervene only if American lives were in danger. The Wessin-y-Wessin faction promptly disclaimed responsibility for American lives and property, the United States ambassador requested U.S. troops, and Johnson, after agonizing over the issues for a few hours, sent in troops and notified Congress, the Organization of American States, and the American public of his action.

Our intervention was publicly justified at first as necessary to rescue and protect United States and other non-Dominican citizens. In fact we served to help the immediate interests of the Wessin-y-Wessin faction party because our intervention separated the combatants. It soon became evident that President Johnson had acted out of fear of another radical revolution like Castro's in Cuba, giving undue weight to exaggerated reports from the U.S. Embassy of threats to the lives of United States citizens and reports of a Communist threat. His anxieties may have been real, but they were not persuasive. Liberals were outraged as much by his explanations as with the actions he had ordered.

The United States now found itself in a situation comparable to the Lebanese crisis. Its forces stood between two national factions, and it was virtually impossible not to favor one side or the other. Our own interests lay in the direction of disengagement. Washington turned first to the OAS, obtaining endorsement for our forces as peacekeepers and receiving help from the OAS, principally from Brazilian troops. A coalition government was painfully put together, and the peacekeeping force was phased out. Eight thousand peacekeepers lingered on, but the United States had extricated itself. A Dominican national election in 1966 brought a competent moderate to the Presidency; Bosch accepted electoral defeat and soon retired to Spain. The Johnson Administration made amends by stressing its preference for support of democratic over non-democratic governments and promising the Dominican Republic additional economic aid. But Mann's initial doctrine of nonintervention lay in shambles.

With the mystique of the Alliance diminished, the level of American economic aid limited by our Vietnam commitment, and Congress again restless about foreign aid, the Administration's emphasis in Latin America shifted back toward the private sector— trade and business development. In Washington the new stance looked like a return to the days of Eisenhower. For Latin America, however, there was no turning back. At a Panama meeting of the OAS in the spring of 1966 Latin American representatives aggressively demanded positive and formal United States commitments to pay higher prices for their principal export products—in effect, U.S. subsidies for Latin American products. Just as the United States resisted European efforts to tie its nuclear arm to NATO, the Johnson Administration withstood Latin American pressures for subsidies and countered with a drive for Latin American economic integration instead. The strategy of great-power diplomacy led Washington to promote the regional integration of our allies both in Europe and Latin America as an alternative to their dependence on the United States.

CHINA AND THE PEACE OF ASIA

There was a good deal of the affected quality of the "good neighbor" in the Alliance, as well as some genuine acceptance of Latin American and other underdeveloped countries as simply different from us and less developed. Yet during the first half of the sixties we had a growing vision of the special power (and sometimes the morality) of the United States position in the world. Our economy leapt forward in the early sixties while economic growth rates in Europe declined and the Soviet Union appeared to be more and more plagued with the common problems of sustaining growth and meeting increased demands for domestic consumption. By the late sixties, moreover, Eastern Europe's unity could no longer be taken for granted, and Soviet power had long since ceased to be measured in terms of the cumulative strength of the Soviet bloc.

Johnson became President at a time when the disunity of Western Europe was growing and De Gaulle's vision of a united Europe was gaining ground with the growth of trade through the thinning Iron Curtain across central Europe. In 1966 Johnson launched a program designed to open contacts with Eastern Europe, following up Kennedy's Test Ban Treaty and wheat deal with the Soviet Union. But, like other potential initiatives, our overtures to the East remained undeveloped because of the Administration's preoccupation with Vietnam.

Not only had the "missile gap" of 1959 evaporated but Mc-Namara had been able to construct force postures and doctrines that reasserted the utility of American nuclear strategic superiority. The United States remained preeminent as a world power, and the Soviet Union and the United States formed a distinct pair as major nuclear powers. The gap between Russia and those countries behind it in nuclear power (the British and French) and in economic size (West Germany, Japan, Britain, and France) was large. The Soviet Union and the United States, by virtue of their nuclear-power relationship if nothing else, shared certain interests not always harmonious with those of their respective allies. Kennedy and Johnson had both asserted the special relationship between the United States and Russia by ending the paralysis in Soviet-American negotiations induced by West Germany's fear of an East-West settlement in which Bonn did not participate. But in the mid- and late sixties it was in Asia rather than Europe that a tacit Soviet-American accommodation seemed to be growing.

The issue did not begin with Vietnam, but with Communist China. During the Korean War American relations with China had frozen into a persistent effort to isolate Peking diplomatically and to institute trade embargoes in order to undermine the technical and economic basis for China's military power. The diplomatic isolation had partially succeeded. Not only had the United States and some of her allies refused to establish diplomatic relations with Communist China, but Peking had been kept from membership in the United Nations. Our attempts at economic isolation, however, did not succeed. By the late sixties, more than 70 percent of China's trade was with the non-Communist world.[2]

The problem of American relations with Communist China has been often a partisan issue, but the positions of the two major political parties have not been far apart. The Eisenhower Administration attached much value to the potential trouble which Taiwan could make for Peking. Yet it was Dulles who in 1958 got Chiang Kai-shek to renounce the objective of invading the mainland. The Kennedy Administration, for all its resolve to recast the Cold War, did not begin to change the relationship between the United States and Communist China.

The alliance structure for Asia, developed by the Eisenhower Administration, reflected our expectation of China's aggressiveness. In the mid-fifties China seemed on its way to becoming a major economic power. The plans for a "great leap forward," announced in 1957, seemed to confirm the impression of phenomenal Chinese development. But the image was inaccurate. By 1959 the Chinese economy was in a tailspin. Natural disasters, Soviet withdrawal of aid, bureaucratic problems, and economic mismanagement had contributed to a major fiasco that changed the whole outlook for China's future. China's foreign trade did not return to its 1959 level until the late sixties.

Having split with Russia, Peking now claimed to be the true spokesman for Communist revolution. Her verbal belligerence sustained her image of potential aggressiveness during a period of actual weakening in her aggressive potential. The attack on India in 1962, although largely defensive in nature, appeared in some capitals—Washington among them—to demonstrate this belligerence. The United States sprang to India's aid. But our involvement led us to take a closer look at the Chinese threat, and we began to realize the limitations of Chinese power in South Asia. India's reaction was profound. China had been considered a friend; now it became the principal threat to Indian security. Gradually, however, New Delhi came to share the American view that the Chinese posed only a very limited direct military threat to India.

In October 1964, when the Test Ban Treaty was hardly more than a year old, China detonated her first nuclear device. In the

2 Edwin O. Reischauer, *Beyond Vietnam: The United States and Asia* (New York: Vintage, 1967), p. 167.

next two years four more detonations occurred, and in June 1967 China tested a hydrogen bomb. The first detonation boosted China's reputation enormously with non-nuclear powers and made it very difficult for nuclear-power aspirants—particularly India—to refrain from turning over their own nuclear-power resources to the development of military weapons.

The Chinese detonations began when the United States was considering a heavy commitment to Vietnam. They added to the fear in Washington and elsewhere that escalating the American commitment—particularly by bombing North Vietnam (begun in February 1965)—would bring China directly into the Vietnam War. Making his own assessment of the risk, Johnson chose a steady increase in the American war involvement, which could have been halted if signs of dangerous Chinese reactions appeared. They did not, perhaps because of Chinese caution, perhaps because its Cultural Revolution was about to be launched.

The Cultural Revolution was a drastic program of reform that turned into an upheaval. It was undertaken by the old revolutionary leaders in the central government of Communist China in order to restore revolutionary enthusiasm and root out what they considered the increasingly harmful influence of the technicians in the bureaucracy. The course of the factional in-fighting was difficult to follow in the West, but the dominant theme of the revolution was clear. It was xenophobic and ideological, evidently resisting trends toward a Communist technocracy that had long been evident in the Soviet Union. In effect, the Cultural Revolution became an internalization of the ideological conflict with the Soviet Union. All indications were that it would cost the Chinese government a high price in future economic development. It was causing substantial civil chaos and evidently the crushing of personal initiative in the administrative apparatus of China. A whole generation of technicians lost a year of their education. One of the targets of the reformist faction (the Maoists) was the professional military. Apparently reluctant to take actions that would lead to a greater dependence on the military, Peking is reported to have notified the United States through indirect diplomatic channels that it would not intervene in Vietnam provided the United States did not invade China or North Vietnam or bomb the Red River dikes in North Vietnam. The United States was reported to have replied that we had no intention of attacking these areas. Following this exchange, war talk in Peking died down.[3]

The Chinese nuclear detonations had given impetus to negotiations for a treaty to prevent the spread of nuclear weapons to states that did not already have them. The nuclear powers pursued the treaty out of mixed motives. The Soviet Union wanted to keep Germany from gaining control of nuclear arms, and she also used the negotiations to divide NATO members over their fears of German military power. Within its own bloc, Moscow could use this fear of Germany to rally Eastern Europe and turn these countries against Communist China's nuclear aspirations. From Washington's viewpoint a nonproliferation treaty would isolate France and Communist China, the newest nuclear powers, and reduce the likelihood that India, Israel, Sweden, and other states would acquire nuclear weapons. In June 1968 the United Nations General Assembly approved a nonproliferation treaty that the Soviet Union and the United States had drafted. France and several nuclear-aspirant powers did not vote for approval, but the heavy majority favoring the treaty assumed that it would bring strong pressure against new national nuclear-weapons programs.

China's growing nuclear power also led to an important new phase in the arms race—the decision in Washington to build a "thin" defense system against nuclear-tipped missiles (a so-called antiballistic missile system, or ABM). McNamara had long delayed the decision to move beyond the development phase of such a system to production and deployment because of the system's limited capability. But with its capabilities gradually improving, with the Russians apparently deploying a thin ABM system of their own, and with considerable pressure in Washington not to hold back any longer, he acceded. The thin ABM, he explained, was intended to eliminate the possibility that the Chinese could coerce the United States with nuclear threats. It was not meant to protect American cities from a Soviet attack. But the ABM decision raised the prospect of a new generation of weapons on both sides.

The nations on the periphery of China manifested mixed developments and expectations in the late sixties. The South Korean economy was booming, and the outlook there was optimistic. The

[3] The report of the diplomatic exchange is in the *U.S. News and World Report*, January 15, 1966.

Philippine economy was chaotic, and its political system was show-ing signs of disintegration. The Philippines were, oddly, only now in the first stages of anticolonial agitation against their ties with the United States.

Indonesia had been rescued from the brink of a Communist takeover in 1965 by a military counter coup and was now being ruled by a Western-oriented military-dominated regime intent upon reform and national reconstruction. Although many prominent Indonesian military officers had received training in the United States, Washington kept somewhat aloof from Indonesia after the coup. The dramatic shift of Indonesia from a leftward drift to a Western orientation seemed to confirm the utility for Washington of a hands-off policy in Asia.

Similarly, when Pakistan attacked India in 1965 in the hope of seizing the disputed territory of Kashmir, Johnson cut off aid to both sides and delayed the resumption of economic assistance even in the face of famine in India. When economic aid was resumed, the precedent of the American cut-off and the conditions of resump-tion indicated that the Johnson Administration was willing to force responses from the Indian government—something the Ken-nedy Administration had not done. American officials recognized that the central government in India, chaotic and sometimes paralyzed, operated under many pressures. In 1966 Johnson used the threat of American economic cutbacks to intensify these pres-sures and thus to get the Indian government to adopt tougher development policies.

The presence in Southeast Asia of Britain—the last of the European colonial powers—had gradually diminished. Britain scheduled the pullout of her remaining military forces in Hong Kong and Singapore first for 1972 and then for 1970. Japanese power, on the other hand, had grown immensely. By 1967 Japan was the third industrial power in the world. Her gross national product was larger than that of all Latin America together. Her population growth was under control, her economic growth rate phenomenal, and she had stemmed a drift toward the left in the late fifties, which might have made Japanese politics vulnerable to Chinese Communist manipulation. The vexing issues for Japan raised by the Chinese nuclear-weapon developments she faced calmly. After two decades Japan had begun in 1966 to assume a role as a regional power in Asia. In doing so, she could balance the hostility generated by her aggressive policies of the thirties and early forties—and the memory of her brutal occupations throughout Southeast Asia—with a residue of good will from the same period for eliminating European colonial rule in much of Asia. In the foreseeable future, Japan could be more powerful in international affairs than Communist China; and by assuming a greater role in Asia, Japan might reduce the pressures on Washington to be the counterweight to China on that continent.

CONCLUSION

The circumstances under which Johnson came to the Presidency heavily predisposed him to emphasize domestic programs from the beginning. Kennedy's legislative program was in the doldrums, and Johnson was confident of his ability to salvage it. Johnson needed continuity with the fallen President and was personally disposed toward domestic-reform legislation anyway. In the first weeks of his Presidency, Johnson asked his cabinet to avoid foreign crises so he could promote Kennedy's domestic legislative program. After winning his own electoral mandate in November 1964, his legislative success continued through 1965, only to be slowed down by growing political opposition to Vietnam and by the war's drain on our resources. But even with the slack years after 1965, Johnson's legislative record was impressive.

As a result, however, he was never able to give foreign policy the priority that it deserved. Kennedy had been able to turn his handling of foreign relations into a means for achieving the national standing that he lacked and needed. Johnson found a comparable vehicle in his extraction of domestic legislation from Congress. He may have intended to give greater priority to foreign relations later, as the momentum of his legislative agenda lagged, but, when this time came, he was in no position to take the initiative in foreign relations.

The secondary status of Johnson's foreign relations meant that his promise as an international negotiator went untested. His Senate record showed that his grasp of political negotiations was extraordinary. Its potential transferability to foreign relations was suggested by Johnson's graceful deflation of the MLF project and other points of confrontation with De Gaulle. Most of all, the promise of Johnson as the great negotiator lay in the development of a détente with the Soviet Union. Kennedy had started a movement in that direction with the Test Ban Treaty, demonstrating the domestic political gains possible from settling issues with the Soviet Union. In addition, as more of a Cold Warrior than Kennedy, Johnson was in a better position to retain the public's trust during such negotiations. His Administration did carry through tortuous negotiations of terms for a treaty—with Moscow, our allies, and other U.N. members—to hinder the spread of nuclear weapons. But Johnson had planned to go further in exploring the grounds of common interest between the two nuclear superpowers. He was hardly a rigid Cold Warrior. (Had Johnson's negotiations with the Soviet Union come to occupy a prominent role in American politics, however, the subtlety of his negotiating skills would probably have been outweighed by his heavy-handed methods of winning public support. At least his handling of Vietnam, covered in the next chapter, suggests this inference.)

Finally, our perspective on Johnson suffers from the aura that sprang up around President Kennedy's achievements after his death —particularly the Alliance for Progress. The change of tone in the Alliance that many observers throughout the hemisphere noted after Johnson took office had really begun before Kennedy died. As we saw in the last chapter, much of the Alliance's appeal lay in the accompanying rhetoric, and Johnson lacked the rhetorical style —and the means or the will to contrive it—that had won sympathy and support for Kennedy among European, Asian, and Latin American leaders and intellectuals.

chapter 9

Vietnam Defeats Johnson

GOLDWATER AND THE 1964 DEMOCRATIC LANDSLIDE

Franklin D. Roosevelt's Presidency fascinated Johnson as it had Kennedy. It was Roosevelt's innovative spirit and his management of presidential power that attracted Kennedy. Johnson, however, was attracted by Roosevelt's methods of aggregating political support, or winning consensus. Johnson's origins were the barren poverty of the Texas hill country—hardly comparable to the genteel prosperity of the Duchess County Roosevelts. Johnson's early success in politics came from identifying with Roosevelt's New Deal. Moving from a congressional constituency to the statewide Senate constituency in Texas, however, Johnson moved to the right politically, winning support from the money and power of Texas business. As his status in the Senate and in national life grew, he was able to move back toward the social values he had supported in the thirties. In identifying with the program of the President, as the Vice-President must, Johnson was also reasserting the values of his earlier years in politics. Furthermore he was adapting to a national constituency, much as Roosevelt had adapted his personal background to the constituencies of New York state and, later, national politics. Roosevelt and Johnson, it would appear, both believed in constructive tactical shifts in national politics.

It was not out of character, then, for Johnson to identify with the Kennedy record in establishing the continuity of the Presidency after Kennedy's assassination. From his first speech to the Congress, in the leaden atmosphere of grief over Kennedy's death, through the election the following November, Johnson's political style placed him in the broad center of American politics. "No memorial oration or eulogy," he had said in that first speech, after reminding Congress of his own record in supporting civil-rights measures in 1957 and 1960, "could more eloquently honor President Kennedy's memory than the earliest possible passage of the civil-rights bill for which he fought."

A few weeks later, in his State of the Union Message in January 1964 Johnson announced his determination to wage a "war on poverty." In the presidential campaign that year he stated his major aspirations for domestic welfare efforts to achieve what he called the "Great Society."

The moderates of the Republican party had not coveted a presidential nomination in 1964 until it was too late. When it became apparent that Goldwater was the Republican front runner, first New York Governor Nelson Rockefeller then Pennsylvania Governor William Scranton tried in vain to head him off.

Once nominated, Goldwater made no attempt to unite his party. He picked two fellow Arizonians with little national political experience for the two key posts in the Republican campaign. He campaigned with a narrowly selected personal staff, directing his campaign to the sector of public opinion most disposed to support him anyway.

Goldwater's campaign included strongly right-wing proposals. In the primaries, for example, he had proposed dismantling some of the social-welfare programs—making social security "voluntary," for instance—and he suggested that not only the President but the NATO Commander should have the right to order the firing of strategic nuclear weapons. Goldwater also revived some of the right-wing rhetoric that Eisenhower had buried—"rollback," "brinksmanship," "total victory"—and brought back a strong ideological version of the Cold War. "We must make clear that until [Communism's] goals of conquest are absolutely renounced and its relations with all nations tempered," Goldwater had declared in accepting the nomination, "Communism and the governments it controls are the enemies of every man on earth who is or wants to be free." He advocated militant assertions of American power, such as ordering the Marines to restore the water supply cut off by Cuba at Guantanamo Bay and bombing of North Vietnam. Yet he asked for an end to the draft and a 5 percent cut in the income tax in each of the next five years.

Johnson's political style would have predisposed him to seek the middle ground in the campaign regardless of his opponent, and Goldwater willingly left the political center to Johnson in both domestic and foreign relations. The Vietnam War, which played a persistent role in the 1964 election, well illustrates this contrast between the candidates.

When Johnson had become President in November 1963 South Vietnam urgently needed a central government that was stable and effective enough to cope with the insurgent threat. As Vice-President, Johnson had recommended a major economic-development program for the Mekong River basin. During his first year as President, however, Johnson wanted to limit American involvement in Vietnam, and this preference ruled out the possibility of our changing the regime or broadening its nation-building programs. Thus in order to promote political stability in South Vietnam it was necessary to support the regime in Saigon—whatever its form.

Kennedy had kept the Vietnam War from general public view, despite his decision to increase the number of American military advisers there and to encourage a change of regime, but Johnson could hardly keep the war from being an issue in the 1964 election. Instead, he posed as the moderate candidate in comparison to Goldwater's belligerence on this issue.

Goldwater began with a question that loomed large on the political horizon: should we escalate the war in order to get it over with? But this issue became lost behind a clutter of related questions. Should the military have authority to use nuclear weapons on their own? Are nuclear weapons "conventional" weapons? Are all Communists automatically our enemies?

Given Goldwater's militancy, the middle ground was a stand against escalation. "We don't want our American boys to do the fighting for Asian boys . . ." Johnson declared at Eufala, Okla-

homa, in late September, paraphrasing a famous campaign statement of Eisenhower's. Two weeks before the election he told a
university audience in Ohio: "There is only one road to peace and
that is to work patiently, deliberately, wisely, step by step, year by
year, never to become weary of the journey and irritated with folks
who may not agree with you the first time you talk with them."

Though Goldwater made Johnson's campaign easier, throughout 1964 the President still faced an intractable problem of mul-
tiple audiences with conflicting needs and goals. Saigon needed to
be told that the United States would stand by our commitment in
Vietnam. And given the evidence available to Johnson of Hanoi's
support for the insurgency in the South, it would be helpful to
tell the North Vietnam regime that its actions could provoke the
United States into increased military opposition. On the other
hand, given Goldwater's belligerence and Johnson's decision not
to escalate the war before the election, Johnson would want to
tell the American public that it would not be necessary to increase
American military action in Vietnam—that Goldwater's belligerence was unnecessary. But Johnson could not say different things
to each audience. In his first major speech on Vietnam as President,
he told the Viet Cong that they were playing a "deeply dangerous
game" and the American public that "the contest in which South
Vietnam is now engaged is first and foremost a contest to be won
by the government and the people of that country for themselves."
Both audiences could hear all that he said. Later, in reassuring his
domestic audience that he would not escalate, he may have re-
assured Hanoi as well.[1]

The main White House objective in Vietnam throughout
1964 was "keeping it quiet," according to one of Johnson's aides.[2]
(He might have added, however, that Johnson was willing to talk
about Vietnam in the campaign in order to improve his advantage
over Goldwater.) There was no assurance, however, that events
would not make a quiet war impossible. One event in particular
did just that.

In early August, an American destroyer was attacked in the
Gulf of Tonkin. Johnson ordered the Navy to destroy such attack-

[1] Too much, as Johnson later came to think, according to Tom Wicker, *JFK and LBJ: The Influence of Personality on Politics* (New York: Morrow, 1968), p. 238.
[2] *Ibid.*, p. 244.

ers in the future. Two days later, when new attacks were reported, he ordered air raids against North Vietnam in retaliation. He also reinforced air and sea units in the Vietnam theater and seized the opportunity to win from Congress a resolution authorizing him to "take all necessary measures to repel any armed attack against the forces of the United States and to prevent future aggression." As Eisenhower had done in 1957 in regard to the Middle East, Johnson used a crisis to associate Congress with our Vietnam military effort.

Johnson won 61.4 percent of the popular vote in 1964. (Roosevelt had barely topped him in 1936.) Substantial ticket splitting occurred among the voters, and some prominent Republicans such as Governors Nelson Rockefeller of New York, George Romney of Michigan, and William Scranton of Pennsylvania and Senator Thomas Kuchel of California refused to endorse Goldwater. Johnson carried thirty-eight more Democrats into the House of Representatives with him, giving Democrats more than a two-to-one ratio over Republicans. In the Senate, already Democratic by two-to-one, the Republicans lost two more seats.

It was a great electoral triumph. But it had been won at great cost to Johnson's political leadership in foreign relations. Not content simply to keep Vietnam from causing a groundswell of public impatience against him in 1964, Johnson had used it as a campaign issue to amass his electoral landslide. Now, as he stepped up the pace in Vietnam, he won the support of the hawks, but his abrupt reversal from dove to hawk laid the basis for the credibility gap— the broadly held suspicion that President Johnson had not been fully honest with the public. This gap was compounded by real disagreement on "facts" about the war and doubtlessly by previous incidents of Cold War dissembling by the American government. Of these, our official lie in the 1960 U-2 crisis and the American-instigated Cuban invasion in 1961 had doubtless attracted the widest public attention. Thus Johnson was now to suffer not only from his own overreach but from the accumulated stresses of our Cold War operations on public confidence.

THE ESCALATION OF 1965

In his State of the Union Message made in January 1965 Johnson sketched the broad scope of his intentions now that he was

President in his own right. Not even the ponderous imagery of the "Great Society" could obscure his enlightened ambition to attack the major recognized social and economic problems of the day. Johnson also indicated that he intended to pursue rapprochement with the Soviet Union—that he envisioned wholesale transformation of the conflictive relationship at the base of the Cold War. In both respects his message was a remarkable vision of the future. But events went in quite a different direction.

Beginning perhaps a month before the presidential election, Johnson came under increasing pressure within the government, primarily from the Joint Chiefs of Staff, it would appear, to authorize bombing raids in North Vietnam. Twice in September, as the Saigon government had assumed different forms, Johnson had promised increased support to stabilize the internal political situation. In December, after our election, a bloodless coup in Saigon brought in new faces and a direct assertion of military power. Washington judged the coup a step backward and put American aid commitments on a standby basis: more than a year after the fall of Diem, the Vietnamese political situation was still highly unstable.

Two days before the election a Viet Cong mortar attack destroyed six B-57 bombers and killed five Americans at a South Vietnamese air base at Bien Hoa. Johnson did nothing. When a similar attack occurred at Pleiku in February 1965 he ordered air strikes against North Vietnam in retaliation and then continued them on a regular basis against a restricted set of targets. The response to Pleiku evidently reflected a decision made weeks and possibly months before it happened. At the same time, McNamara announced a major expansion of the South Vietnamese army and a small increase in the number of American advisers in Vietnam.

The bombing lifted the morale of the beleagured Saigon government, but stability was still needed. The situation, as it appeared from Washington that spring, could not be saved with halfway measures. The United States would have to make a major commitment of forces to eliminate serious doubts about the future of the South Vietnamese government. If the American public reaction to another major commitment on the Asian mainland was to be ridden out successfully, moreover, it seemed advisable to secure a quick military victory, possibly before the congressional elections in 1966 or at least before the 1968 presidential election. Johnson decided on a buildup of American ground forces in Vietnam on a scale so large that we would have to assume an important share of the fighting burden.

The buildup of ground forces, like the air attacks, became incessant. In May 1965 American forces numbered 35,000; by September they totaled 130,000; by the end of the year, more than 180,000; by mid-1966, 270,000; by year's end, 380,000. In 1967, they increased another 100,000, and in the first half of 1968, another 60,000.

The escalation was by no means one-sided, although the steps taken by Hanoi are more difficult to specify. An important phase in the escalation from the North began in 1964 when organized units of North Vietnamese regulars became the major manpower traffic southward. The rate of infiltration from the North has always remained a matter of dispute and revision. Despite heavy losses (according to American claims) the total number of North Vietnamese troops in the South continued to increase, sometimes faster than the U.S. buildup.

The Administration planned a continuing American buildup in Vietnam from mid-1965 on in order to show Hanoi and the National Liberation Front that time was not on their side—that the United States intended to increase the engagement of our own vast military power until the insurgent conflict in Vietnam was stopped.

The size of the American ground-force commitment eliminated the possibility that the Viet Cong would win a military victory over the United States. Two other outcomes remained possible, however, and both posed grave implications for American interests. First, even if overwhelming U.S. military strength could "defeat" the Viet Cong, we could not provide a stable political order for South Vietnam. Unless the political situation improved considerably, the United States would face the difficult choice between a long and unpleasant occupation and a pullout, followed by the collapse of the South Vietnamese government.

Hanoi clung to the second possibility: that domestic political pressures could force the United States, as it had the French, to give up and pull out. Hanoi made no secret of these expectations. Washington's demonstration of resolve by escalation could easily be offset by signs of serious division at home about the war. The Johnson Administration listened to the rising domestic criticism of its expanding air and ground operations, aware of their implications for the strategy of coercion it had adopted. Johnson, in fact, told his critics that they were comforting the enemy. His remarks added to their alienation from his Administration.

THE DOMESTIC IMPASSE OVER VIETNAM

Vietnam spelled trouble to any American politician with a memory of Korea. A continuing if limited war inflicting U.S. casualties, requiring increased draft quotas, producing daily newspaper reports and radio and television broadcasts penetrates public consciousness as nothing else does while offering little gratification. Depicting the violence of war may gratify, but it also becomes frustrating and irritating as the coverage becomes monotonous.

Moreover, a gradual entanglement threatens: the otherwise preoccupied voter perceives that somehow American national security is at stake, yet the issue—whatever it is—remains unsettled. On a more personal level, the war threatens to involve family and friends in dangerous military service. Its electoral consequences for the incumbent government are ominous. In the short run, public opinion can be rallied by a vigorous response to a threat, as Kennedy showed with the Berlin crisis in 1961 and during the Cuban missile crisis in 1962. But a protracted threat, requiring a persistent and costly response, can be expected to produce a wide mood of dissatisfaction; and dissatisfaction expressed as electoral behavior becomes a vote against the incumbent.

Doubtless the men of the Kennedy and Johnson Administrations knew that a protracted war in Vietnam would hurt them politically. Johnson minimized the threat of Vietnam until after the 1964 election and then, it would appear, tried to end it with a quick victory.

The Johnson Administration suffered from other problems with Vietnam as well. There was an appalling lack of knowledge in our government as to precisely what was happening there—what American and South Vietnamese operations were accomplishing, what the situation was on the other side, and so forth. This official ignorance and misperception had been demonstrated as early as 1962 by the journalists in Saigon. Symptoms of it were the numerous revisions of our military estimates and the inaccurate predictions about the course of the war that persisted through March 1968. These symptoms had already created a credibility gap between government statements and those from other sources in Vietnam before the 1964 election. The gap was to widen as the Administration unconvincingly tried to depict its decisions to increase American commitments in Vietnam as dramatic responses to dramatic threats.

As it had during the Korean War, the press failed to consider the pressures on the field operators—General MacArthur's command in Korea, the U.S. Embassy and the military headquarters in Saigon—to prove they were succeeding in order to justify a larger American commitment. Their foolishness continued to be mistaken for knavery by many American journalists in Saigon.

Inaccurate reporting within the government had plagued Kennedy as well as Johnson. The problem was closely linked to the difficulties of working through a client regime—particularly one dependent upon the United States for its very existence. For Kennedy these difficulties had largely coincided with Diem. For Johnson the problems shifted with the changes in Saigon's government, settling eventually upon young military men of narrow perspective and experience. The most prominent of them was a Northerner, Marshal Nguyen Cao Ky, Premier in the military junta in 1966 and Vice-President after the national election in 1967. During the American congressional election campaign in 1966 Ky publicly refused to negotiate with the National Liberation Front (NLF)—the political arm of the Viet Cong—and called for an invasion of North Vietnam, indicating that if the Chinese came into the fight it would be better to deal with them now than later. Ky's statement greatly embarrassed the Administration both at home and abroad. Under American tutelage he backed away from that position. But his statement indicates a gulf in purpose between the United States and the client government of South Vietnam which persisted, much as the Formosa Strait crisis in 1958 had etched the difference between Nationalist Chinese and American purposes in dealing with Communist China.

The bombing of North Vietnam that began in February 1965 cut the ground from under Johnson's opposition on the right, but it opened a large fissure within his own party on the left—in what became the peace wing of the Democratic party. It centered, as one might expect, in Congress. Senator Church of Idaho had registered a strong dissent against American policy in Vietnam as early as the summer of 1963 when he proposed a resolution calling for U.S. withdrawal from South Vietnam if Diem's "cruel repressions" of the Buddhists continued. In an address in March 1964 Senator Fulbright had labeled as "old myths" a great many established tenets of American foreign policy. But though Fulbright's speech attacked many popular Cold War tenets, the public reaction to it was only moderate. This temperate public response stood as an invitation for Johnson to move left, away from the Cold War. But Fulbright's speech was poorly timed. With a presidential election eight months away, Johnson was not inclined to open up the range of issues that a thawing of our frozen hostility to Red China would raise.

When the bombing of North Vietnam began a year later, fifteen Democratic Senators signed an appeal to Johnson to stop it; many more shared the view. A similar protest came from the House. Much criticism clustered around the argument that if the bombing stopped Hanoi would negotiate. Johnson stopped it for eight days in May but resumed it when he concluded that Hanoi remained unwilling to negotiate.

Johnson coupled the resumption with another call for negotiations—"unconditional discussions," as he put it. Hanoi refused in September, charging bad faith on Johnson's part. In December Ho Chi Minh and Johnson exchanged charges about negotiations via press interviews. An important propaganda duel had developed, with both sides no closer to serious negotiations than their firing of broadsides indicated.

In mid-December the first air strikes against major industrial targets occurred near Haiphong. The bombing of North Vietnam, taking place within target restrictions carefully set by McNamara, was designed to reduce the flow of supplies and men to the South and coerce Hanoi into a settlement. Yet both sides observed a thirty-hour Christmas and New Year cease-fire and Johnson extended the bombing pause against the North from December 24 through January.

The Truman Administration had, in Churchill's phrase, "armed to parley," but it had never really parleyed or indicated under what circumstances it wished to. Dulles had turned the Churchillian dicta into "arm and beware!" Kennedy had actually followed Churchill's motto by arming *and* parleying. Johnson, the extraordinarily able parleyer in American politics, now found himself fighting while wanting very much to parley.

But regardless of his preferences, by 1966 Johnson had alienated vital congressional supporters. Looking back on the way Johnson had won the Gulf of Tonkin resolution from them and the way he had escalated the war, they resented his obvious manipulation of them. Congressional leaders came to believe that Johnson had violated the rules of behavior that underlie executive-legislative trust. In his efforts to cope with a public opinion that was expected to be hostile to the war, Johnson had lost the support of the men he knew how to handle best—his Senate colleagues.

THE LINK BETWEEN VIETNAM AND DOMESTIC ISSUES

A radical left had already formed in this country on behalf of civil rights, drawing whites as well as Blacks from the staffs and students of the northern colleges, from the clergy, the arts, and other sources. The civil-rights movement recruited members for closely knit political activity and, increasingly, for direct political action. Vietnam and civil rights were issues that had been linked on the college campuses before 1965, but the bombing drew the two issues closer together. The humanitarian concerns of domestic affairs were now directed toward the victims of American bombing in North Vietnam.

The civil-rights movement had developed methods of peaceful resistance in the mid-fifties as a means of legally challenging state and local laws in the federal courts. Its methods were initially nonviolent, though necessarily coercive. But they did not always remain nonviolent, particularly under the provocation of white supremacists. Moreover, the civil-rights movement generated a revolution of rising expectations among Blacks that had helped produce explosive conditions in the Black urban ghettos of the North by the early sixties. Demonstrations were peaceful there at first, too, but by 1963 they had become angry melees in which lives were lost. In the summer heat of 1965 violent anomic rioting burst out in Los Angeles, followed by riots in other cities during that and successive summers.

College students from northern campuses, applying what civil-rights workers had learned in the South, attempted a more calculated program of nonviolent coercion. At Berkeley in 1964 students (and nonstudents) first demonstrated that a major university could be easily paralyzed. Direct action, in the tradition of the Abolitionists, became a familiar form of political action in protest over the war and other issues. Draft cards were burned, marches and demonstrations staged, and public assemblies picketed and disrupted. Civil rights and the war in Vietnam had politicized the college student.

Johnson coped with his antiwar critics by agreeing to bombing pauses and offering to negotiate. His negotiating posture, however, quickly became entangled in a nettle of issues. He was criticized for excluding the NLF from negotiations, for claiming he would negotiate unconditionally when he would not, and for changing the conditions he had originally set for negotiations.

Johnson also continued his plans for the Great Society, and his executive budget for 1966 was an ambitious guns-and-butter program. But Vietnam cost him support in Congress. Legislators could hardly fail to honor his requests for authority, men, and war material, but they could resist his domestic program, and they did. The Administration's domestic program was also hampered by severe fiscal constraints, so that expenditures for Vietnam could be approved only at the expense of the war on poverty and other domestic welfare programs: urban renewal, health, education, and efforts to offset race-based inequities. By 1967 he had considerably lowered his sights for domestic legislation and expenditures, and even then he encountered strong opposition on Capitol Hill. 1965 had been a vintage year for presidential programs in Congress; 1967 was a mediocre one, and 1968 no better.

The balance-of-payments problem had persisted since 1958. Kennedy had attempted to deal with it by expanding our rate of economic growth. Johnson adopted Kennedy's objective of managing the economy for a high rate of expansion. During the Korean War the Truman Administration had begun with a very strong balance-of-payments position, a slack economy, and modest consumer expectations. In that situation it was possible to allocate resources to the war and permit private consumption to grow without interruption while holding back public-welfare programs only a little. In 1965, however, not only did the economy have little slack, but the public increasingly expected that the federal spending power would be used to deal with a large agenda of domestic welfare problems. It would have been possible to meet the public's expectations about domestic programs, but the war was another matter.

The direct costs of the war rose rapidly in 1965 to more than $25 billion per year. Johnson's guns-and-butter assumptions that year had rested on a serious underestimation of the costs of the war and a miscalculation about the inflationary impact of defense spending. The Administration persistently assumed that the war would be over within six months. Also, the counter-inflationary measures—a squeeze on credit and a tax increase—came too late.[3] As a result, a sustained attack on the dollar grew to crisis proportions by the end of 1967. On New Year's Day 1968 President Johnson announced an emergency program to cope with it, including temporary mandatory controls on domestic investments abroad and an unprecedented plan for the control of a major source of dollar exports—American tourist expenditures abroad.

With diminishing congressional support for his Administration, Johnson was unable to gain approval for an income-tax increase in 1967. He had already reduced his annual domestic-budget requests for the second time. To gain the tax increase in 1968 he had to permit still deeper congressional slashes in domestic programs.

HOLDING THE EXECUTIVE BRANCH TOGETHER

Johnson's most effective demonstration of leadership in the growing crisis over Vietnam was his command of the executive branch. In the United States no administration is a monolith. The President must live with men of independent political means who

[3] The inflationary pressure had begun much earlier than anticipated, well before fiscal disbursements were made, at the time that orders were placed. See Murray Weidenbaum, *Economic Impact of the Vietnam War*, Center for Strategic Studies, Special Report Series No. 5 (Washington, D.C.: Georgetown Univ. Press, 1967).

have direct access to the press and Congress. Yet Johnson managed to deny his critics outside the government any rallying point within his Administration.

A likely potential critic around whom to rally was the field commander of the Vietnam military operation from 1963 to 1968, General William C. Westmoreland. War puts the military commanders under tremendous pressure to perform, and in a protracted war the commander is likely to be embarrassed by a disparity between his resources and the performance expected of his forces. A commander who is unable to achieve military success tends to defend himself by questioning the adequacy of the forces assigned to him. MacArthur's role in the Korean War indicates that an administration runs a considerable political risk when it permits military disgruntlement to grow, and Westmoreland had reportedly asked for and been refused an increase of 200,000 troops in early 1965. In mid-1965, however, Johnson began a troop buildup partly as a concession to Westmoreland, which gained Johnson the general's support. In return, Johnson made Westmoreland Army Chief of Staff in 1968, and until that year the American military persistently demanded and received growing resources for the Vietnam War.

The Johnson Administration was able to keep all prominent executive-branch officials from joining the ranks of its critics. Though executive-branch officials hardly reflected the full range of the controversy that raged outside the Administration, there is evidence of a schism between the military chiefs and commanders and some civilian hawks on the one hand, who drove for a military solution, and a civilian faction, on the other, that was increasingly skeptical of miltary claims and military solutions. Secretary of State Dean Rusk aligned himself with the hawks, and Robert McNamara, Secretary of Defense until February 1968, was evidently a civilian skeptic; his successor, Clark Clifford, also joined the skeptics.

Escalation of the war began with no intention of allowing the military to dominate the solution of the conflicts; yet the decision resulted in doing precisely that. When the bombing did not bring the desired results immediately, the Administration next tried the vast troop buildup. As the size of the American troop commitment grew, the influence of the military grew commensurately, at the expense of our political and economic instruments and objectives in Vietnam. Johnson did not successfully resist this imbalance of influence in a situation fraught with political and economic as well as military problems.

Johnson also failed to hold the support of Congressional leaders, particularly of those in the Senate. Mike Mansfield, the Senate Majority leader, and J. William Fulbright, the Senate Foreign Relations Committee chairman, were early skeptics, though their dissents were constrained at first by the logic of Johnson's coercive strategy. Neither of them condemned the resumption of the bombing of North Vietnam in January 1966; yet both called for more vigorous efforts to negotiate, and Fulbright conducted televised hearings in which he pitted himself against government spokesmen. From there Fulbright came into open opposition to the Administration, carrying many Senators with him.

Robert Kennedy, the first of his brother's cabinet officers to leave the Johnson Administration, had won a Senate seat from New York in the 1964 election. He now became a rallying point for disgruntled Democrats, although Fulbright had criticized the Administration's foreign policy more systematically.

The American effort in Vietnam had focused on avoiding a setback to military security commitments. But as the war became a major issue in American politics, a whole range of associated controversial issues emerged.

The first issue raised was that of American association with a repressive and unpopular government in South Vietnam. The Administration was often mistaken about the degree of indigenous support for the war and the strength of the Viet Cong in South Vietnam. For this reason and because it supported Diem and his successors, the Administration would not acknowledge their limitations. The antiwar critics, free to condemn the government in Saigon, were often quite accurate in depicting its shortcomings and weaknesses, but they in turn overestimated the popular support for the NLF, and hence they underestimated NLF dependence on the North.

Bombing North Vietnam had been resisted within the government, as well as outside it, on the grounds that such a step might bring Communist China into the war. This was not the result, and the Administration soon found itself on the defensive against a quite different charge—that it had overestimated Chinese aggressiveness.

There were also the unavoidable humanitarian issues that grew with the application of mechanized American firepower. The suffering of civilians in North Vietnam from the air strikes, and the cost in lives and property from the American methods of war in the South as well were demonstrably high. By 1968 critics were pressing their case hard: that even a Communist puppet government would be more desirable than the destruction caused by the war.

The Tet offensive in February 1968 brought the antiwar criticism into sharper focus. The Viet Cong had carefully built up their forces and supplies for months in advance while the American military command in Saigon claimed that the enemy threat was diminishing. The insurgents struck at the cities in South Vietnam during the Chinese New Year truce. Their attack demonstrated a surprising strength. It forced South Vietnamese and American forces to abandon rural areas in order to recover control in the cities, and it brought urban populations under greater threat than ever before, forcing an application of American firepower that caused heavy destruction of urban property in an attempt to root out the Viet Cong. The destructive costs of the war, the credibility and competence of the American effort, and the complicity of the Veitnamese population in the preparations for the Viet Cong's offensive now became an embarrassment to the Administration's case for "seeing the war through."

The Tet offensive cost the Viet Cong heavy casualties; it cost the Johnson Administration substantial political support at home; and it hurt the Saigon government by demonstrating that the regime could not guarantee the security of its own urban areas. Moreover, Tet was only the beginning of a new phase in the war. The offensive spent itself in a few weeks, but the attacks on the cities soon resumed. At first it appeared that the Viet Cong intended to concentrate on turning the urban population against the Saigon government by forcing the South Vietnamese and American forces to destroy the cities. Later attacks were less severe and concerted but demonstrated a formidable staying power in the face of the American buildup.

THE DOVES DEFEAT JOHNSON

The Administration suffered no more than expected setbacks in the 1966 congressional elections. If anything, the electoral results lent support to its Vietnam policy by putting into office new Representatives who favored stepped-up operations. The slowdown of Johnson's legislative program that year and the next, the increasingly vocal opposition to the war, and the public-opinion surveys indicated growing public concern over the war, though no clear trend in opinions on what to do about it.

Draft calls and casualty rates had risen considerably since 1964. Monthly draft quotas averaged 4,000 in the first three months of 1965—16,000 from April through August and 28,000 for the rest of the year. In 1967 they averaged just over 30,000; through May 1968, 38,000. At the end of May 1965 American troop casualties in Vietnam stood at 400 killed and 2,000 wounded. At this time, U.S. commanders in Vietnam were authorized to commit American ground troops to combat. Three years later casualties had risen to more than 20,000 killed and 130,000 wounded. Press coverage, if not pervasive, was incessant. By early 1966, as a careful opinion survey sponsored by a group of Stanford experts indicated, the public had a fairly high level of information about the issues associated with Vietnam.[4]

Johnson had evidently expected that his greatest difficulties would come, as they had in the 1964 election, from hawks. It was not an absurd expectation: during the Korean War the opposition had come mainly from that direction. Yet the Korean settlement produced contrary indicators as well. General MacArthur, the leading advocate of escalation, won public acclaim but not support, and the public accepted the modest gains of a negotiated settlement in 1953 with barely a murmur. As domestic and foreign criticism mounted, Johnson claimed that he was doing no less than the public demanded of him. In fact, public support was not confined to a particular course of action but rather placed considerable value on changes in government policy. The Stanford study showed that

[4] S. Verba, R. A. Brody, et al., "Public Opinion and the War in Vietnam," *American Political Science Review*, 61 (June, 1967), pp. 317–333.

the President could not justify his war decisions on the grounds that his hand was forced by public opinion.

The monthly polls had shown Johnson that he could win public support by being firm. He could also win support by trying new alternatives as well. If nothing else, the Administration could present visible action, even if it was without substance. Presidential popularity had shot up, for instance, when Johnson met with Premier Kosygin of the Soviet Union during Kosygin's visit to the United Nations in June 1967.

On the other hand, a considerable number of constraints limited Johnson's choices by early 1968. Among foreign-policy opinion leaders the record of handling the war in Vietnam and the manner of Johnson's switching from a peace candidate in 1964 to a get-it-over-quick Commander in Chief in 1965 had built up hostility and suspicion, and the President had alienated even his old friends in the Senate. He had camouflaged the decisions to escalate the ground war by using piecemeal announcements of troop assignments and initial claims that the air strikes were retaliatory. His object had been to forestall the groundswell of public response to the war. He had seemed the master of public arousal in 1964 with little competition. As the groundswell developed, he was no longer masterful. He displayed a personal uncertainty about public arousal that may have derived from his experience with the relatively private politics of the South and the Senate.

Late in 1967 Senator Eugene McCarthy of Minnesota, who had been an unannounced candidate for the Vice-Presidency at the Democratic nominating convention in 1964, declared that he would challenge President Johnson in five primary elections in 1968. Vietnam was the main issue that led him into a grass-roots confrontation with Johnson. McCarthy made a surprisingly strong showing in the March New Hampshire primary, demonstrating both considerable public dissatisfaction with the Administration over Vietnam and McCarthy's political potency. With these results published, Robert Kennedy declared his own candidacy, competing with McCarthy for leadership among strong antiwar Democrats. Johnson now faced open challenges to his control of the Democratic party.

Any President has formidable assets in winning the renomination of his own party. Truman had demonstrated this fact in 1948, as had William Howard Taft in 1912. No President in the twentieth century has failed to win renomination when he sought it. Yet Johnson announced at the end of March 1968 that he would not seek or accept renomination.

We will never know whether he would have been renominated and reelected had he chosen to run. He was undoubtedly in deep political trouble. His Gallup Poll rating had fallen from more than 80 percent public approval of his performance in early 1964 to 36 percent in March 1968. His rating on the handling of the war had fallen even lower that month, to 26 percent. In addition, a White House poll in Wisconsin showed Johnson running behind McCarthy two to one, and far behind Kennedy in California. The primary elections promised considerable embarrassment for him, but they hardly foreclosed his renomination and reelection.

The more serious trouble that lay ahead was in Vietnam. After the New Hampshire primary, Johnson could hardly expect that his threats and promises about Vietnam would carry much credibility either in Saigon or Hanoi, at least until the 1968 presidential succession had been settled in November. His withdrawal from the campaign hardly took Vietnam off the political-campaign agenda, but it did strengthen the credibility of the Johnson Administration's resolve to coerce Hanoi into negotiations that would permit the survival of the Saigon regime after a reduction in the American military effort.

Johnson's withdrawal had been coupled with an announcement of limited deescalation of the air war against North Vietnam and a renewed effort to parley with Hanoi. The withdrawal may have been the more important disclosure to Hanoi. At any rate, in May spokesmen for the United States and for North Vietnam began negotiations openly for the first time in Paris, while the Viet Cong pursued their attacks on the cities in South Vietnam and the American forces kept up their own pressure against the enemy.

Johnson's Vietnam entanglement cut off his presidential tenure at five years instead of a possible nine, after quenching a brilliant legislative record that had lasted nearly two years. By early 1968 the Vietnam War had badly split the Democratic Party, and Hubert Humphrey's nomination on the first ballot of the presidential convention in August left the party in disarray because of Humphrey's identification with the Johnson Administration. The election campaign of 1968 aired the mood of wide public alienation over Vietnam, but it also demonstrated once again the tendency of domestic issues to preempt foreign issues: law and order rather than Vietnam became the most prominent subject of the campaign.

CONCLUSION

The international consequences of Vietnam came to dominate Johnson's foreign policy and the domestic consequences, his domestic political position. Our Asian policy, particularly our ability to adapt our diplomacy to China's changing role in Asia, became frozen by the requirements of the war. In Europe, a similar paralysis developed. Our relationships had been in visible flux over the prospects of a détente in 1964, but they soon congealed, partly over Vietnam. In August 1968 Moscow reoccupied Czechoslovakia and began the suppression of a surprisingly resilient national Communist regime that had been liberalizing rapidly. Had we been strengthening our bridges to the East instead of abandoning them for two years, the fate of Czechoslovakia might have been different. Such speculations suggest the possible effects on our worldwide interests of Johnson's concentrating our resources and diplomacy in one peripheral area.

The legacy that Johnson inherited from Kennedy in Vietnam strongly disposed him toward greater military involvement there, but it did not predetermine his decisions to increase our military commitments or his persistent preference for military means over other strategies. These decisions were more the product of the domestic political costs of protracted wars, so clear since the Korean War. Johnson attempted to cope with these inevitable costs by undertaking an urgent solution to the Vietnam War—and this meant committing our forces to a relatively conventional military solution, despite our talk about the peculiar requirements of a counterinsurgency campaign and the need to "win the hearts and minds of the people." As a result, the political conditions in the Vietnamese countryside continued to be neglected, since the achievement of political objectives would not fit into a time-table.

Vietnam, then, did not just happen to Johnson; he helped it to happen. He dealt with the problem of a growing political opposition at home by manipulating the press to be more reassuring in its reporting and by manipulating Congress to support him, yet leave him a free hand. The conventional military solutions held the support of American military leaders, but they depended on the false premise that South Vietnam could be supported with a client government.

Johnson's manipulations of Congress and the press nourished public distrust. But the President must have expected public opposition to grow with the protraction and visibility of the war, and evidently these expectations steeled him against political adversity, so that the growing opposition did not persuade him to reconsider his strategy. Johnson was less critical of military enterprises than he should have been, and he was not the master of the broader forums of presidential politics that he was of the Senate. Yet it is not at all clear that another President would have altered the main elements of his Vietnam strategy—to reassure the public while trying to end the war quickly. It is, however, quite certain that future Presidents will avoid committing military forces to an area if they foresee being drawn into a protracted conflict.

chapter **10**

Where Have We Been and What Lies Ahead?

"The Administration has failed to prove," Senator Fulbright declared in an almost vacant Senate Chamber in December 1967, "that the United States will stand by its commitments to defend other nations against wars of 'national liberation.'" The "extravagance and cost of Vietnam" to Americans, he said, are "likely to suggest to the world that the American people will be hesitant indeed before permitting their government to plunge into another such costly adventure."[1]

The war brought the United States up against the political and economic limits of its international power as nothing else in the twentieth century had, and for the first time since World War II it posed a fundamental question about the morality of our intervention in foreign affairs. By the end of 1967 the course of the Vietnam War had indicated that convincing the United States to aid one's country against a Communist insurgency does not necessarily mean that the recipient will be saved from the national tragedy. Indeed, American intervention itself could have tragic consequences for the nation being aided.

Like Korea, Vietnam concentrated vast American resources and

---

[1] *Congressional Record*, Vol. 113, No. 201 (December 8, 1967), S18179.

attention on the problem. Yet the United States was a great power with worldwide interests and commitments. If Vietnam was simply one of many interests, the United States was far off balance devoting a half-million men there and incurring costs of nearly $3 billion per month on the war. On the other hand, if Vietnam had special significance—if winning or losing there would have wide ramifications elsewhere—then the United States was using a grand strategy in the best sense, *providing it could win.* As Fulbright indicated at the end of 1967, however, the failure of American arms to achieve our goals in Vietnam had already deprived the American stand there of its intended exemplary role: Vietnam had cost the United States too much materially and politically to serve as evidence that we would undertake comparable efforts in the future. Political authority in South Vietnam, moreover, remained vested in a narrowly based and shoddy regime.

Vietnam brought into question the capacity of the United States to apply its power productively and with discrimination in its foreign relations. It exposed American foreign policy as a somewhat indiscriminate reaction to perceived threats in which we sometimes used means incommensurate with our ends. As we saw, the American effort to reconcile foreign policy with the demands imposed by domestic public opinion and politics helps explain the basic stance of the United States in the postwar world.

The internationalists had asserted at the end of World War II that the United States ought to be concerned with foreign affairs, without specifying any order of priority or principle of discrimination for our involvement after saving Europe. By substituting anti-Communism for the moral imperative of internationalism in the first postwar years they clinched their argument at a time when foreign intervention could be quite clearly defined as helping European states under threat. Our concentration on Europe was a temporary substitute for discrimination. By the time the threat in Europe faded, the United States had entered a period of economic growth and prosperity that sustained an illusion of omnipotence associated with nuclear-power status. Even the Korean War did not force many Americans to face the realization that the United States in fact had finite resources that required us to make basic choices in our pursuit of foreign interests.

Two conditions, then, prevented a thoughtful sifting of American interests and opportunities after World War II: the need to mobilize American political consent for an international role and the obtrusiveness of the Soviet Communist enemy. Furthermore, it became prudent for every presidential administration to adopt a cover-all-bets strategy toward the Communist world, which included support of anti-Communists all over the globe. The political costs the Truman Administration incurred by appearing to let Nationalist China fall proved that a public sufficiently aroused about an external threat (as they perceived it) to support foreign-policy commitments could also be highly critical of the government when it avoided making or executing such commitments.

Truman, Eisenhower, and Johnson—every President until 1969 except Kennedy—each left office suffering from widespread public alienation over his conduct of foreign relations. Truman suffered at first from public anxieties that his Administration was not tough enough in fighting Communism abroad. After 1948 criticism focused on Truman's Asian policies, and the suspicion of Communist subversion in Washington supplemented and aggravated public distrust.

The Korean War first drew a positive public response, but as the war drifted into stalemate, public awareness and impatience grew. Political discussions turned on particulars. Should MacArthur have been fired? Should the United States bomb Communist China? Who were the Communists in the government who let China fall? The war's important political effect, however, was a general decline of public confidence and support that damaged the Truman Administration's legislative program after 1950 and diminished its authority in foreign relations.

Behind the foreground of Dulles' scurrying about, the Eisenhower Administration stood self-possessed for more than five years. It operated with a sense of restraint in foreign relations that was closely related to its view about limited national government in domestic affairs. In part as a result of this restraint, public confidence in Eisenhower's conduct of foreign and domestic affairs remained high through his first term, although during that period he lost the support of some foreign-policy spokesmen he had had in the beginning who wanted stronger leadership from him. The election of 1956 indicated a broad public confidence in Eisenhower, a feeling of security in knowing that he was President when the

Suez War occurred. Yet Eisenhower's critics were able to capitalize on public anxieties over his apparent complacency about foreign developments that Sputnik triggered in 1957.

A reassessment of foreign relations followed the launching of Sputnik. The Eisenhower Administration now acted in response to its critics and to its own new perceptions of external conditions. Among these conditions were problems of political unrest in Japan and Latin America and the political stakes seemingly involved in Southeast Asia, the diverging interests of the newly prosperous NATO member nations, the new strengths and weaknesses of the Soviet Union, and changing perceptions throughout the world about the nature of the Cold War.

The 1960 election reflected the corrosive effects of these anxieties on public confidence: the nomination of two young candidates, Nixon and Kennedy, and the theme of renewal and reinvigoration expressed by both.

Kennedy came to the Presidency without the political stature that Eisenhower had possessed in 1953: Kennedy's popular majority over Nixon was tiny; Eisenhower's victory had been a landslide. Kennedy was young and partisan; Eisenhower had been a national hero enjoying wide extrapartisan confidence.

But though Kennedy lacked political status, he was favored by purpose and circumstance, which permitted him to use foreign policy as an opportunity. The widespread public anxiety about Eisenhower's seemingly underactive stewardship in foreign relations, coupled with Kennedy's own activism, allowed him to capitalize on the demands of foreign policy, quickly expanding his popularity. By the time of his death in 1963, however, some dissatisfaction, particularly on foreign aid, had set in from his politics of arousal in the first two years. He had, moreover, demonstrated an odd sense of proportions. He had drifted into the Bay of Pigs debacle with his attention on the wrong issues. He had laid the basis for further involvement in Vietnam while worrying about the Test Ban Treaty. He had devoted such generous attention to the public-relations component of an aid program for Latin America that misapprehensions developed on both sides about what the Alliance for Progress would and would not do.

We will never know what Johnson—or Kennedy, had he lived— might have been able to accomplish in foreign relations without the burden of Vietnam. Its massive political effects have dwarfed the consequences of all other foreign-policy issues. Yet even without Vietnam Johnson might well have suffered the public alienation that was the pattern for Truman and Eisenhower.

Johnson confronted—and contributed to—a revolution of rising domestic expectations that put heavy pressure on the government to limit our external commitments in order to give domestic reforms higher national priority. Johnson's style of national politics often alienated the very opinion leaders he was attempting to persuade, as his handling of the Dominican intervention (to say nothing of Vietnam) showed. The legacy of Kennedy's politics of arousal and his priorities in foreign relations that Johnson inherited included some formidable problems: high expectations and growing discontent about the Alliance for Progress; a settlement in Laos that helped Hanoi support the insurgency in South Vietnam along the Ho Chi Minh Trail; an unstable and inept regime in Saigon with no arrangements for reform in it; a European alliance that had put aside the political logic of its function to pursue a narrower, more efficient, and more disruptive military logic; a new military link to India (after the Chinese attack) that had already been handed over to the economic and military technicians; and a minor détente with a Soviet Premier who would soon be succeeded by a less amenable group.

Several factors, then, hampered the Johnson Administration: the legacy of Kennedy's activist foreign policy, Johnson's own presidential style of foreign relations and domestic persuasion, and the lengthening domestic agenda. But the worst problem was Vietnam. By 1966 Johnson had given his Administration over to a military solution in Vietnam. Everything else became secondary. By 1968 Vietnam had become deeply imbedded in the public's awareness, arousing widespread concern and doubt.

The postwar era had begun with bipartisanship in foreign relations as a solution to America's isolationist past. In effect bipartisanship was the product of collusion among Democratic and Republican leaders to prevent partisan controversy—and thus public arousal—on foreign-policy issues. The collusion worked imperfectly at best, and the Republicans abandoned bipartisanship over the Korean War. The rising public awareness of our foreign policies proved bipartisanship was unsuccessful anyway. And by the time Vietnam was an issue, dissident Democrats were more willing to arouse public attention and recommend changes than were many Republican leaders.

The Vietnam issue, by appealing to the broad public, shattered the postwar leadership consensus about foreign relations, polarizing foreign-policy leadership opinion far more than had Goldwater's effort to provide "a choice, not an echo" in 1964. The classical questions about morality, national interest, and power, quiescent since the Korean War, now drew attention, with critics at once demanding that the United States turn to the achievement of its own domestic objectives first and that it be consistent in applying moral standards both at home and abroad. By raising the possibility of a major reduction in our foreign commitments, these critics forced the country's leadership to examine the fundamental question of what American interests really consisted of—particularly when the claim that we had a vital interest in Vietnam had soured so badly.

Well before the presidential nominating conventions of 1968 the statement "the United States is not the policeman of the world" had become a leading cliché of the political season. The statement reflected the impression that our Vietnam entanglement was the result of indiscriminate involvement in external problems, and to some degree this impression was doubtless correct. Settling Vietnam, however, would still leave the United States puzzled about its role in the world. Universalism had been thrown into disrepute because it seemed to be a license for nonselective involvement abroad. The world-policeman statement, indeed, could be interpreted as an attack against the idea that the United States had an interest in every part of the globe, an argument in favor of dividing the world into spheres of influence. Since Washington stood silently by in July 1968 while Czechoslovakia openly challenged Soviet hegemony, one could view American behavior as confirmation that Eastern Europe was not within the sphere of influence of the United States.

Despite official denials, the idea of establishing certain spheres of influence for Soviet and American interests now came to enjoy a new vogue on the political scene. Since 1945 it had lost the melancholy association with unsuccessful Old World diplomacy. But even this criterion for discrimination in American involvement abroad seemed less likely to prove fruitful than the exercise of thoughtful choice and skillful management by the President and his Administration.

The Nixon Administration may have a wide choice in foreign-policy leadership strategies. It can temporize about other foreign-policy issues, liquidate the Vietnam commitment, await the decline in public attention that would follow disengagement in Vietnam, and then proceed to fashion foreign policy in cooperation with the limited public-opinion élites whose attention would remain. Or, it can refashion foreign policy while holding public attention to foreign affairs through Vietnam. If a President expected to find a solution to contemporary problems in the craftsmanship of foreign-policy experts, he would want to let public attention to foreign affairs die down. On the other hand, a President who wished to rely on widespread public support to maintain his foreign policies would seek to keep the public's attention focused on these issues. Yet the aroused public has clamored for the very thing that would end its arousal, and the dissenting politicians have demanded the very thing that would blunt the edge of their dissent: a settlement in Vietnam.

The early strategy of the Nixon Administration seemed to encourage a reduction of public attention to specific foreign-policy issues and a return to the deferential public attitudes that prevailed during Eisenhower's first term. Nixon's evident purpose was to gain latitude in handling the complex foreign-policy issues that greeted him on taking office by cultivating general public confidence rather than seeking public endorsement of specific proposals.

The early results of the Nixon Administration's effort are indicated by comparing public-opinion surveys about how President Nixon was "handling his job as President" during his first month in office with surveys on President Kennedy during a similar period. According to the Gallup Poll published in February 1969, 59 percent of the public approved of Nixon's conduct, 3 percent disapproved, and 36 percent had no opinion, while in 1961 72 percent approved of Kennedy's conduct, 6 percent disapproved, and 23 percent had no opinion.

When the Cold War began President Truman responded by invoking the threat of Soviet expansion in order to arouse public support for our economic and military programs to combat Communism abroad. Perhaps, then, if the United States is to move beyond the Cold War it must do so with a President whose style of leadership in foreign relations is less given to the politics of arousal than either Truman's or Kennedy's was.

In any case Nixon has what no President since the fall of China has had: a justification for *not* getting involved somewhere. Whatever else Vietnam has done, it has provided a counterexample to the debacle in China that the Republicans hung around the neck of the Truman Administration. Rather than "covering all bets" for fear that something will go wrong and it will be accused of being insensitive to national-security threats, the Nixon Administration can invoke a new popular mythology—that in saying "no" it is simply avoiding another Vietnam.

Bibliographical Essay

AMERICAN FOREIGN POLICY: AN OVERVIEW

Public-opinion surveys are compiled by issue in each number of the *Public Opinion Quarterly*. In addition, several extensive works treat American public-opinion behavior as it pertains to foreign relations on the basis of numerous opinion and voting surveys:

* Alfred O. Hero, *Americans in World Affairs* (Boston: World Peace Foundation, 1959), is an excellent summary of how voting studies structure the electorate. * Gabriel A. Almond, *The American People and Foreign Policy*, rev. ed. (New York: Praeger, 1960), provides an important description of the social structure of public-opinion formation and his new introductory essay comments on public-opinion behavior during the 1950s. H. Bradford Westerfield, "Congress and Closed Politics in National Security Affairs," *Orbis* (Fall, 1966), pp. 737–753, describes foreign-policy making as an example of "secret politics."

The intrepid reader can go further. V. O. Key, Jr., *Public Opinion and American Democracy* (New York: Knopf, 1961), maps the dimensions of public opinion and adduces its rationality. Samuel Stauffer, *Communism, Conformity and Civil Liberties* (New York: Doubleday, 1955) relates public perceptions of external threats to political belief and behavior during the Korean War red scare; * Lloyd A. Free and Hadley Cantril, *The Political Beliefs of Ameri-*

* Asterisk indicates this book is also available in paperback edition.

cans: A Study of Public Opinion (New Brunswick: Rutgers Univ. Press, 1968), analyzes the basis of American public-opinion reactions on specific issues; Hadley Cantril, *Patterns of Human Concerns* (New Brunswick: Rutgers Univ. Press, 1966), uses cross-national surveys with basic-issue categories to provide extensive evidence of broad public perception about public issues. Archibald T. Steel, *The American People and China* (New York: McGraw-Hill, 1966), uses survey techniques to examine public awareness, perception, and information levels about China as a foreign-relations issue. * Bernard R. Berelson, Paul F. Lazarsfeld, and William N. McPhee, *Voting: A Study of Opinion Formation in a Presidential Campaign* (Chicago: Univ. of Chicago Press, 1954), is a panel study of the 1948 election. * Kenneth N. Waltz, *Foreign Policy and Democratic Politics: The American and British Experience* (Boston: Little, Brown, 1967), develops criteria for foreign-policy performance and thoughtfully compares the postwar performance of the two countries.

THE TRUMAN ADMINISTRATION

For the origins of the Cold War the best single source is still * William H. McNeill, *America, Britain and Russia: Their Cooperation and Conflict, 1941–1946* (New York: Johnson Repro., 1953). Reflecting more recent concerns about the subject and also excellent are Louis J. Halle, *The Cold War as History* (New York: Harper & Row, 1967), and * William L. Neumann, *After Victory: Churchill, Roosevelt, Stalin and the Making of the Peace* (New York: Harper & Row, 1967).

A full and sober revisionist statement about the Cold War—arguing that it was an avoidable tragedy—is Denna F. Fleming, *The Cold War and Its Origins, 1917–60,* 2 vols. (New York: Doubleday, 1961). A recent compilation on the subject is * David Horowitz (ed.) *Containment and Revolution* (Boston: Beacon Press, 1967). See also * David Horowitz, *The Free World Colossus* (New York: Hill & Wang, 1965), * William A. Williams, *The Tragedy of American Diplomacy,* rev. ed. (New York: Dell, 1962); * Walter LaFeber, *America, Russia and the Cold War 1945–1966* (New York: Wiley, 1968). A more plausible revisionist position, though less authoritative and thorough, is*Ronald Steel, *Pax Americana* (New York: Viking, 1967).

Indispensible on the Truman Administration are * Harry S Truman, *Memoirs, Vol. I: Years of Decisions;* Vol. II: *Years of Trial and Hope* (New York: Doubleday, 1958). The best account is now * Cabell B. Phillips, *The Truman Presidency: The History of a Triumphant Succession* (New York: Macmillan, 1966).

Seyom Brown, *The Faces of Power: Constancy and Change in U.S. Foreign Policy from Truman to Johnson* (New York: Columbia Univ. Press, 1968), Part II, concentrates on the perceptions of policymakers in the Truman Administration. Edward S. Flash, Jr., *Economic Advice and Presidential Leadership: The Council of Economic Advisors* (New York: Columbia Univ. Press, 1965), traces the development of the CEA, an important agency that first came into its own during our Korean War rearmament. Warner R. Schilling, Paul Y. Hammond, and Glenn H. Snyder, *Strategy, Politics and Defense Budgets* (New York: Columbia Univ. Press, 1962), pp. 1–378, is valuable on congressional and presidential policy-making.

Arthur H. Vandenberg (ed.), *The Private Papers of Senator Vandenberg* (Boston: Houghton-Mifflin, 1952) provides a rich view of bipartisanship in action by a Senate Republican statesman. H. Bradford Westerfield, *Foreign Policy and Party Politics* (New Haven: Yale Univ. Press, 1955), examines bipartisan cooperation on foreign policy from Pearl Harbor to Korea.

Harry B. Price, *The Marshall Plan and Its Meaning* (Ithaca: Cornell Univ. Press, 1955), assesses the European Recovery Program in retrospect; Coral Bell, *Negotiations from Strength* (New York: Knopf, 1963), advances interesting interpretations of the Cold War stance of the Truman Administration; and * Joseph M. Jones, *The Fifteen Weeks* (New York: Harcourt, Brace & World, 1955), and George F. Kennan, *Memoirs, 1925–1950* (Boston: Little, Brown, 1967), Chaps. 11–20, both provide accounts by State Department participants of how the Marshall Plan was mapped out in Washington.

* Tang Tsou, *America's Failure in China, 1941–1950*, 2 vols. (Chicago: Univ. of Chicago Press, 1963) treats its subject definitively. Trumbull Higgins, *Korea and the Fall of MacArthur* (New York: Oxford Univ. Press, 1960), is clever and quite sound; Walter Mills,

et al., Arms and the State (New York: Twentieth Fund, 1958), surveys the military side of the U.S. response to the Cold War, including an interesting treatment of MacArthur (Chap. 7).

THE EISENHOWER ADMINISTRATION

Robert J. Donovan, *Eisenhower: The Inside Story* (New York: Harper & Row, 1956), is an account of Eisenhower's first term by an independent journalist with special access to the White House. *Dwight D. Eisenhower, *The White House Years, Vol. I: Mandate for Change, 1953–1956* (New York: Doubleday, 1965), reveals little but is a valuable and authoritative survey. *Vol. II: Waging Peace, 1956–1961,* recounts events of Eisenhower's second Administration from the President's vantage point. Sherman Adams, *First-hand Report* (New York: Harper & Row, 1961), is sometimes quite revealing, though less comprehensive and orderly. *Arthur Larson, *Eisenhower, the President Nobody Knew* (New York: Scribner, 1968), is candid and often revealing. * Richard E. Neustadt, *Presidential Power: The Politics of Leadership* (New York: Mentor, 1960), diagnoses Eisenhower's leadership problems through comparisons with Truman. Louis L. Gerson, *John Foster Dulles* (New York: Cooper Square Pub., 1967), is highly informed but cryptic. Richard Goold-Adams, *The Time of Power: A Reappraisal of John Foster Dulles* (London: McClelland, 1962), is a superb appraisal and keen explanation. Emmet J. Hughes, *The Ordeal of Power* (New York: Atheneum, 1963), is a revealing critical memoir.

Glenn H. Snyder, "The 'New Look' of 1953," in Schilling, Hammond, and Snyder, *op. cit.,* pp. 379–524, is illuminating and definitive on the changes in our strategy and defense postures during this period. * Samuel P. Huntington, *The Common Defense* (New York: Columbia Univ. Press, 1961), is a scholarly work on defense policy and politics throughout the Eisenhower Administration; and Maxwell D. Taylor, *The Uncertain Trumpet* (New York: Harper & Row, 1960), and Matthew B. Ridgway and H. H. Martin, *Soldier: Memoirs of Matthew B. Ridgway* (New York: Harper & Row, 1956), discuss defense-policy making from the viewpoint of two generals.

*Adam B. Ulam, *Expansion and Coexistence: The History of*

Soviet Foreign Policy, 1917–1967 (New York: Praeger, 1968), is comprehensive and scholarly. * Philip E. Mosely, *The Kremlin and World Politics* (New York: Random House, 1960) is a collection of essays by a scholar-diplomat. Arnold L. Horelick and Myron Rush, *Strategic Power and Soviet Foreign Policy* (Chicago: Univ. of Chicago Press, 1966) discusses Soviet policy since 1954 and includes a provocative account of how the Russians exploited Sputnik. See also Lincoln P. Bloomfield, Walter C. Clemens, Jr., and Franklyn Griffiths, *Khrushchev and the Arms Race: Soviet Interests in Arms Control and Disarmament, 1954–1964* (Cambridge: Mass. Institute of Technology, 1966). Bernard G. Bechoefer, *Postwar Negotiations for Arms Control* (Washington: Brookings, 1961) is a major work on disarmament negotiations by a participant. Leonard Beaton and John Maddox, *The Spread of Nuclear Weapons* (New York: Praeger, 1962) is an early, somewhat alarmist survey of nuclear proliferation.

Many books offer valuable insights into the Eisenhower Administration's policies in specific areas of the world: On the Eisenhower policies in the Middle East, see John C. Campbell, *Defense of the Middle East: Problems of American Policy,* rev. ed. (New York: Praeger, 1960), is a solid account of the Eisenhower period. * Anthony Eden, *Full Circle* (Boston: Houghton Mifflin, 1960), is the British Prime Minister's memoir on the Suez crisis. Herman Finer, *Dulles Over Suez: The Theory and Practice of His Diplomacy* (Chicago: Quadrangle, 1964), is angry and unfair but nonetheless illuminating. Terence Robertson, *Crisis: The Inside Story of the Suez Conspiracy* (New York: Atheneum, 1965), is cool and independent inside journalism. Anthony Nutting, *No End of a Lesson* (London: Potter, 1967), is a revealing memoir.

* Melvin Gurtov, *The First Vietnam Crisis* (New York: Columbia Univ. Press, 1967), is sound and definitive on the 1953–54 period. Morton H. Halperin and Tang Tsou, "United States Policy Toward the Offshore Islands," in John D. Montgomery and Albert O. Hirschman (eds.), *Public Policy, 1967* (Cambridge: Harvard Univ. Press, 1967), pp. 119–138, recounts the Formosa Strait crisis. American relations with Europe are analyzed by an American, Robert E. Osgood, *NATO: The Entangling Alliance* (Chicago: Univ. of Chicago Press, 1962), and by a European, Jacques Freymond, *Western Europe Since the War* (New York: Praeger, 1964). * Theodore Dra-

per, *Castroism: Theory and Practice* (New York: Praeger, 1965), is a thoughtful account of the Cuban Revolution of 1959 and the Castro regime.

THE KENNEDY ADMINISTRATION

On the 1960 election, see * Theodore H. White, *The Making of The President 1960* (New York: New Amer. Lib., 1967), which emphasizes Kennedy's campaign, and Richard M. Nixon, "The Campaign of 1960," in his *Six Crises* (New York: Doubleday, 1962), pp. 293–426.

Indispensable on Kennedy are three memoirs: * Arthur M. Schlesinger, Jr., *A Thousand Days* (Boston: Houghton Mifflin, 1965), * Theodore C. Sorensen, *Kennedy* (New York: Harper & Row, 1966), and * Roger Hilsman, *To Move a Nation* (New York: Dell, 1967). Seyom Brown, *op. cit.*, is a valuable analysis.* John F. Kennedy, *The Strategy of Peace,* edited by Allan Nevins (New York: Harper & Row, 1960), presents Kennedy's early foreign-policy views. In Seymour E. Harris, *Economics of the Kennedy Years, and a Look Ahead* (New York: Harper & Row, 1964), a modern if venerable economist surveys economic policy.

On our defense policies under the Kennedy Administration, William W. Kaufmann, *The McNamara Strategy* (New York: Harper & Row, 1964), is authentic McNamara. Maxwell D. Taylor, *Responsibility and Response* (New York: Harper & Row, 1967), is a memoir from Kennedy's closest military adviser.* William B. Bader, *The United States and the Spread of Nuclear Weapons* (New York: Pegasus, 1968) is especially valuable on the diplomacy of the test ban and nuclear proliferation during the Kennedy and Johnson Administrations. See also Bloomfield, Clemens, and Griffiths, *op. cit.,* and Horelick and Rush, *op. cit.* on the Soviet Union's foreign relations and views on arms control.

On the Kennedy Administration's policies in specific areas of the world, several works are valuable. Jean Edward Smith, *The Defense of Berlin* (Baltimore: Johns Hopkins, 1963), thoroughly examines the Berlin crisis. On the Cuban missile crisis see two excellent analyses: Arnold L. Horelick, "The Cuban Missile Crisis: An Analysis of Soviet Calculations and Behavior," *World Politics*

(April, 1964), pp. 363–389, and Albert and Roberta Wohlstetter, "Controlling the Risks in Cuba," *Adelphi Papers* (London, 1965). Elie Abel, *The Missile Crisis* (Philadelphia: Lippincott, 1966), gives excellent detail.

John C. Dreier (ed.), *Alliance for Progress* (Baltimore: Johns Hopkins, 1962), records the origins of the Alliance and the early expectations for it, but William D. Rogers, *Alliance for Progress* (New York: Random House, 1967), is a more thorough survey and appraisal.

On the background of American intervention in Vietnam and developments in Asia see Gurtov, *op. cit.,* * Edwin O. Rischauer, *Beyond Vietnam: The United States and Asia* (New York: Random House, 1967); * Arthur M. Schlesinger, Jr., *The Bitter Heritage: Vietnam and American Democracy, 1941–1966* (Boston: Houghton Mifflin, 1966); and * George M. Kahin and John W. Lewis, *The United States in Vietnam* (New York: Dell, 1967). Of particular value is * Robert Shaplen, *Lost Revolution: The U.S. in Vietnam* (New York: Harper & Row, 1965). David Halbertstam, *The Making of a Quagmire* (New York: Random House, 1965), is a journalist's account of the Buddhist uprising and American operations during the Kennedy Administration. * Donald S. Zagoria, *Vietnam Triangle: Moscow/Peking/Hanoi* (New York: Pegasus, 1967), examines the problems faced by the principal foreign supporters of the insurgency.

THE JOHNSON ADMINISTRATION

Eric F. Goldman, *The Tragedy of Lyndon Johnson* (New York: Knopf, 1969), the first memoir on the Johnson Administration to appear, probes personalities and examines Johnson's fall from popularity. In addition, three valuable works by journalists are * Rowland Evans and Robert Novack, *Lyndon B. Johnson: The Exercise of Power* (New York: New Amer. Lib., 1966), especially strong on Johnson's Senate experience; Philip L. Geyelin, *Lyndon B. Johnson and the World* (New York: Praeger, 1966), a reflective contemporary interpretation; and * Tom Wicker, *JFK and LBJ: The Influence of Personality upon Politics* (New York: Morrow, 1968), valuable on Johnson's handling of Vietnam. On the 1964 election see*Theodore

H. White, *The Making of the President, 1964* (New York, Atheneum, 1965).

On the Vietnam War a number of works are illuminating. Bill D. Moyers, "One Thing We Learned," *Foreign Affairs* (July 1968), pp. 657–664, offers the reflections of a former close adviser to Johnson on the relationship of public opinion to the Vietnam War. Sidney Verba, Richard A. Brody, Edwin B. Parker, Norman H. Nie, Nelson W. Polsby, Paul Ekman, and Gordon S. Black, "Public Opinion and the War in Vietnam, *The American Political Science Review* (June, 1967), pp. 317–333, demonstrates that the public is concerned but deferential. Seymour M. Lipset, "Doves, Hawks, and Polls," *Encounter* (October, 1966), pp. 38–45, surveys the polls to make a similar point. Press coverage of Vietnam is described in John Hohenberg, *Between Two Worlds: Policy, Press and Public Opinion in Asian-American Relations* (New York: Praeger, 1967), Chap. 6. * J. William Fulbright, *The Arrogance of Power* (New York: Random House, 1967), is an angry and eloquent attack on the Administration's Vietnam policies by a leading Senate critic. * Staughton Lynd and Thomas Haydon, *The Other Side* (New York: New Amer. Lib., 1967), is the account of New Left visitors to Hanoi.

Several works are valuable on other aspects of Johnson Administration policies: On the Dominican crisis, see Theodore Draper, "The Dominican Crisis: A Case Study in American Policy," *Commentary* (December, 1965), pp. 33–68, and * Tad Szulc, *Dominican Diary* (New York: Dell, 1966). Alastair Buchan (ed.), *China and the Peace of Asia* (New York: Praeger, 1965), is a competent survey. Karl H. Cerny and Henry W. Briefs, *NATO in Quest of Cohesion* (New York: Praeger, 1965), Part III, is a collection of essays on recent NATO problems. See Bader, *op. cit.*, on negotiations with the Russians on arms control under the Johnson Administration.

Appendix: Maps and Chart

The Course of the Korean War

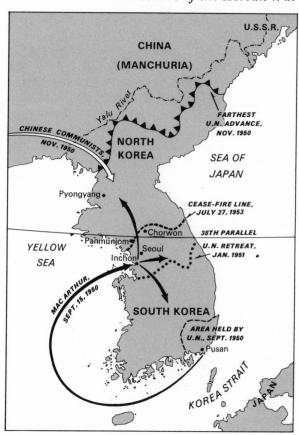

Europe, North Africa, and the Middle East

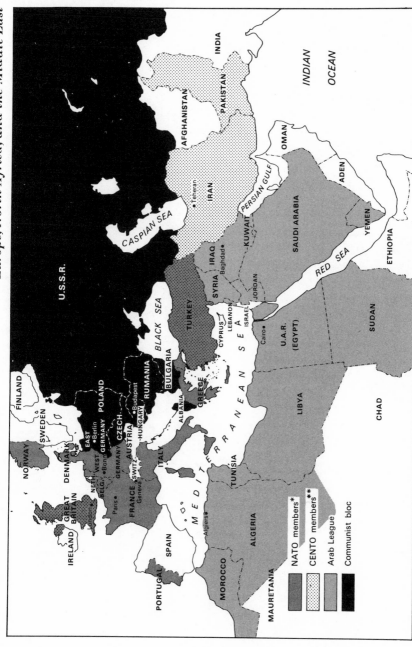

NATO members* — CENTO members** — Arab League — Communist bloc

*All European NATO members were Marshall Plan recipients.
**Iraq withdrew from CENTO in 1959.

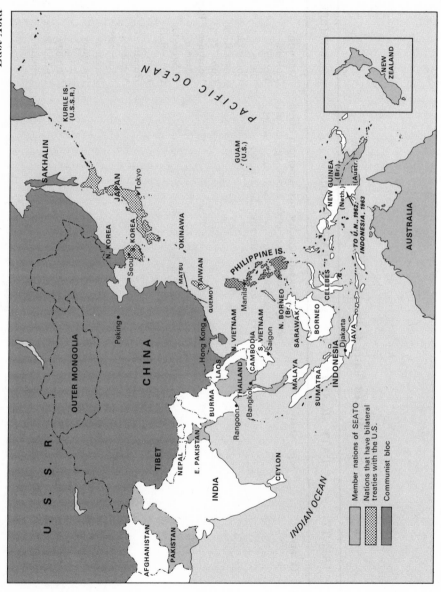

PACIFIC OCEAN

KURILE IS.
(U.S.S.R.)

SAKHALIN

GUAM
(U.S.)

JAPAN
Tokyo

NEW ZEALAND

NEW GUINEA
(Neth.)   (Austr.)

TO U.N. 1962;
INDONESIA, 1963

N. KOREA

S. KOREA
Seoul

OKINAWA

AUSTRALIA

MATSU

TAIWAN

PHILIPPINE IS.

CELEBES

QUEMOY

Manila

N. BORNEO
(Br.)

OUTER MONGOLIA

Peking

CHINA

Hong Kong

N. VIETNAM

SARAWAK

BORNEO

U. S. S. R.

LAOS

S. VIETNAM
Saigon

Djakarta

JAVA

TIBET

BURMA

THAILAND

CAMBODIA

MALAYA

INDONESIA

Rangoon

Bangkok

SUMATRA

NEPAL

E. PAKISTAN

AFGHANISTAN

PAKISTAN

INDIA

CEYLON

INDIAN OCEAN

Member nations of SEATO

Nations that have bilateral
treaties with the U.S.

Communist bloc

255

United States Collective Defense Arrangements

TREATY	DATE SIGNED	TREATY TERMS	MEMBERS
Rio Treaty*	September 2, 1947	An armed attack against any American State "shall be considered as an attack against all the American States" and each one "undertakes to assist in meeting the attack...."	Argentina Bolivia Brazil Chile Colombia Costa Rica Cuba** Dominican Republic Ecuador El Salvador Guatemala Haiti Honduras Mexico Nicaragua Panama Paraguay Peru Uruguay United States Venezuela

*The Organization of American States, called for by the Rio Treaty, was established in April 1948.
**Suspended from the OAS in 1962.

North Atlantic Treaty* April 4, 1949

"The parties agree that an armed attack against one or more of them in Europe or North America shall be considered an attack against them all;" and each party "will assist the...attacked by taking forthwith, individually and in concert with the other parties, such action as it deems necessary including the use of armed force...."

Belgium
Canada
Denmark
Federal **Republic of** Germany††
France†
Great Britain
Greece**
Iceland
Italy
Luxembourg
Netherlands
Norway
Portugal
Turkey**
United States

*The North Atlantic Treaty Organization was established in September 1950.
**Joined in 1951.
†Joined in 1954.
††Withdrew forces by 1967 but still a NATO member.

Philippine Treaty August 30, 1951

Each party recognizes that "an armed attack in the Pacific Area on either of the parties would be dangerous to its own peace and safety" and each party agrees that it will act "to meet the common dangers in accordance with its constitutional processes."

Philippines
United States

(Continued next page)

United States Collective Defense Arrangements (*Continued*)

TREATY	DATE SIGNED	TREATY TERMS	MEMBERS
ANZUS	September 1, 1951	Each party recognizes that "an armed attack in the Pacific Area on any of the parties would be dangerous to its own peace and safety," and each party agrees that it will act "to meet the common dangers in accordance with its constitutional processes."	Australia New Zealand United States
Republic of Korea Treaty	October 1, 1953	Each party recognizes that "an armed attack in the Pacific Area on either of the parties ...would be dangerous to its own peace and safety," and each party agrees to "act to meet the common danger in accordance with its constitutional processes."	Republic of Korea United States
Southeast Asia Treaty*	September 8, 1954	Each party "recognizes that aggression by means of armed attack in the treaty area against any of the parties...would endanger its own peace and safety" and each will "in that event act to meet the common danger in accordance with its own constitutional processes."	Australia France Great Britain New Zealand Pakistan Philippines Thailand United States

*The Southeast Asia Treaty Organization was established in September 1954.

Republic of China Treaty	December 2, 1954	Each party recognizes that "an armed attack in the West Pacific Area directed against the territories of either of the parties would be dangerous to its own peace and safety" and that each would "act to meet the common danger in accordance with its constitutional processes." (The territory of the Republic of China is defined as "Taiwan and the Pescadores.")	Republic of China United States
Japanese Treaty*	January 19, 1960	Each party recognizes that "an armed attack against either party in the territories under the administration of Japan would be dangerous to its own peace and safety" and each party would "act to meet the common danger in accordance with its own constitutional provisions and processes."	Japan United States

*Replaced the bilateral security treaty of 1951.

Index